RESEARCH IN CORPORATE SOCIAL PERFORMANCE AND POLICY

Volume 5 • 1983

RESEARCH IN CORPORATE SOCIAL PERFORMANCE AND POLICY

A Research Annual

Editor: **LEE E. PRESTON**
College of Business and Management
University of Maryland

VOLUME 5 • 1983

 JAI PRESS INC.

Greenwich, Connecticut   *London, England*

CONTENTS

LIST OF CONTRIBUTORS

Diane Biernot-Fawkes

TCS Management Group
Nashville, Tennessee

Raj Chaganti

School of Business Administration,
Department of Management,
Temple University

James L. Chan

Department of Accounting,
University of Illinois at
Chicago Circle

Katherine Maddox McElroy

TCS Management Group
Nashville, Tennessee

William C. Frederick

Graduate School of Business,
University of Pittsburgh

Barbara Gray Gricar

College of Business Administration,
Pennsylvania State University

Stefanie Lenway

School of Business,
Washington University
St. Louis

John F. Mahon

School of Management,
Boston University

Ian Maitland

School of Management,
University of Minnesota

Neil Mitchell   Department of Political Science,
                                        Grinnell College
                                        Grinnell, Iowa

Mildred Myers   Department of Communications,
                                        Robert Morris College
                                        Pittsburgh

Arvind Phatak   School of Business Administration,
                                        Department of Management,
                                        Temple University

John J. Siegfried   Department of Economics,
                                        Vanderbilt University

James E. Stacy   School of Management,
                                        State University of New York
                                        at Binghamton

EDITOR'S INTRODUCTION

The ten papers drawn together in this volume continue the development of empirical research on corporation and society interactions to which this publication series is dedicated. The authors include both senior scholars and newcomers; at least five of the papers had their origins in doctoral theses. The papers continue the case study orientation characteristic of many past contributions, although the "cases" selected for study have grown to include some important examples of corporate activity examined in the aggregate and in large samples, and the investigations of individual firms are now extended to yield multi-case, comparative analyses. Only one paper in this volume reports on a single case investigation, and in that instance primary interest attaches to the character of the decision-making observed rather than the topical issues.

The first three papers present important new perspectives on the role of business in the political arena. Maitland notes the recent expansion of business political activity, and focuses on the widely-held view that there is a contradiction between an espoused ideology of laissez-faire and actual business pursuit of protective and supportive actions by government. In an analysis of recent business lobbying, he contrasts a collective interest in broad principles with a particularistic interest in special support policies and finds that broad-based organizations tend to support the former and individual industries and firms the latter. The study serves to confirm Maitland's hypothesis that the business community is, indeed, a house divided.

The influence of business interests on foreign policy—one of the best established and most important topics in the corporation-society literature—is the subject of an impressive comparative case analysis by Lenway. She finds that in three major instances, involving textiles, autos, and telecommunications equipment, U.S. adherence to the multilateral free trade principles of the General Agreement on Tariffs and Trade has served to blunt the force of protectionist and self-promotive policies advocated by business and labor groups. Her careful investigations seriously qualify widely held views as to the decisive influence of parochial economic considerations on public policy.

Frederick and Myers report a meticulously documented analysis of public policy advertising by business during the 1980 presidential election. They found, contrary to common impressions, that such advertising never amounted to a very large share (less than 10 percent) of all comparable ads included in their sample, and that the volume of such advertising did not vary significantly between pre-election and post-election periods. Trade associations were responsible for a substantially larger volume of policy advertising than individual companies. Their content analysis confirmed that business advertising overwhelmingly supported the policy views of candidate Reagan, as opposed to those of President Carter or neutral positions. Their detailed report contains information of considerable intrinsic interest and also establishes a benchmark and methodology that will guide future studies of this important subject.

Corporate philanthropy is another subject with a long and interesting historical literature, but authoritative information about its scope and practice has been extremely limited. It is generally believed that philanthropy is now more professionally managed and less subject to executive whim, but both the management processes involved and their impact on the volume and pattern of contributions are little understood. Siegfried, McElroy, and Biernot-Fawkes report on an interview study of 240 corporations in 14 different locations and provide a statistical basis for describing philanthropic activities and analyzing changes over time. Their multi-industry sample extends the earlier findings of Levy and Shatto, reported in Volume 2 of this series, which related to firms in the electric utility industry alone.

Two major areas of current public concern about corporate performance—and hence of extensive government regulatory activity—are occupational health and safety and environmental protection. Each of these is the focus of a pair of papers in this volume, and these topical studies complement each other effectively. Chan presents an overview of the health and safety issue, an analysis and critique of the available aggregate data, and a discussion of some of the barriers to easy problem resolution among business, labor, and government. He strongly favors an informational strategy, as opposed to conventional "command and control" techniques, as a means of achieving social objectives in this area. Gricar reports on a detailed study of OSHA compliance response by a sample of 34 firms in a single industry. She finds that regulatory response was strongly influenced by the ideological views of top management, by firm size, and by several other organizational characteristics. Her study is representative of the new and rigorous types of empirical work now emerging in the organizational behavior literature.

The two papers dealing with environmental protection issues offer a different contrast. Mahon focuses on the external strategies of several of the leading chemical companies with respect to the creation of a "superfund" for environmental cleanup. His research shows the variety of political goals and strategies pursued by various companies, arising from their own particular circumstances and previous experiences. His observations underscore Lenway's conclusion that even vigorously pursued political tactics do not necessarily result in corporate dominance of the public policy process. Chaganti and Phatak examine internal aspects of the environmental issue in a study of the evolution of the environmental affairs function in a sample of four companies. Their research confirms a "stage" model of organizational change, and they describe the variety of activities carried out by fully developed units of this type within major companies.

Mitchell examines an empirical issue of great historical importance—the separation of ownership and control—and presents a major summary and critique of the available data and interpretations. In addition, he looks for implications of ownership/control separation for corporate social policy, as reflected in an unusual collection of data from the 1920s. This analysis reveals that there is no discernable effect of control type on social policy, and Mitchell suggests that both increasing management control and social policy development are responses to growth in the size of large corporations.

A central question in the study of corporate social policy is the extent to which decisions that have social impact are made in a different fashion, and according to different criteria, than other important business decisions. There is some impression that major business decisions are based entirely upon economic criteria ("the bottom line") and that one problem in dealing with corporate social policy is that the relevant decisions depend primarily on political considerations and personal values, allegedly unfamiliar criteria in the executive suite. Stacey's case study of the commitment to nuclear power by an electric utility company reveals a "social" decision in the broadest sense. Not only would the outcome have widespread and multi-dimensional impact, but the decision-making process itself hinged on judgments about social value—in this case the value of nuclear power development—rather than on "bottom line" considerations. Once the nuclear option had passed an "economic gate" of feasibility, its support and implementation appear to have been guided primarily by political and ideological considerations.

I owe a word of thanks to all of these contributors for their interest in this series and for their patience in responding to questions and suggestions. Thanks are also due to several future contributors whose papers could not be completed in time for inclusion here. Papers and abstracts for consideration for future volumes are warmly solicited. In addition, it has been suggested that from time to time an established scholar might develop a plan for an entire volume, or portion thereof, based on a unifying theme—either topical or methodological—and take responsibility for gathering a collection of papers to fulfill that purpose. I am enthusiastic about this idea, and I invite interested parties to be in touch with me as to their interests and intentions.

Lee E. Preston
Series Editor

HOUSE DIVIDED:

BUSINESS LOBBYING
AND THE 1981 BUDGET

Ian Maitland

There is a natural tendency to equate the growth of political involvement by business over the past decade—through expanded corporate presences in Washington, PAC contributions, well-orchestrated grass-roots lobbying, etc.—with the growth of business influence within our political system. In this paper I argue that this view is logically and empirically flawed.

The logical error of this view lies in its confusion of the interests of business as a whole—i.e., a coherent set of interests distinct from those of, say, labor or consumers or the general public—with the sum of the interests of individual firms. It cannot be assumed *a priori* that individual firms and trade associations promote the common interests of business when they pursue their own particularistic ends in the political marketplace. Indeed, it is possible that the pursuit of particularistic ends may actually undermine business's common interests. In

Research in Corporate Social Performance and Policy, volume 5, pages 1-25
ISBN: 0-89232-412-0

this paper I argue that such a result is not uncommon. By contrast, broad-based business confederations or "encompassing organizations" are very likely to work for the collective interests of business or, at least, not to injure them. However, the political effectiveness of these organizations is the subject of controversy.

Thus, before the outcomes of business political activity can be predicted, it is necessary to know something about the structure or pattern of business interest representation. It makes a great deal of difference whether business's political power is highly centralized (as in Sweden, for example) or highly fragmented (as in the U.S.). Such differences affect the political agenda of business (exactly which interests are served?) and, in turn, the relationship between business and government (Beer, p. 50; Dahl, pp. 68-80 and 191-193).

The importance of the organization or structure of business interest representation in shaping the political behavior of business is often neglected. Lindblom (p. 206), for example, takes as axiomatic that business is united and highly effective at protecting its interests when it comes to the "grand issues" (viz., the fundamentals of the politico-economic order) in spite of findings that firms have been really influential participants in the political process only when the stakes have been "hard, specific matters of immediate concern" (McConnell, p. 293). Lindblom entirely overlooks Olson's argument that it is precisely at the level of grand issues or "collective goods" that the political mobilization of the members of a large group is hardest to achieve. Where the political power of business is dispersed, we should not expect it to be used to further a collective interest, because "however valuable the collective good might be to [business] as a whole, it does not offer the individual [firm or association] any incentive. . . to bear. . . any of the costs of the necessary collective action" (Olson, 1965, p. 50-51).

In this paper I examine business lobbying in connection with the 1981 Budget and Tax Acts with a view to characterizing the different stands taken by different levels of interest representation in the business community. I expect the encompassing business organizations will have adopted positions broadly in keeping with the "collective" interests of business, while more narrowly-based coalitions of firms will have lobbied for particularistic interests.

My concerns are to distinguish between the "collective" interests of business and the "particularistic" interests of sections of the business community and to examine empirically the following propositions:

- The pursuit of particularistic interests may be inimical to business's collective interests.
- Lobbying by narrowly-based business coalitions is likely to be oriented to particularistic goals while that by encompassing business organizations is likely to be directed toward more collective ends.
- Encompassing business organizations can effectively act as representatives of business's collective interests.

COLLECTIVE AND PARTICULARISTIC INTERESTS

In view of the extreme heterogeneity of the business community, it may be questioned whether business has any collective interests at all. Certainly many businessmen would dispute the idea that "business" is an entity with a monolithic set of interests distinguishable from the conditions that promote national prosperity and freedom. It remains true, however, that businessmen are in substantial agreement regarding the proper relationship between business and government. In his study of the ideology of American business leaders, Vogel concluded that "the most characteristic, distinctive and persistent belief. . . is an underlying suspicion and mistrust of government" (Vogel, 1978, p. 45).

Nevertheless, the sincerity of business's commitment to *laissez faire* has evoked widespread skepticism, largely because of the failure of business to practice what it preaches. Vogel himself noted the tendency for executives' "hostility to government. . .to vanish when their profits are at stake" (p.51). Ideology has conspicuously failed to restrain corporations and trade associations from lobbying for protection from foreign competition, preferential tax treatment, subsidies and loan guarantees, etc. As a result many observers have dismissed businessmen's professions of faith in the free market as hypocritical rhetoric (McConnell, p. 293; Moore, p. 278).

Vogel rejected this conclusion. His extensive interviews with chief executives during 1974 and 1975 convinced him that their public commitments to the market faithfully reflected their private sentiments:

> In fact, the gap between what executives or their spokesmen say in public and in private is far less than most students of business appreciate.. . . Executives tend to believe their own propaganda.. . . If anything, the private views of corporate executives are more critical of government than their public statements. The lack of acceptance of a large and powerful state is also not confined to small businessmen or reactionary sunbelt capitalists. It also dominates the political and social outlook of the top managers of 'Fortune 500' firms. [A central belief of] virtually all American businessmen. . . is the notion of governmental involvement as inimical to a sound economy and incompatible with a free society (pp. 45-6).

If the beliefs publicly professed by executives are sincere, then how do we account for business's continual backsliding? I believe that this question can most satisfactorily be resolved by distinguishing between what is in the collective interest of business and what is in the individual interest of a firm or industry group. It is in the rational self-interest of executives to urge government non-interference in the economy if they believe that a more prosperous economy will result and they will participate in that prosperity; but, at the same time, it is no less rational to urge government intervention when that will benefit them. (To say that this behavior is rational does not of course absolve it of a certain hypocrisy.)

Accordingly, this analysis is based on a distinction between collective and particularistic interests of business. I assume that "collective interests" involve the limitation or rollback of government intervention in the economy, while "particularistic interests" involve specific benefits procured through government action by a corporation, industry, or set of industries. An important implication of this distinction should be noted: The pursuit of particularistic goals may injure business's collective interests.

While lip-service is paid to the ideal of the free market, it remains a "collective good" in Olson's (1965) sense of the term. That is, individual corporations and trade associations have little incentive to work for it since its benefits will accrue to them irrespective of whether or not they contribute to providing it; moreover, their own specific contributions will have little or no perceptible effect on the free market's existence. Conversely, these organizations have a strong incentive to try to obtain government intervention in their favor, even if they deplore government intervention in principle, because the incremental influence of government in the economy will be minuscule, while the benefit to them could well be substantial.

In this way it is quite possible for the separate, uncoordinated actions of different firms, taken to advance their immediate interests, to lead cumulatively to outcomes which none of them would have desired, e.g., the election of a Congress hostile or lukewarm to the market, or large-scale government allocation of credit.

Nevertheless no individual firm has a realistic option to show restraint or to try unilaterally to advance the collective interests of business. To do so would be simply to place oneself at a competitive disadvantage while having a negligible impact on the health of the free market. In this fashion government intervention in the economy feeds on itself. "Dependence [on government] creates a vicious circle of dependence.. . .When one sector of the economy is subsidized, others are forced to seek comparable participation" (Reich, p. 737; see also Thurow, p. 33).

It follows that increased political resources, if they are in the hands of narrowly-based business interests, may not result in increased corporate domination of the polity in the aggregate, but rather in the further politicization of the economy in all of its parts. This will be the case if firms employ their newfound resources to achieve particularistic goals through the political marketplace instead of the economic marketplace.

THE POLITICS OF ENCOMPASSING BUSINESS ORGANIZATIONS

In these pages I will examine the political activity of the U.S. Chamber of Commerce, the National Association of Manufacturers (NAM), the Business Roundtable (BRT), and the National Federation of Independent Businessmen

(NFIB). We should expect these organizations to adopt positions broadly consistent with the collective interests of business as a whole. Olson has described the incentives facing such encompassing business organizations as follows:

> The incentives facing an encompassing special-interest organization are dramatically different from those facing an organization that represents only a narrow segment of society.. . .The members of the highly encompassing organization own so much of the society that they have an important incentive to be actively concerned about how productive it is; they are in the same position as a partner in a firm that has only a few partners.. . . In [this] way national confederations of business or labor organizations can also introduce a more nearly national perspective on political issues.. . . [They] should on average take a somewhat less parochial view than the narrow associations of which they are composed (1982, pp. 47-53).

Assuming for the moment that encompassing business organizations have the *incentive* to represent business's collective interests, there still remains the question of their *capacity* to do so. Wilson has pointed out that such organizations face acute problems of organizational maintenance. The "free-rider" problem identified earlier applies *a fortiori* to them—"no single businessman has an incentive to contribute to the attainment of what all will receive if the organized political efforts are successful." Moreover, the collective interests of business are highly general and can easily lead to inconsistent policy positions. Any concrete political choice typically involves divisive trade-offs (p. 153).

If encompassing organizations must constantly be looking over their shoulders, can they be effective spokesmen for business's collective interests? Some political scientists say no. Epstein concluded that "because [such organizations] must represent the views of a wide range of constituents, they must necessarily take positions of consensus on general issues" (p. 51). In their study of business and tariffs, Bauer et. al. found that "quasi-unanimity" on the part of membership was a precondition of political action by any business organization (pp. 332-340). The major business confederations were ineffectual on the tariff issue because their heterogeneity meant that any forthright stand was bound to antagonize some part of their membership. In Malbin's view, the U.S. Chamber's "growth and their self-limiting agenda are intimately connected" (Kirkland, p. 158).

However, there are other findings that at least partially contradict this view of the political ineffectiveness of encompassing business organizations (Wilson, p. 311). On certain kinds of issues, the Chamber and the NAM appear to have been active and successful advocates. In general these issues tended to be bills that affected business as a whole (e.g., minimum-wage, tax, antitrust, right-to-work, or picketing legislation). On broad issues of social welfare, consumerism, or ecology, the two organizations spoke up forcefully, but without the same degree of success.

In recent years encompassing business organizations have occasionally overridden the wishes of minorities of their memberships. Thus the BRT opposed

legislation that would have subsidized the merchant marine industry by requiring
that a percentage of imported oil be carried in American ships; and it opposed
the Chrysler bailout, prompting Chrysler to resign from the organization (Vogel,
1980). NAM also opposed the Chrysler bailout and endorsed trucking deregulation over vehement objections from members who manufactured truck frames
(Kirkland, p. 156; Keller, 1982, pp. 121-122).

RESEARCH SITE: THE 1981 BUDGET

The growth of government since the 1960s has not come about as part of a grand
design to socialize the commanding heights of the economy; rather it has been
the culmination of a series of pragmatic responses to social pressures and demands
(Aharoni, p. 7). A fragmented Congress has proved unable to resist the lobbying
of different groups for special interest legislation. Bell has pointed out that the
"public household"—meaning the management of public revenues and expenditures—has become.

> . . .the arena for the expression not only of public needs *but also of private wants*. This
> takes the form of governmental responsibility for economic growth, or of various social
> claims on the community. . . .Above all, the basic allocative power is now *political* rather
> than *economic*. And this raises a fundamental question of restraints. The economic constraint
> on private wants is the amount of money that a man has, or the credit he is able to establish.
> But what are the constraints on political demands? (Bell, p. 226; see also Brittan).

In the past, business lobbies have generally participated only as special interests
in the budget process, pressing for preferential tax treatment or for specific
spending programs. In this they have also, of course, contributed to government
encroachment on the market. However, the budget of 1981 presented a uniquely
favorable setting for business solidarity in support of collective priorities, particularly limiting the growth of public spending. First, although Reagan had been
the second choice of important parts of the business community (John Connally
was their favorite), his election was seen as providing an opportunity—perhaps
a last chance—to arrest the drift toward a state-dominated economy. While there
was ambivalence towards the proposal for sweeping personal income tax cuts,
business was sympathetic to the broad thrust of the president's program.

Second, an exceptional conjunction of events boded well for the program: For
the first time in thirty years Republicans controlled the Senate, business appeared
to have forged an unprecedented degree of unity in the congressional battles of
the 1970s, and the public mood seemed to be receptive to the need for spending
cuts. An NAM vice president said: "This time, with the president and this
Congress, and the current mood in the public at large, we can do these things"
(Keller, 1981a; Edsall, 1982).

In these circumstances, how did the lobbyists for business special interests react? Did they suspend their lobbying for parochial advantage in favor of the president's program? And were the encompassing business organizations markedly more supportive of the program than the more narrowly-based business lobbies? We now look at the role played in the 1981 budget process by four encompassing organizations and at eight cases of lobbying that undermined the Reagan administration's plans for a "clean" budget.

BUSINESS LOBBYING AND THE 1981 BUDGET

The president's four-part "Program for Economic Recovery," announced in February 1981, provided for a sharp slowdown in the growth of federal spending, major tax reductions for individuals and businesses, regulatory relief, and slow and steady growth of the money supply. Even before many of the details were known, the program had been endorsed by all four major "encompassing" business organizations.

This united front masked misgivings about some aspects of the program. The Business Roundtable (BRT) had reservations about the proposed cuts in the lending authority of the Export-Import Bank. Both the BRT and the NAM were skeptical about the across-the-board, Kemp-Roth individual tax cuts. Even small business executives, in response to an NFIB poll in January 1980, had by better than 2-1 favored deferral of tax cuts until the budget was balanced. Only the U.S. Chamber, of the four, unreservedly supported them (Kirschten; *Business Week*, December 22, 1980). But all these organizations quickly rallied behind the president's program because they were in agreement with its overall thrust.

The Spending Cut Package

The four encompassing business organizations did not take positions on the specifics of the spending cut package; they simply declared their outright support for it. This appears to have been part of a strategy to prevent the package from unraveling and to avoid divisive confrontations with their own memberships. A Chamber spokesman said, "Our goal is to keep a united front within the business community so that we don't start tearing the package apart. Every time the administration has tried to make cuts in the budget, people have started protecting their own particular interest. There just isn't any way a member of Congress can resist that kind of pressure" (Keller, 1981a). The BRT acknowledged that the Ex-Im Bank cuts "could be a negative factor for our competitiveness in world markets and the creation of jobs," but added that "business must not join in the tendency to say, 'Cut government expenditures but don't cut those that affect us.' That could help scuttle a package that is good for all Americans" (Kirschten).

As later with the tax bill, business unity was facilitated—perhaps even orchestrated—by a coalition of business federation staff people and Washington corporate representatives. The "Budget Control Working Group," in which staff of the four organizations played a strategic role, formulated the business view on spending cuts and presented it to Congress. The group was not in a position to instruct its members but provided a forum in which a consensus was arrived at.

The principal focus of the group was not substantive, i.e., who should get cut by how much, but procedural. It concentrated on how to preserve the integrity of the congressional budget process, especially "reconciliation." This is the procedure by which authorizing and appropriating committees are required to cut back expenditures to meet ceilings mandated in the initial budget resolution. Thus Keller (1981a; see also McClenahen) reports that the business organizations believed that if they could stick together until Congress had committed itself to specific spending levels, the scope for special interests to pick the budget cuts apart would be sharply reduced.

When the budget proposals went to Congress, business unity in support of the spending cuts held remarkably firm. Writing in March, Keller (1981a) noted "the early intensity of business lobbying for Reagan's budget, including cuts that may inconvenience the business sector, and. . .the low-key and sometimes half-hearted efforts of special pleaders trying to salvage their portions of the budget." However, there was some slippage: Even before the budget had been unveiled Congressional supporters had won reprieves for three major synthetic fuels projects. Congress also thwarted the administration's plans to reduce funding for the Export-Import Bank. The administration's half-hearted fight to save the Ex-Im cuts was portrayed as "a retreat from earlier vows to hit harder at 'haves' " (*Wall Street Journal*, May 1, 1981), and as a consequence "the program Reagan picked to prove that business must suffer alongside social programs ended up showing just the opposite" (Keller, 1981c). In short, these cuts had acquired a symbolic importance that transcended their dollar impact on the budget; and the administration's failure to follow through with them may have robbed its mission to bring federal spending under control of much of its moral force.

The administration's package triumphed in the House on June 25, assuring its final victory. The support of the major business organizations, especially the Chamber, was described by the White House's chief lobbyist as crucial (Kirkland).

The Tax Cut Package

The Reagan administration hoped to get approval of a "clean" tax bill containing only across-the-board rate cuts for individuals (30 percent over three years) and accelerated depreciation for business (known as 10-5-3 because it contemplated write-offs of three years for vehicles, five years for most equipment, and ten years for buildings). In the event, the act the administration got contained a 25 percent cut in individual rates and an accelerated depreciation schedule providing a 15 year write-off period for buildings. But the act was also overloaded with tax breaks for special interests granted during a violent bidding war for the votes of a handful of conservative House Democrats. In the space of a few short weeks "the new political climate dissolve[d] rather rapidly and [was] replaced by the reflexes of the old politics. Every tax lobby in town. . .moved in on the legislation, and pet amendments for obscure tax advantage and profit became the pivotal issues of legislative action, not the grand theories of supply-side tax reduction" (Greider, p. 51). What role did business lobbies play in the unraveling of the administration's tax bill?

Once again the four encompassing business organizations had quickly united around the president's plan. This unity is remarkable when seen against the backdrop of bitter disagreement that had marked earlier tax bills. In 1978 this disagreement had surfaced in an especially acrimonious dispute over the bid to cut the capital gains tax rate from 48 to 28 percent. The proposal had been championed by the U.S. Chamber, while the NAM had remained lukewarm and the BRT had tried to persuade businessmen to forgo capital gains tax relief in return for a Carter administration promise to cut the corporate income tax rate (Kirkland, pp. 156-158). Following this wrangle the initiative for working out a common business stand on taxes actually came from politicians rather than the business groups themselves. The two architects of the cut for capital gains, Reps. James Jones (D.-OK) and the late William Steiger (R.-WI) began to meet with key representatives of business and encouraged them to reach agreement on a new tax bill which they undertook to sponsor. After Steiger's death his place was taken by Barber Conable (R.-NY).

In response to this prompting a group of tax lobbyists, including representatives of the four major business organizations, began what were to become weekly breakfast sessions in the Sheraton Carlton Hotel in Washington. Thus was born the "Carlton" group which forged a consensus in support of 10-5-3 (Edsall). As the de facto chairman of the Carlton group, Cliff Massa of NAM, recalled: "At the end of 1978, Jones and Conable said they'd like to do something on depreciation if the business community had a united position. The organization sat down to work out a common point of view. That hadn't been done before in an offensive manner. Business had always splintered up" (Bacon, 1981a).

When Reagan adopted 10-5-3, business leaders swallowed their misgivings about Kemp-Roth and embraced the administration's tax plan (Mark I). From this point on the Carlton group served as a clearinghouse for legislative intelligence and as a means for the loose coordination of business lobbying in support of the tax plan.

In interviews with journalists, Carlton group members took pains to dispel any impression that they made legislative policy, set strategy, or imposed discipline. They preferred to characterize their activities as "information sharing" (Cowan, 1982). Nevertheless, the group not only performed the crucial task of shaping a tax plan behind which business could unite, but helped to keep business in line behind that plan. Keller (1982) reported that the group "persuaded most of the business lobbying community—often by appealing to the solidarity of their superiors in corporate headquarters—to postpone their more parochial legislative wishes."

Congressional Action and Reaction

Even with the support of the major business organizations, however, the president's tax cut plan was from the beginning in more trouble than the budget cuts had been. An early rebuff came when the Senate Finance Committee rejected the plan after the defection of conservative Republicans alarmed at the size of the projected deficits. As a result, administrative officials began to explore the possibility of a compromise with House Ways and Means Democrats. By late May, however, these negotiations were broken off when chairman Rostenkowski (D.-IL) was unable to get bargaining authority from his committee majority.

After this failure the administration turned to the conservative Democrats who had provided it with its margin of victory on the first budget resolution. These negotiations led to a revised tax plan (Mark II), announced on June 4, which included a variety of tax breaks designed to attract broad support. Notable among these was a tax credit for holders of small gas and oil royalties. Reagan was apparently eager to top an offer the oil-state Democrats had received from Rostenkowski.

In order to finance these tax breaks the administration modified its original depreciation plan, cutting the projected business tax benefits by almost 30 percent. Business lobbyists had not been party to the negotiations between the administration and the conservative Democrats, and when the new plan was announced it was greeted with a sense of betrayal. The Chamber's chief economist called it "a breach of faith with the business community" (Keller, 1981b; see also Tate; Bacon, 1981b).

The president's announcement of his revised tax plan on June 4 unleashed intense lobbying by the Carlton group and other business leaders during the so-called "Learjet weekend" (Edsall). The administration realized that it had blundered and hurried to heal the breach. On June 9 a third tax plan (Mark III) was introduced in the House which restored most of the original business cuts. By June 11 all four major business organizations had publicly endorsed this plan.

The administration's actions had temporarily thrown the business community into disarray and left the door ajar for the Democrats. Carlton group members were contacted by House Ways and Means Democrats soliciting support for their own tax proposals. But no Carlton member broke ranks. According to the group's de facto chairman, "That was an option no one wanted to take. . .; the group believed a 'bidding war' over tax legislation could lessen the chances of winning what it wanted" (Bacon, 1981a). On the other hand, one anonymous lobbyist whose organization renewed its support reportedly felt that more could have been gained by waiting (Keller, 1981b).

The Carlton group's resoluteness notwithstanding, a bidding war was underway. The president's most recent bill (Mark III) retained a number of popular tax breaks for individuals carefully tailored to attract the votes of conservative House Democrats, e.g., easing of the marriage penalty, estate tax relief, and reduction of income tax on overseas earnings. In response the House Ways and Means Democrats started to draw up a bill with which they hoped to drive a wedge into the coalition of Republicans and conservative Democrats. For this purpose they not only matched the administration's incentives to individual taxpayers, but added inducements to the business community as well. Writing in June, Keller noted that "while the public rhetoric of the president and many Democrats has emphasized the shape of tax cuts for individuals. . . . the competition for votes in the House has been waged primarily on the question of business cuts."

The bidding war presented many business lobbies that had been waiting in the wings with temptations they were unable to resist. "Reagan's negotiating signaled to some industries and their allies in Congress that it was now acceptable to step up efforts for their provisions." Although the major business organizations continued to urge restraint, business's united front in support of a clean tax bill was irretrievably breached. "The private lobbyists had forgone a lot of opportunities to lobby out of a feeling they had an understanding with the administration," that they would wait for a separate bill that would address their concerns, a Senate aide told Keller. "As time goes by, people are sensing more and more that they have a chance of getting their amendments accepted" (Keller, 1981b).

In spite of the technical requirement that revenue bills originate in the House, the Republican-dominated Senate Finance Committee had gone ahead and completed marking up its own tax bill by mid-June. This bill differed in only a few respects from the one proposed by Reagan. Several of the provisions added at this stage will be examined later in this paper—a tax-free savings certificate for S&L's, elimination of the commodity straddle tax loophole, liberalization of the tax laws regarding stock options, and refunds of unused investment tax credits to ailing industries. The committee also raised the credit for oil royalty owners to $2500, as proposed in the administration's bill. (With the exception of stock options, all of these provisions had also been approved by Ways and Means or were under consideration by it.)

The House Ways and Means Committee's deliberations wore on through June and most of July. On July 22 the committee completed writing up its bill. It had delayed to the very last its decision on whether or not to include generous tax relief for independent oil producers. After lengthy negotiations with conservative Democrats it went ahead and did so. The bill also contained a number of provisions designed to woo business support, such as:

- In place of 10-5-3, a one year write-off of new equipment, called "expensing."
- Refundability of unused investment tax credits.
- A tax-free savings certificate for S&L's.
- A tax break for public utility shareholders to encourage them to reinvest their earnings in the companies.
- Reductions in corporate income tax for small business.
- A 25 percent tax credit for new R&D expenditures. ,
- A drop in top tax rate on investments from 70-50 percent.
- A less stringent limitation than the Senate on the use of commodity tax straddles for tax avoidance.
- A more generous reduction in estate and gift taxes than that approved by the Senate.

Liberal Democrats on the committee were dismayed by many of the provisions but then held their noses and voted for the bill anyway (Keller, 1981b). Business lobbyists reacted to the Ways and Means proposals with astonishment and not a little suspicion. A chemical company tax expert was quoted as saying, "People are a little nervous about it. It's almost like Greeks bearing gifts" (*Chemical Week*, July 1, 1981).

The administration responded to the House Ways and Means bill by hastily revising its own bill to forestall potential defections. The new administration bill (Mark IV) incorporated many of the features of the Ways and Means bill and added some extra inducements. It did not quite match the Democrats' generosity in cutting oil taxes, but it included annual indexation of tax rates to offset inflation, relief from estate and gift taxes, increased charitable deductions, and a variety of other measures. Both sides admitted their bills were more products of political bidding than blueprints for economic recovery (Fessler). Jim Jones (D.-OK) said: "We're in a bidding war. Any economic foundation for the tax bill has been abandoned" (Cowan, 1981a).

On June 29 the administration bill triumphed in the House. This left the House-Senate conference conferees to reconcile two bills that both enjoyed the president's support. The conference bill was acknowledged by Treasury Secretary Regan as the administration's: "We are willing to stand behind this bill and say we got what we wanted" (*Wall Street Journal*, Aug. 3, 1981).

SPECIAL INTEREST BUSINESS LOBBYING

We now turn to a detailed examination of eight cases of special interest business lobbying, summarized in Table 1, that endangered Reagan's comprehensive spending and tax packages.

Table 1. Special Interest Lobbying: Analysis of Cases

Issue	Principal Lobbies	Principal Congressional Supporters*	Victory (V) or Defeat (D) for Business Lobby
Synfuels Funding	National Council for Synthetic Fuels Production	D	V
Ex-Im Bank Funding	Coalition for Growth through Exports; American League for Exports and Security Assistance (aircraft and nuclear Industries)	D	V
Oil Tax Relief	Independent Petroleum Producers Association of America (independent oil producers, *not* majors)	B	V
All-Savers Certificate	U.S. League of Savings (S&L's)	B	V
Aviation User Taxes	Aircraft Owners & Pilots Association (AOPA); General Aviation Manufacturers' Association; Air Transport Association	B	V
Commodity Tax Straddle Loophole	Chicago Mercantile Exchange; Chicago Board of Trade	D	D
Stock options-Tax Liberalization	American Electronics Association; American Business Council (growth industries)	B	V
Safe-harbor Tax Leasing Amendment	American Council for Capital Formation (distressed Industries)	D—(Refundable Investment Tax Credit) R—(Leasing provision)	V

*D = Democrat; R = Republican; B = Bipartisan.

The Synfuels Program.

In 1980 Congress passed the Energy Security Act establishing a Synthetic Fuels Corporation (SFC) authorized to hand out $20 billion in subsidies, with the possibility of $68 billion more to come later. Until the SFC was operational the Department of Energy (DOE) had limited authority to subsidize synfuels production. These subsidies became a target of Budget Director Stockman's budget-cutting zeal.

Stockman's leaked "black book" of cuts drew a swift reaction from synfuels supporters in Congress. Even before the budget had been officially unveiled, the House Democratic leadership had written to the president denouncing the cuts as a false economy. A week later three leading Senate Republicans informed Reagan of their opposition to the cuts.

In his February 18 budget message the president scaled back Stockman's cuts. In spite of this victory, the supporters of synfuels still had to pry the funds loose from the administration. Congressional leaders brought intense pressures on the White House, including holding Reagan's nominations for the SFC board hostage. On the day the cabinet met on the subsidies, the House voted to approve funds for a synfuels plant in Kentucky (89 Republicans joined most of the House's Democrats). In late summer the president approved the award of funds to the three major projects.

Finally, in October Congress reaffirmed its commitment to synfuels by rejecting an amendment by Senator Proxmire (D.-WI) to delete funds earmarked for the Kentucky plant. The vote was 40-57, with Proxmire winning the support of Republican Senators 29-23, but failing to carry his Democratic colleagues 11-34.

Export-Import Bank

The proposed cutbacks in the lending authority of the Export-Import Bank were depicted by the administration as proof that its budget cuts would not spare "profitable corporations."

The Bank provides direct loans and other forms of loan assistance at subsidized rates to overseas purchasers of U.S. goods and services. The loans have enabled U.S. exporters to compete with foreign companies that are helped by their governments' export subsidy programs. Two-thirds of the Bank's loans have benefited seven large corporations exporting airplanes, nuclear power plants, and other big ticket items. David Stockman said: "If we are ever caught not cutting this while we're biting deeply into the social programs, we're going to have big problems. . . . I've got to take something out of Boeing's hide to make this look right" (Greider, pp. 34-35).

Before the cuts officially became part of the administration's program, corporate lobbyists brought pressure on Stockman to leave the Bank alone. When this failed to sway him, however, the corporations called off their campaign and promised their support for the package of spending cuts as a whole.

The administration suffered its first reversal in March when Senator Nancy Kassebaum (R.-KS) won an amendment in the Senate Budget Committee to restore about one third of the cuts. Supporters of ExIm encountered little administration resistance, and word got around that the administration was not really in earnest.

By May much of the industry's reticence had faded, and the major Bank users mounted a campaign in Congress. A coalition including Boeing, Westinghouse, and the Machinists Union sent industry-labor lobbying teams to Capitol Hill. Subcontractors were mobilized to counteract the impression of ExIm as "Boeing's bank."

On May 12 the House accepted an amendment by David Obey (D.-WI) to give the Bank what the president had requested. But the very next day, following intense lobbying, the House reversed itself and voted to exceed the president's ExIm budget by $400 million. The overnight lobbying, focusing on the jobs issue, changed about 70 votes. (Republicans voted against the Bank 91-86; Democrats for it 151-71.)

A final threat to the Bank arose when the House Banking Committee was forced by the budget reconciliation process to choose between the Bank and subsidized housing, and tried to cut the former. The Republican reconciliation alternative, put together with administration help and with an eye on conservative Democratic votes, restored the Bank's funding. This triumphed and was included in the final budget package.

Oil Tax Relief

The breakdown of the administration's negotiations with the House Democratic leadership over the 1981 tax bill ignited a bidding war for the votes of a handful of conservative Democrats. On June 4 Reagan announced a revised tax bill which included a $2,500 exclusion for royalty owners from the windfall profits tax. This apparently followed a similar offer oil-state Democrats had received from House Ways and Means chairman Rostenkowski.

Not content with the credit for royalty owners, oil-state Democrats in the Senate began a drive to give the independent producers relief from the windfall profits tax. After initial stonewalling, Senator Dole (finance chairman) met with Democrats and worked out a deal to drop the tax rate on newly discovered oil. The administration looked the other way. Nevertheless, the independents scorned the proposed amendment as a "sop." On July 9 Dole took representatives of the independents to a meeting with the president "to cool them off so they wouldn't be here pushing for [a] 1,000 barrel exemption," but they were not mollified.

Meanwhile Rostenkowski had been exploring ways to improve upon the relief given the independents by the Senate Finance Committee. By mid-July there were reports that southern Democrats had been approached with a proposal to exempt up to 1,000 barrels of new oil from the tax in return for their support for the Ways and Means plan. They were also offered a $3,000 tax credit for oil royalty owners, $500 more than the Administration had proposed. Rostenkowski told restive Democrats on his committee that the choice was "whether you want to lose courageously, or to win. I'd like to win."

In the closing hours of its deliberations, Ways and Means adopted extra windfall profits tax breaks for independents and royalty owners.

Not to be outbid, the White House and House Republicans hastily redrafted their bill. While the new bill did not match the Democrats in cutting taxes on oil, the improved breaks were clearly designed to neutralize the appeal of the Democrats' oil tax sweeteners.

On July 29 the House voted to adopt the revised Republican bill; 48 Democratic defections carried the day for the president. Of the 30 Democrats in the three big oil-producing states, Texas, Louisiana and Oklahoma, 12 voted with the Republicans. (For a detailed chronology, see Corrigan.)

The All-Savers Certificate

The 1981 tax act included a provision that allowed banks, credit unions, and savings and loan institutions to issue one-year tax-exempt certificates ("all-savers" certificates) that would earn 70 percent of the interest on a one-year Treasury bill. This provision was intended to lower the cost of money for these institutions, and its passage was widely credited to the vigorous lobbying of the U.S. League of Savings (which represents most of the country's 4,700 S&L's). A congressional tax specialist called the campaign "one of the finest grass roots lobbying jobs done in a long time."

Before the all-savers campaign, the U.S. League had considered other ways of staunching the S&L's hemorrhage of red ink. An effort to obtain restrictions on money market mutual funds had been abandoned when the funds' customers had deluged Congress with postcards protesting any restrictions. A proposal that government take over or "warehouse" low-yielding mortages had met with stiff opposition from the administration.

The concept of a tax-exempt certificate first surfaced in January 1981. In the following two months it was fleshed out by various League committees and finishing touches were added by the League's Washington staff who coined the "all-savers" label. Even before this process was complete, the League's Political Liaison Committee (made up of state league executives and politically well-connected members) had begun the job of selling the certificate to Congress. The committee's efforts were rewarded on May 6 when the all-savers bill was introduced in the House. On May 21 Senator Danforth (R.-MO) overcame his initial reluctance to oppose the president's wishes for a "clean" bill and introduced the bill in the Senate (with David Pryor, D.-AR).

While the industry's lobbying campaign was making headway in Congress, the administration was turning a deaf ear to the S&L's appeals for help. The Treasury had denied the FSLIC an increased line of credit and had generally shown itself hostile to any form of aid to the industry. "Well the thrifts are losing money. So what?" said Treasury Secretary Regan.

Accordingly, in early June the League wrote off the administration and concentrated its lobbying efforts on Congress. These quickly bore fruit as members flocked to sign on as co-sponsors. On June 22 the Senate Finance Committee voted unanimously to include the all-savers provision in the tax bill. The following day the administration formally abandoned its opposition to the provision.

The only remaining stumbling block was the House's wish to tie the certificates to home loans, which could have denied the bill's benefits to commercial banks. This endangered the coalition that had been assembled behind the bill. Danforth rescued the provision by adding a housing link to the Senate bill, but one so broad that it included banks and credit unions. With the provision in both House and Senate bills, passage was now certain. (See also Kulczycky)

Aviation User Taxes

The administration's budget plans, announced in February, provided for substantial tax increases for aviation users. The increases were in keeping with the administration's philosophy of making users pay for benefits received from the Federal Government.

The administration estimated that in recent years only 40 percent of the cost of operating and maintaining the air traffic control system had been defrayed by aviation tax revenues; the balance had come out of general revenues. The Administration proposed to raise the share contributed by user taxes to 85 percent (15 percent was imputed to defense-related purposes) by increasing the ticket taxes paid by commercial airline passengers from 5 to 9 percent, the fuel taxes paid by general aviation from 4 cents per gallon to 20 cents, and by raising other aviation taxes.

These proposed increases were greeted with dismay by the airlines and the general aviation industry. But it was general aviation which stood to suffer the larger increases, and its opposition was vehement. It was particularly incensed by the concept of a percentage tax that would increase as the cost of fuel rose. Lobbying by the Aircraft Owners and Pilots Association (AOPA) led the administration to abandon the percentage tax method in its March 10 budget. At the Office of Management and Budget (OMB), there was bemusement: "All of a sudden the word came down that percentage taxes were absolutely verboten. I don't know what happened."

The administration's March budget plans replaced the 20 percent tax with a

12 cents per gallon tax rising to 36 cents in 1986, and they rolled back the proposed airline passenger ticket tax from 9 to 6.5 percent. Although delighted with its victory, the AOPA still opposed the tax increases as too high, and it countered with a detailed list of cuts that it said could be made in the FAA's $3.3 billion budget.

By the end of the year Congress had still not acted on the administration's proposals. Instead it had passed stopgap measures to keep the system running. Meanwhile at least one other bill had been introduced in Congress proposing tax increases smaller than the administration's. (See also Feaver)

Commodity Tax Straddles

The 1981 Tax Act closed a tax loophole which had permitted individuals to defer or lessen tax payments by buying offsetting commodity futures contracts. At any time one contract reflected a loss and the other a gain; taxes were avoided by declaring the loss one year and the gain in the next. Straddles were used to defer tax liability or even roll it over indefinitely, or to convert ordinary income into capital gains.

Congress halted this practice by requiring that at year-end all of a taxpayer's futures contracts be lumped together, using the fair market value of the contracts as of December 31, and that the resulting net profit be taxed even though it had yet to be realized.

Although known to industry insiders for at least thirty years, this device had gained notoriety only recently as it began to be exploited by wealthy outsiders. At first commodity industry leaders claimed that tax-motivated trading was an insignificant part of their business. But when congressional studies disputed this claim, the industry accepted the need for reform but lobbied for an exemption for professional commodity traders.

In mid-June the industry suffered a setback when the Senate Finance Committee adopted a proposal, supported by the Treasury Department, to end tax straddles without any exemption for traders. On July 10, however, the House Ways and Means Committee accepted an amendment by Marty Russo (D.-IL) that allowed traders to continue to make use of straddles.

The Ways and Means vote followed an intense lobbying campaign by the Chicago-based industry executives which Robert Merry of the *Wall Street Journal* called an "old style, big money approach." "The New York boys were down, the Chicago boys were down," a congressional staffer told him.

When the Senate and House adopted their respective committees' versions of the bill, the scene of the industry's lobbying shifted to the conference committee. In a last-ditch effort to have Congress adopt their plan, top officials of the Chicago exchanges came to Washington to press their views on the conferees. New evidence was offered to show that the Senate approach would severely curtail futures trading. On July 31 industry officials waited in vain outside the conference chamber where the Senate's version was adopted. (See Merry, Prinsky, and Knight)

Incentive Stock Options

In 1978 the American Electronics Association (AEA) had started lobbying for a liberalization of the tax treatment of stock options. Specifically, the AEA wanted the taxation of stock options granted by companies to executives to be deferred until the sale of the stock (instead of when the option was received or exercised) and it wanted profits taxed as capital gains rather than as ordinary income. Congress had proved receptive, but the administration's tax plan contained no provisions regarding stock options.

Although the industry groups interested in liberalization, foremost among them the AEA and the American Business Conference (ABC), generally endorsed the president's plan, they maintained a low-key campaign. In May, for example, the ABC brought 18 corporate chairmen to Washington to meet with congressional leaders and Treasury officials.

At the end of May, with the administration still insisting on a "clean" tax bill, the groups turned their attention to Congress. The AEA initiated a letter-writing campaign and brought 160 electronics executives to Washington. Some member companies began calling the association to ask, "What's this grass roots lobbying? I thought we were supporting the president." The association's chief lobbyist explained that the president himself had opened the bidding. "The turning point was when the president officially began negotiating. . . . It was obvious that the only things that would have a chance of getting in [the bill] were things that people had an opportunity to hear about" (Keller, 1981b).

Having heard about the industry's interest, on June 23 the Senate Finance Committee adopted an amendment offered by Senators Packwood (R.-OR) and Bentsen (D.-TX) over the opposition of the administration. This amendment was in due course accepted by the Senate-House Conference Committee. (See Bacon, 1981b)

"Safe-Harbor" Tax Leasing

The 1981 Tax Act liberalized the rules regarding equipment leasing so that distressed companies would be able to "sell" tax breaks to profitable companies. Unprofitable (and low-profit) companies complain that they are discriminated against by tax incentives for investment. Without profits they have no corporate income tax liabilities against which to offset their credits. Moreover, Reagan's proposal to allow companies to write off their capital investments over shorter periods of time (10-5-3) threatened to aggravate this situation.

Lobbyists for "distressed" industries had long pushed for the "refundability" of investment tax credits (ITC's). When the administration's February budget plans failed to address this concern, executives met with Treasury Secretary Regan. He offered them no encouragement, but an administration task force was formed to study the matter.

In June, over heated Republican opposition, the House Ways and Means Committee approved a proposal to allow companies in six distressed industries to reclaim unused ITC's. The administration responded by dangling the prospect of liberalized leasing rules before lobbyists for the industries, apparently in a move to head off defections by major money-losing companies tempted by the Ways and Means bill.

On June 4 Reagan announced a revised tax cut plan which instantly drew the anger of the business community. That was replaced on June 9 by another plan that for the first time contained provisions to liberalize leasing rules. It was reportedly "one of the key concessions. . . to keep the business community fully behind the Reagan tax plan" (Edsall).

INTERPRETATION

The Reagan administration's budget plans enjoyed solid support in the business community, but at the same time they were undermined by lobbying by business interests. As anticipated, the more encompassing business organizations played a crucial role in mobilizing business support behind the president. By contrast, the lobbying that endangered the budget plans involved more narrowly-based business interests—trade or industry associations, ad hoc industry coalitions, and/or individual firms.

Not all narrow business interests undertook such lobbying. The majority of firms and business associations did not succumb to the bidding war for their support—though obviously they were not all exposed to the same degree of temptation. Some firms were conspicuous supporters of the president's program. Speaker Tip O'Neill (D.-MA) complained to the House that corporate giants such as "Philip Morris, Paine Webber, Monsanto Chemical, Exxon, McDonnell-Douglas. . .were so kind as to allow the use of their staff to the president of the United States in flooding the switchboards of America" (Wehr). This study has not tried to characterize the behavior of the universe of firms and associations, nor has it tried to quantify the extent of the erosion of business solidarity under the pressure of the bidding war. It has simply established that where slippage of support did occur it involved narrowly-based interests with fairly concrete legislative objectives. Meanwhile, the principal architects of the business coalition supporting the president were the major business organizations. These encompassing organizations played an indispensable role by resolving intrabusiness conflicts and formulating a coherent stand to which the administration and Congress could respond.

Eight cases of "special interest" lobbying were examined in detail in order to uncover the reasons for their defections from the business coalition supporting the president's budget plans. Three findings deserve mention. First, the defections did not result from any ideological repudiation of the budget plans. The special interests generally acknowledged the vital importance of passing the president's economic program, but they pressed ahead with their own provisions regardless. The following comments typify this reaction:

> The Boeing Company recognizes the need to reduce government spending and curb inflation. However, the company is concerned that the severe cuts being recommended for the Export-Import Bank may be counterproductive (Boeing's chairman, Brophy, p. 82).
>
> We support the president's program in general, but we can't support this (Edward Stimpson, president, Gen. Aviation Manufacturer's Assn., *CQ*, 1981, p. 408).
>
> A spokesman for the American Electronics Association commented that while 10-5-3 is 'important to the nation's economy and business' the association has 'an idea or two peeking out of our sleeve' about how to help hi-tech firms in particular (*Washington Post*, May 12, 1981, p. A5).
>
> In March, 1982, oblivious to any inconsistency, the thrift industry called on President Reagan to cut the federal budget and asked Congress for $10 billion in immediate aid (*Wall Street Journal*. March 4, 1982).

Second, each special interest lobby was caught in a prisoner's dilemma: If it passed up the opportunity to obtain a long-coveted amendment, it ran the risk that Congress would instead woo some other business interest which might not resist so hard. Consequently even the president's backers often expressed only conditional support for the administration's package. They made no secret of their skepticism about its chance of passing intact, and so they remained poised at the first sign of its unraveling to make sure they got their share. This point was made by various lobbyists: Clyde Farnsworth of the *New York Times* was told that if the administration's package of spending cuts "breaks apart on the Hill, and I'm not so sure it won't, then we'll fight tooth and nail to rescind the Ex-Im cuts." A spokesman for the independent oil producers said, "We probably had been as supportive of the president's economic program as any group in America, but everyone was getting his tax problem addressed except us. It became obvious we had to start a ruckus about this" (*Oil and Gas Journal*, July 20, 1981, p.25). The Aircraft Owner's chief lobbyist said, "I can't think of any scenario where Congress is going to pass this as a package. I think if things start dropping out, we've got to be on the top of the list" (*CQ*, 1981, p. 408). The American Electronics Association started a full-scale campaign for stock options because "it was obvious that the only things that would have a chance of getting in [the bill] were things that people had heard about" (Keller, 1981b).

Third, the political "balkanization" of American business presents politicians with the temptation to court segments of the business community. Thus, it appears from the case-studies that the initiative for the special interest provisions often originated in Congress rather than with the lobbyists, and it was generally the Democratic House leadership that made the running. For example, the bidding war over the tax bill can largely be understood as a result of the Democrats' strategy of trying to pry loose individual interest groups from the business coalition supporting the president (Keller, 1981b, pp. 1136-1137). Consider the part played by the Democrats in the cases examined in this paper:

- The first shot across the administration's bow in the war over synfuels was fired by the House Democratic leadership, and in two votes on funding for the Newman, Kentucky, plant, one in the House and the other in the Senate, Republican majorities opposed funding while Democratic majorities supported it. (Key Senate Republicans also provided crucial support for the industry.)
- In the decisive vote on Ex-Im Bank funding, Democrats voted 2-1 to restore funding, Republicans voted by a slim margin against it.
- The House Ways and Means bill allowed commodity traders to continue to make use of tax straddles. The president did not miss this opportunity: "Of course they're offering the poor man's tax bill and we're out to favor the rich, that's why they've gone out of their way to offer 2,500 commodity speculators a tax break of $400 million" (*New York Times*, July 15, 1981).
- The liberalization of stock options enjoyed bipartisan support in Congress. According to the American Electronics Association's chief lobbyist, "The Republicans have so many contacts with business that we find ourselves locked out sometimes. The liberals know they're bankrupt more than the conservatives. They're open to new ideas" (Hagstrom, p. 865).
- The all-savers bill also garnered bipartisan support. The chief Democratic fundraiser, Tony Coelho (D.-CA) said, "All-savers was a way to help the savings and loan industry. I appealed to them by saying they had to keep us alive" (Drew, p. 88).
- Although the safe-harbor leasing provision originated in the Treasury, it was designed to counter the House Ways and Means' proposal to refund unused Investment Tax Credits (ITCs). The retroactive ITC was denounced as a bailout by one Republican congressman: "You guys have come a long way toward being Republican on taxes, but this goes too far (*Washington Post*, June 11, 1981).

On both the oil issue and aviation user fees the parties appear to have been equally eager to win business support.

Business unity proved unable to withstand the spiral of lucrative offers and counter-offers targeted at discrete interests. The "defectors" were not opposed to the president's economic program—most enthusiastically endorsed it. But its payoff must have seemed rather remote and speculative as compared with, say, the immediate and tangible relief available from passage of an amendment addressing some specific need or grievance. In any case, no single defection by itself was going to cause the program to unravel, and if large-scale defections occurred then forbearance would have been futile anyway. It is striking that despite this logic many interests did in fact restrain their lobbying for parochial provisions in the larger interest of getting the president's program approved. That restraint dissolved with the outbreak of the bidding war for the votes of conservative Democrats and its accompanying temptations.

CONCLUSION

This study has focused on the political behavior of different levels of business interest representation. In examining business lobbying in connection with the 1981 budget, it uncovered differences between the behavior of encompassing business organizations and more narrowly-based business interests (firms, trade and industry associations, and coalitions of industries). The administration's principal allies in trying to get passage of a "pro-business" budget were the major business organizations. Although the budget also enjoyed broad support among firms and business associations, this coalition began to disintegrate under the pressure of the "bidding war" for the votes of a handful of conservative Democrats.

The study has also highlighted the strengths and weaknesses of encompassing business organizations in the United States. These organizations played an indispensable part in working out a consensus within the business community on budgeting priorities; however, even in the exceptionally hospitable political climate of 1981, they could not restrain the endemic sectionalism of American business.

What difference does it make if encompassing and more narrowly-based business organizations pursue different political agendas? After all, most firms are well aware of the potential friction between their parochial interests and the interests of the business community as a whole. That is why they typically use a variety of means of political participation, e.g., a corporate government relations office, trade association memberships, and membership in national business organizations. The profusion of forms of political involvement reflects the many-sided nature of business's political interests; the different specialized means of political representation each reflect different facets of concern. Variety is the natural spice of life.

What this argument overlooks is that there is no necessary correspondence between business's interests and the existing structures of their political representation. The collective interests of business are likely to be systematically underrepresented because of the free-rider problem. Additionally, a variety of political, social, and legal forces can influence the system of political representation independent of the underlying structure of business. Thus countries at similar stages of economic development and with similar industrial structures exhibit very dissimilar patterns of interest representation. In other words, the concrete political objectives pursued by business do not necessarily mirror business's actual interests.

This discussion has refocused attention on the *structure* of business interest representation as an independent source of variation in business's political behavior. Specifically, it has shown that business's political program may vary depending on whether business's political power is centralized or decentralized. Where that power is centralized it is likely to be used to further business's collective interests, and where decentralized to serve the particularistic ends of various sections of the business community. This proposition needs to be tested in other contexts. In particular, one intriguing implication deserves further study: It is that the U.S.'s political pluralism may make the American economy especially vulnerable to political encroachment, while corporatist political systems (such as are found in Austria and Sweden) may be more hospitable to business autonomy and freedom from detailed political interference in the market.

NOTE

In addition to the sources specifically cited below, the case studies were developed from other periodicals and newspapers, viz., *Congressional Quarterly Weekly Reports* (CQ), *Aviation Week, Industry Week, Inquiry, Iron Age, Newsweek, Oil and Gas Journal*, and *U.S. News and World Report*.

REFERENCES

Aharoni, Yair. *The No-Risk Society*. Chatham, NJ: Chatham House, 1981.

Bacon, Kenneth H. "In Tax Cut Fight, 'No-Name' Group Lobbies Hard for Business Viewpoint." *Wall Street Journal* (June 23, 1981a):23.

———. "Lobbyists Say Tax Option Break is Needed." *Wall Street Journal* (July 1, 1981b):27.

Bauer, R., I. de S. Pool, and L. Dexter. *American Business and Public Policy*. New York: Atherton, 1963.

Beer, Samuel H. *Britain Against Itself*. New York: Norton, 1982.

Bell, Daniel. *The Cultural Contradictions of Capitalism*. New York: Basic, 1976.

Brittan, Samuel. "The Economic Contradictions of Democracy." *British Journal of Political Science* 5 (1975): 129-159.

Brophy, Beth. "Political Credit." *Forbes* (June 22, 1981):78-82.

Corrigan, Richard. "Tax Relief for the Oil Interests--How the Battle Was Won." *National Journal* (August 15, 1981):1454-1460.

Cowan, Edward. "A Tax Bill 'Bidding' War Seen." *New York Times* (July 9, 1981a).

———. "GOP's Tax Strategy in House: All or Nothing." *New York Times* (July 24, 1981b):D1.

———"Carlton Group Spurns Lobbying Limelight." *New York Times* (March 18, 1982):D1, D5.

Dahl, Robert. *Dilemmas of Pluralist Democracy*. New Haven, CT: Yale University Press, 1982.

Drew, Elizabeth. "A Reporter at Large: Politics and Money--1." *New Yorker* (December 6, 1982):54-149.

Edsall, Thomas. "How a Lobbyist Group Won a Business Tax Cut." *Washington Post* (January 1, 1982):G1.

Epstein, Edwin. *The Corporation in American Politics*. Englewood Cliffs, NJ: Prentice-Hall, 1969.

Farnsworth, Clyde. "Washington Watch." *New York Times* (February 3, 1981).

Feaver, Douglas. "Pilots' Group Shoots Down Air Fuel Tax Hike." *Washington Post* (March 15, 1981):A11.

Fessler, Pamela. "Reagan Tax Plan Ready for Economic Test." *Congressional Quarterly Weekly Reports* (August 8, 1981):1431-1436.

Greider, William. "The Education of David Stockman." *Atlantic Monthly* (December 1981):27-54.

Hagstrom, Jerry. "High-Tech Leaders Have Their Own Ideas of What Government Can Do For Them." *National Journal* (May 5, 1982):861-865.

Keller, Bill. "Business Tries to Cool Its Back-street Romance with Federal Spending." *Congressional Quarterly Weekly Reports* (March 7, 1981a):406-408.

———. "Democrats and Republicans Try to Outbid Each Other in Cutting Taxes for Business." *Congressional Quarterly Weekly Reports* (June 22, 1981b): 1132-37.

———. "Jobs Appeal, Business Lobbying, Save Export-Import Bank Funding." *Congressional Quarterly Weekly Reports* (July 18, 1981c):1276-1277.

———. "Coalitions and Associations Transform Strategy, Methods of Lobbying in Washington." *Congressional Quarterly Weekly Reports* (January 23, 1982): 119-123.

Kirkland, Richard I. "Fat Days for the Chamber of Commerce." *Fortune* (September 21, 1981):144-158.

Kirschten, Dick. "Reaganomics Puts Business on the Spot." *National Journal* (December 19, 1981):2229-2232.

Knight, Jerry. "Lobbyists Fight for Tax Tricks in Commodities." *Washington Post* (May 31, 1981):E1.

Kulczycky, Maria. "All Savers Bill: From Long Shot to Big Winner." *Savings and Loan News* (September 1981):52-58.

Lindblom, Charles E. *Politics and Markets*. New York: Basic, 1977.

McClenahen, John S. "Business Coalitions: More Clout in the Capital." *Industry Week* (December 14, 1981):81-85.

McConnell, Grant. *Private Power and American Democracy*. New York: Vintage, 1966.

Merry, Robert W. "Yacht Parties and Heavyweight Lobbyists Help Commodities Interests on Capitol Hill." *Wall Street Journal* (July 14, 1981):33.

Moore, Wilbert. *The Conduct of the Corporation*. New York: Vintage, 1962.

Olson, Mancur. *The Logic of Collective Action*. New York: Schocken, 1965.

———. *The Rise and Decline of Nations*. New Haven, CT: Yale University Press, 1982.

Prinsky, Robert. "Tax Bill Backed by Commodity Industry Clears House Panel, Angering Treasury." *Wall Street Journal* (July 13, 1981a):6.

———. "Industry Pushes to Persuade Congress to Accept Its Tax Straddle Proposals." *Wall Street Journal* (July 31, 1981b):30.

———. "New Taxes on Futures Profits Elicit Ire." *Wall Street Journal* (August 4, 1981c):46.

Reich, Charles. "The New Property." *Yale Law Journal* 73, No. 5 (April 1964).

Tate, Dale. "Reagan and Rostenkowski Modify Tax Cut Proposals to Woo Conservative Votes." *Congressional Quarterly Weekly Reports* (June 6, 1981):979-980.

Thurow, Lester. *The Zero Sum Society*. New York: Basic, 1980.

Vogel, David. "Why Businessmen Distrust Their State: The Political Consciousness of American Corporate Executives." *British Journal of Political Science* 8 (1978):45-78.

———. "Businessmen Unite." *Wall Street Journal* (January 14, 1980).

Wehr, Ellen. "White House's Lobbying Apparatus." *Congressional Quarterly Weekly Reports* (August 1, 1981):1372-1373.

Wilson, James Q. *Political Organizations*. New York: Basic, 1973.

THE IMPACT OF AMERICAN
BUSINESS ON INTERNATIONAL
TRADE POLICY

Stefanie Lenway

The extent to which corporations possess political power continues to elude analysts in their attempts to evaluate the ability of business to influence public policy. Business appears to be a very powerful political actor. Corporations are highly complex institutions capable of mobilizing vast numbers of people (employees and stockholders) to participate in the political process. Corporate representatives also gain access relatively easily to the political process because of the importance of business to the government. If for some reason this access is not readily available, corporations also can aggregate money in political action committees and make campaign donations to those political candidates who are or will be in a position to further their interests.

Before concluding that it is obvious that business is easily able to influence public policy and that most policy outcomes reflect business preferences, the above observations need to be embedded in a theoretical framework. Two prom-

Research in Corporate Social Performance and Policy, volume 5, pages 27-58
Copyright © 1983 by JAI Press Inc.
All rights of reproduction in any form reserved.
ISBN: 0-89232-412-0

inent approaches to the question of corporate political power offered by the business and society literature include Edwin M. Epstein's *The Corporation in American Politics* and Charles Lindblom's *Politics and Markets*. Epstein uses the classical pluralist approach to understand corporate political activity. This theory assumes that business as an interest group is not different from other interest groups. Thus business does not have a disproportionate amount of political power and is not in a position to dominate the political process. Instead, it is one among many interest groups attempting to influence policy. In contrast Lindblom, who offers a critique of classical pluralism, argues that business is a preeminent interest group which is able to prevail in policy disputes a disproportionate part of the time. Neither Epstein nor Lindblom, however, can account for policy outcomes in the area of U.S. international trade policy.

The politics of U.S. international trade policy poses a dilemma for interest group political analysis. This dilemma stems from the observation that while the interest group activity which surrounds the decision to impose trade restraints is dominated by industry interest groups (or industry in coalition with labor organizations) and thus seems to lend support to Lindblom's basic argument with respect to the ability of business to influence public policy, the actual policy outcomes are not always congruent with the interests of these dominant interest groups and thus appear to reflect the presence of countervailing interest groups. In the case of the political decision to impose import restraints, interest group political activity is dominated by a relatively small number of producer (and labor) organizations which will benefit from a reduction of foreign competition. The costs in turn are spread among all consumers. Thus while the concentrated benefits act as incentives for producer groups to organize to obtain protection, there is very little incentive among consumers to organize to oppose trade restraints.

This asymmetry of interest group pressures violates a major assumption inherent in Epstein's work (and in all interest group pluralism) that interest groups will organize on all sides of an issue so that the policy outcome will reflect a political "equilibrium." In spite of this asymmetry in interest group political pressure, producer groups actively attempting to persuade the government to impose import restraints do not appear to be able to dominate the policy process. What is particularly interesting about trade policy is that notwithstanding the fact that the benefits are concentrated while the costs are diffuse, industry requests for trade protection are not always granted by the government. Thus while Epstein's framework cannot incorporate the asymmetry of interest group pressures by virtue of his basic assumptions, Lindblom's analysis cannot account for the fact that business does lose political battles even when issues involving business performance are at stake.

THESIS AND EVIDENCE

The primary goal of this paper is to reconcile this dilemma and explain why American trade policy has not been more protectionist in the post World War II period, given that the incentives for interest groups to organize in favor of protection are very strong while those which exist to oppose trade protection are weak. The thesis here is that the international institutional context in which trade policy is formulated, the General Agreement on Tariffs and Trade (GATT), has constrained the ability of the U.S. government to protect industries impacted by imports.[1] The U.S. government agrees to limits posed on its autonomy by this international institution and agreement because the aggregate economic benefits from trade were defined by policy makers after World War II to be in the national interest of the United States. Although the status of the United States as the hegemon in the international economic order has declined considerably since the GATT was created, the U.S. is still committed to GATT membership and to abide by GATT rules, norms and procedures.

The following analysis is not an attempt to predict whether the U.S. will continue to go along with the GATT. The argument here only suggests that as long as the United States is a member of the GATT, it will be difficult for specific protectionist sectors of the economy to prevail over this commitment. The implication of this argument for corporate political power is that, at least in the case of trade policy, business interests do not always prevail. Thus, there appear to be limits on the ability of business to influence public policy in the absence of countervailing interest groups when the policy issue has an international dimension.

The evidence for this contention is contained in the following analysis of three case studies. Each case study focuses on a trade decision which involves a specific sector of the U.S. economy. The first case involves an attempt by the U.S. textile and apparel industry to insulate the domestic market from any increases in import competition during the Tokyo Round negotiations of the GATT.[2] This analysis concerns specifically the negotiations between the industry and the U.S. government over the Carter Administration's White Paper on Textiles (made public March 1979). This statement was devised in order to obtain the support of the textile and apparel industries for the congressional ratification of the Tokyo Round Multilateral Trade Agreements. The international context for this analysis is the Multifiber Arrangement.[3]

The second case concerns the auto industry. It focuses on an attempt by the Ford Motor Company and the United Auto Workers Union to obtain temporary import relief from Japanese imports during the period between 1978 and 1980. The GATT context for the request to limit imports is Article 19 of the Charter, the escape clause.[4]

The third case, which deals with the telecommunications industry, differs from the first two in that it does not involve a direct request made by American industry for trade protection. Instead, it looks at pressure on the U.S. government brought by U.S. telecommunications producers to pry open the Japanese telecommunications equipment market. The GATT context for this case is the government procurement code negotiated during the Tokyo Round.[5] This case, although explicitly concerned with the question of trade expansion, also relates back to the question for trade protection in two respects. First, the U.S. firms were prepared to ask the government for import restraints in the absence of concrete possibilities of increased export markets. Secondly, for the U.S. to maintain the political viability for its support of an open trade policy it needs to obtain increased access to foreign markets for those goods in which it has a comparative advantage.

In this paper I will explicate the theoretical framework used to structure the case studies. Secondly, I will describe the methodology involved in piecing together the three cases. Finally, I will present the three case studies. The intent in each is to demonstrate the way in which the GATT agreement as embedded in the U.S. policy process acted as a constraint on the demands made by business for protection from foreign competition.

BUSINESS AS A POLITICAL ACTOR

Traditionally the field of business and society has adopted theory from other disciplines to help analyze the interaction between business and the environment in which it operates. In looking at the impact of business on public policy, interest group politics presented itself as a logical point of departure as it provides a theoretical framework within which to consider the degree to which interest groups influence the governmental decision-making process. As the ability of a given interest group to dominate the policy process is a function of whether one posits the political efficacy of countervailing interest groups, I will briefly review the debate within this literature (Truman, Epstein, Lindblom, and Olson) with respect to the role that either real or potential countervailing groups are expected to play in the political process.[6]

One of the most comprehensive statements of interest group politics is found in David Truman's *The Governmental Process*. Here Truman elaborates the basic assumptions inherent in interest group (or pluralist) political analysis:

- When groups have a common interest, they will organize and become politically active;
- potential interest groups exist to act as countervailing pressures to constrain the demands made by dominant interest groups; and
- the size of an interest group does not make a difference in terms of the ability of different groups to organize around a specific issue.

Truman is thus able to conclude, given the above assumptions, that policy outcomes reflect a political equilibrium. Specifically, he argues that the widely held but unorganized interests or values of the potential interest groups "serve as a balance wheel in a going political system like that of the United States'' (Truman, p. 514).

Edwin M. Epstein adopts this model in his analysis of the role that economic groups, pimarily business and labor, play in American political life. Here Epstein argues that business is not a uniquely powerful political actor and that ''the current power relationships among major social interests indicated that the outlook for corporate political control is. . . bleak'' (Epstein, p. 175). To support the contention that corporate interests will not dominate the political process Epstein relies on the notion of potential interest groups. He suggests that in fact business will never become politically dominant because ''competing interest groups would be quick to oppose, from the very inception, any efforts by business corporations to achieve hegemony in the political arena'' (p. 175).

The significance of potential interest groups has been challenged by Charles Lindblom in *Politics and Markets*. Here Lindblom contends that corporate autonomy poses an institutional barrier to a more representative democracy and that business interests in fact dominate the public policy process. Business is able to prevail in part because it is able to ensure that the potential interest groups do not challenge the principle of corporate autonomy. In addition, since the government relies on business for the health of the economy, the government has very high incentives to cater to the demands made by business groups, especially when jobs are at stake. Finally, business groups have more access to politicians than other political interest groups as a result of the government's need for business to perform to sustain economic growth. To enhance this access, business groups can also use corporate funds and the corporate organization to bring influence to bear on the political process.

For Lindblom no other interest groups have the strength to limit the ability of business to dominate the policy process. Thus public policy does not reflect a political equilibrium representative of a broad array of interests. Even the values of potential interest groups are manipulated by business through its ability to persuade citizens not to raise certain issues. Thus in Lindblom's framework it is unlikely that potential interest groups will spring into life to protect their interests as they are not even aware of what these interests are.

In *The Logic of Collective Action*, Mancur Olson offers yet another critique of potential interest groups. Olson explicitly treats participants in interest group politics as rational self-interested individuals who engage in politics to maximize their economic welfare. He argues that just as interest groups organize and enter the political process to serve their own best interests, individuals participate in these groups to further their own self-interest. The point of departure for this analysis is that ''organizations typically exist to further the common interest of groups of people'' (Olson, p. 7). This common interest consists for the most part in the provison of ''public'' or collective goods for the members of the group. He goes on to argue that although all the members of the group ''have an interest in obtaining this collective benefit, they have no common interest in paying the costs of providing the collective good'' (p. 21).

Assuming rational self-interest is the primary motivation for political action, Olson argues that large potential groups are unlikely to organize. He calls these ''latent groups'' and argues that ''however beneficial the function large voluntary associations are expected to perform, there is no incentive for any individual to join such an organization'' (p. 58). There is no incentive to join because in a large group the costs of joining for any given individual will most likely outweigh the benefits to the individual provided by the group. Even if a group is formed Olson suggests that it is unlikely to accomplish anything because ''if one member does or does not help provide the collective good, no other one member will be significantly affected and therefore no one has any reason to react'' (p. 9). He then concludes that the difference in size is crucial to an understanding of interest group formation.[7] He states:

> For the small privileged group one can expect that its collective needs will probably be met one way or another, and that voluntary action will solve its collective problems, but the large latent group cannot act in accordance with its common interests so long as the members of the groups are free to further their individual interests (Olson, p. 58).

As a result, Olson argues that there is no reason to believe that latent groups will coalesce around an issue and prevent policies from becoming overly biased in favor of certain interest groups. Instead, he suggests:

> The distinction between the privileged and intermediate groups, on the one hand, and the latent group, on the other, also damages the pluralistic view that any outrageous demands of one pressure group will be counterbalanced by the demands of other pressure groups, so that the outcome will be reasonably just and satisfactory. Since relatively small groups will frequently be able voluntarily to organize and act in support of their common interests, and since large groups normally will not be able to do so, the outcome of the political struggle amoung the various groups in society will not be symmetrical (Olson, p. 127).

Olson's analysis of the dynamics of interest group formation provides a framework upon which to base a typology of the interest groups involved in the trade policy process. Those sectors threatened by import competition fall into Olson's category of privileged (small) or intermediate groups. The collective good these groups are attempting to obtain from the government is a tariff increase or the imposition of another kind of trade barrier, e.g., a quota. The financial benefits of this increase in trade protection are sufficiently high to producer groups to provide incentives for members to contribute toward the costs of maintaining an organization to further their interests. Thus, using Olson's analysis one would expect producer groups to organize to obtain trade protection due to their small size relative to the number of consumers.

The group with the greatest interest in opposing increased trade protection is consumers. Consumers have an economic interest in opposing trade protection because they are confronted with higher prices and less choice as a result of increased trade restraints. Consumers, however, fall into Olson's category of latent groups. Thus, there is little basis upon which to expect consumers to organize in opposition to industry pressure for protection.

Although Olson's framework is useful in terms of predicting which interest groups will be active in the trade policy process, it cannot explain why those groups which do participate are not more successful. Thus, the politics of trade policy poses problems for Olson as well as for Epstein and Lindblom. Epstein's framework (as representative of interest group pluralism) would suggest that countervailing interest group activity is present in the trade policy process when in fact there is little empirical evidence for this. In contrast both Lindblom and Olson discount the political efficacy of countervailing interest groups and would lead one to expect that the interest groups which are active should prevail. Yet if they did prevail, given the amount of political activity in the U.S. in support of trade protection, U.S. trade barriers should be much more restrictive than they currently are.

Thus, the problem for analysis posed by the politics of trade policy is that while the policy outcomes are not consistently protectionist and appear to reflect the presence of countervailing interest groups, actual interest group pressure is significantly biased towards trade protection. In order to explain why interest group pressures do not play a more determinant role in U.S. trade policy, I will suggest that the international political environment has to be taken into account. In this paper I will argue specifically that the General Agreement on Tariffs and Trade, which specifies a set of constraints on the ability of contracting states to act autonomously, has led to a reduction of the ability of pressure groups within the United States to obtain the degree of protection they believe necessary.

This is not to imply, however, that U.S. interest groups will never obtain any protection from rapidly increasing foreign imports. Embedded in the GATT is the recognition that governments cannot allow market forces to undermine the social stability of regions of the country in which declining industries provide the major source of employment. Some restrictive trade agreements are very likely to accompany the underlying commitment of the United States to a liberal trading system. I will contend, however, that the degree of import restraint the U.S. industry receives from the government is less than it would have been in the absence of the GATT. The primary evidence of this contention is that in all three cases the final action taken by the U.S. differs significantly from the preferred policy of the industry.

Opposition in the United States to trade restraints is based on the belief that protectionism will retard industrial adjustment in declining sectors and lead to the loss of export markets for U.S. producers thereby resulting in a reduction of aggregate U.S. economic growth. Thus the GATT, while holding the U.S.

to agreements which appear to run counter to the interests of specific sectors in the U.S. economy, is defined to reflect the overall national interest of the United States.

METHODOLOGY

Post and Andrews in their overview of research in the business and society field argue that "case research remains a vital form of inquiry" (p. 2). Case studies can provide detailed information useful for both testing hypotheses and building theory. They go on to suggest two dimensions along which research in business and society can be organized. The first specifies whether the primary focus of the research is on the corporation or the environment in which the corporation operates. The second dimension divides research in business and society into those works which adopt an applied approach and attempt to suggest how firms can best respond to social and political pressures and studies which are more theoretical in scope. The intent of the theoretical studies is to explain different aspects of the relationship between business and society rather than to suggest ways in which the corporation can more effectively manage environmental pressures.

In terms of the above framework, the cases in this study have as their research focus the interaction between business and society (here, specifically the government). In addition, the research orientation is theoretical. The intent of the cases is not to advise management in terms of how to manipulate the political process more effectively in order to obtain trade restraints. Instead, the motivation for undertaking the case studies was to explain why the three sectors representative of American industry in general were not more successful in obtaining the protection they believed to be necessary.

The cases were structured around three different bodies of theory which are summarized in Exhibit 1. These cases are grounded in international economics which explains the basis for trade between countries in terms of the theory of comparative advantage. In general this theory, which provides the basis for most neo-classical international economics, suggests that if nations can organize an international market for goods, they will be able to increase substantially the level of both domestic and international aggregate economic efficiency through exporting those goods which they can produce more cheaply relative to other countries and importing those goods which they produce at above market prices. In terms of the factor endowments of the United States this would imply that the U.S. should specialize in the production of goods which are relatively capital-intensive and which embody a high degree of technological sophistication. In terms of this perspective the telecommunications industry is a sector in which the U.S. should attempt to expand its export markets. The theory of comparative advantage further suggests that the U.S. should not produce goods which are

Exhibit 1. Economic and Political Context of the Case Studies

Industry	Factor Intensity	U.S. Comparative Advantage	Future as Prescribed by International Economics	Political Position of the Industry On Trade Policy
Textiles/Apparel	Labor-intensive	Declining vis à vis LDC producers	Mostly replaced by imports	Strongly protectionist
Autos	Capital-intensive, but labor costs make a difference (U.S. labor is expensive)	Momentarily the U.S. industry is not competitive because of gasoline price increases	Restructure the industry; it may become smaller but will again be competitive	Ford and the UAW argue for temporary import restraints
Telecommunications	Capital/technology-intensive	U.S. currently competitive	Try to expand export markets through changes in government procurement policy	Split— part wants to isolate U.S. market —other segment interested in expanding export market

35

labor-intensive because the high labor costs in the U.S. relative to less developed countries make these goods non-competitive on the international market. In the context of the case studies, this implies that the U.S. should restructure its textile/ apparel industry in order to phase out the labor-intensive production of textile and apparel goods. Finally, the theory of comparative advantage also indicates that the U.S. has temporarily lost is competitive edge in some sectors due to outmoded production process and products; but that with new investment and considerable restructuring of the industry, the U.S. once again can become competitive internationally. This is the international economic context within which the auto industry found itself when the UAW and the Ford Motor Company requested temporary relief from imports.

The three sectors were chosen so that each represents a different part of the spectrum of the international competitive posture of the U.S. industry. Although the experience of these three sectors may not be generalizable to American business as a whole, this collection of cases should capture the basic political conflict in the United States between free trade and protection. James Kurth provides some support for looking at these three sectors in his contention that "the political outcomes of the next decade. . . may be shaped by the conflict between protectionist industries (textiles, steel, and recently chemicals) and free trade ones (aerospace, computers, telecommunciations), with a swing position being held by the automobile industry whose interests are divided and conflict-ing" (p. 33).

The second kind of theory used in structuring and interpreting the materials upon which the case studies were based is taken from international politics. International relations theory was used to explain why the United States was willing to collaborate over the norms and rules of international trade as embodied in the GATT charter. Ernst Haas suggests that "the need for collaboration arises from the recognition that the costs of national self-reliance are usually excessive" (p. 357). In the context of trade policy this implies that states will agree not to impose trade restrictions on a unilateral basis because they recognize that they will be better off if each agrees not to engage in restrictive trade practices. The emphasis on international collaboration is introduced into the three cases through a discussion of the international agreements and negotiations which put con-straints on the autonomous actions states can take in trade policy.

OVERVIEW OF THE CASES

The core of the cases consists of the domestic politics of each decision. Interest group analysis directed the research on the cases towards identifying the dominant interest groups involved in each, the government agency where they chose to make their case, and the arguments made in defense of their position. The analysis, however, does not attempt to explain the outcomes of the three cases

Exhibit 2.   Aggregate vs. Group Interests in U.S. Trade Policy

	International[1] *Economics*	*Interest Group*[2] *Politics*
Textiles/ Apparel	The U.S. is loosing its comparative advantage to low cost LDC producers. Non-competitive U.S. producers should be phased out.	As the competitive pressures from imports increase, the industry demands more protection.
Auto	U.S. producers have been making the wrong product for current market conditions. For the U.S. industry to regain its position in the international market, it needs to be subject to foreign competition.	The industry asks for protection to reduce the financial risk involved in the conversion process to front-wheel-drive cars.
Telecommunications	The U.S. is a leader in technological innovations (the digital switch). The U.S. should attempt to gain access to foreign markets and keep its own open.	As the U.S. market is the largest in the world, a segment of the industry has tried to isolate it from foreign competition.

Notes:
[1]Assumes the primary value is economic efficiency.
[2]No apriori hierarchy of interests.

in terms of the differences among the various political actors. In each case the interest groups involved differ from one another. The textile/apparel cases involves a coalition of several industry trade associations and labor unions while the auto case involves one firm, the Ford Motor Company and one union, the United Auto Workers Union. The Electronic Industries Association (EIA) was the most visible interest group in the telecommunciations case. It is perhaps a shortcoming of interest group political analysis and of this study that these various political actors are considered to be in this context relatively homogeneous. The intent in each of the three cases is to demonstrate how the international political framework in which trade policy is conducted constrains the ability of these domestic interest groups to dominate the policy process.

While Congress is the most vulnerable branch of the government to pleas for import restraint, as producers in declining industries and workers displaced from their jobs are also constitutents, the Executive branch tends to rely more on international economics rather than interest group pressures as the basis for formulating trade policy. The tension between the policy outcomes which would result from interest group pressures and those which are informed by international economic theory can be seen below.

Congress' recognition of its vulnerability to interest group pressures for import protection led it to delegate to the Executive branch the authority to engage in trade negotiations on behalf of the United States in 1934. The Executive branch, however, is not uniformly committed to an open trading policy. The primary agencies in the Executive branch involved in trade policy are the Departments of State, Treasury, Commerce, Labor, the Office of the Special Trade Representative, and the Council of Economic Advisors (CEA). The Treasury Department has the reputation of supporting liberal trade policies because they are anti-inflationary. The Council of Economic Advisors tends to agree with the Treasury, again because of its concern with the cost of protection. The State Department also supports open trading policies, but for reasons different from the Treasury and the CEA. It identifies the national interest with the international stability in economic relations of the United States. Thus it opposes most potential import restraints which would disrupt the trade flows of other nations. The Commerce Department in contrast is more likely to support an industry in its pleas for import restraints because it considers U.S. business to be its primary constituency. The Department of Labor, given its concern with American jobs, tends to side with the Commerce Department in discussions over whether the U.S. should impose trade restraints. The Office of the Special Trade Representative sees Congress as its main constituency. Its overall concern is with the maintenance of an open trade regime, although the STR negotiators are always sensitive to the Congressional reaction to a particular trade policy. Thus, they appear to be willing to make exceptions if necessitated by domestic political pressures.

The three studies indicate that in spite of industry pressure for protection, the U.S. has basically adhered to the GATT agreement. Currently, however, in the United States political pressures for trade protection are increasing. While the cases help to explain the way in which the GATT has helped to sustain a commitment to an open trading system in the U.S., they cannot be used to predict future developments in U.S. trade policy.

TEXTILES AND APPAREL: THE POLITICS OF PROTECTION

As the Tokyo Round negotiations began to draw to a close late in 1978, the U.S. textile/apparel industry threatened to use its political clout to block the congressional ratification of the agreements. The opposition of the textile/apparel industry to trade agreements stemmed from the willingness on the part of U.S. negotiators to include tariff reductions in textile and apparel products as a concession to the European Community. To obtain the industry's support for ratification, the Carter administration decided to devise a program for the textile/apparel industry which was made public in the form of a White Paper. There was a belief within the Administration, especially within the Office of the Special Trade

Representative, that the opposition of the textile/apparel industry to the Tokyo Round agreements would be sufficient to block their ratification, thereby threatening the stability of the international trading system. Robert Strauss, the chief STR, saw the White Paper as a way of eliminating this possibility. The Textile White Paper was a part of a larger strategy orchestrated by Strauss to obtain widespread support for the ratification of the Tokyo Round Agreements.

The first draft of the Textile Industry White Paper was formulated in a series of meetings between industry representatives and Alan Wolff, a high ranking STR negotiator, during January 1979. This initial draft was then revised in meetings of the interagency Trade Policy Committee in which the Treasury Department and the CEA played a large role in reducing the strength of the trade restrictions which the government agreed to in the White Paper. The significance of the White Paper, in the context of this study, is that although it did offer the textile/apparel industry some additional protection from rapidly increasing imports, the final version did not include any of the industry's demands that would have caused the U.S. to abrogate the terms of the Multifiber Arrangement (MFA). The MFA, first negotiated September 14, 1973, regulates trade in textile products of wool, man-made fibers, and cotton and is administered under the auspices of the GATT.

In order to place the White Paper in the context of the MFA, I will first briefly review the changes in textile trade which led to the negotiation of the MFA, those aspects of the MFA relevant to the White Paper, and the ways in which the initial draft of the White Paper involved violating the basic tenets of the agreement. Finally, I will demonstrate how the demands made by the industry that would have involved breaking the MFA were not incorporated into the final version of the White Paper.

U.S. Trade Policy in the Textile/Apparel Industry

Since the 1930s the U.S. textile/apparel industry has argued for restricting imports. The first formal agreements to restrain trade in textile/apparel products in the United States were negotiated in 1937 between representatives of the U.S. and Japanese industries. The U.S. industry raised the question of the need for quantitative restrictions on textile/apparel products in the mid 1950s after U.S.-Japanese negotiations at the GATT resulted in a steep reduction in the U.S. tariff on these products.

Competitive pressure within the textile/apparel industry became intense as a result of the post-World War II diffusion of standard technologies which did not have high skill requirements. Because of this diffusion of technology, countries with low labor costs developed a strong competitive advantage in the production of textile and apparel products. In response to the increase in foreign competition, the U.S. industry has been very successful in persuading the government that these rapid increases in imports from low wage countries will force the majority of U.S. textile and apparel producers out of business.

The industry argues that increased imports of textile and apparel products are devastating as a result of the magnitude and composition of the workforce. The textile and apparel industries together employ two to three million workers in primarily labor-intensive jobs. Representatives of both industries suggest that these jobs are threatened by any increase in textile apparel imports to the United States because of the high cost of American labor relative to other textile and apparel producers. They further contend that it is important that imports do not reduce employment opportunities in these sectors because textile and apparel jobs provide employment for women and minorities in regions of the United States where there are few sources of alternative employment.

In order to reduce the degree of social dislocation attributed to imports of cotton textile and apparel products, in 1961 the first multilateral negotiations were held between importing and exporting countries to establish quotas on these products. Although these quotas represented a significant concession on the part of the exporting countries, they were considered to be preferable to the unregulated proliferation of trade restraints, the most likely alternative. In return for this concession, the importing states agreed to ensure the orderly growth of trade.

In 1973 the multilateral agreement regulating trade in cotton textile/apparel products was expanded to cover trade in manmade fibers, wool, and silk and renamed the Multifiber Arrangement (MFA). The MFA regulates a series of bilateral restrictive trade agreements in textile/apparel products within a framework designed to ensure the continual growth of trade in the sector. The MFA is restrictive in that it has led to the creation of a legal framework within which importing countries could establish quotas on imports to avoid "market disruption." Market disruption was defined as a sudden increase in imports of specific products from specific countries which are sold at prices substantially lower than the prevailing market prices for similar goods in the importing country.

The quotas sanctioned by this agreement were aimed at reducing the potential disruptive effects of rapid increases in trade. They were not, however, designed to seal off producers in the importing countries from competitive pressures. In order to ensure the continual growth in trade, the restrictions which were allowed by the MFA included strict growth and flexibility provisions.

In the Multifiber Arrangement the importing countries agreed that the annual quota could not be set at levels less than the level of trade in the prevous 12 months and must be increased by six percent per year. The importing countries also agreed to certain flexibility provisions which allow suppliers to ship at above quota levels in products in which they have a strong market. These flexibility provisions include swing, which allows exporters to move yardage from one category to another; carryover, which allows shortfalls in one year to be transferred to the next year; and carryforward, in which yardage can be borrowed from the next year. The combination of the quota restrictions with the growth and flexibility provisions was to allow for the natural dynamic growth of the textile industry and textile trade while at the same time provide some protection for importing countries from the social dislocation caused by rapid increases of low cost imports.

The White Paper

In the initial negotiations over the White Paper, the textile/apparel industry hoped to eliminate the growth and flexibility provisions from U.S. textile/apparel policy. In these negotiations with the government, the industry suggested that the United States

1. impose a global import quota;
2. tie the increase in all quotas to the rate of growth of the U.S. market;
3. reduce the flexibility provisions through a reduction of unfilled quotas; and
4. reduce aggregate imports from Hong Kong, Taiwan, and Korea to allow more room for new suppliers.

The initial version of the White Paper drafted by the STR office gave the head of the STR the personal responsibility to carry out a global import evaluation which would involve an analysis of the impact of textile and apparel imports from all countries in terms of market growth of the United States. In this statement, the industry was trying to extract two policy changes from the government.

The first was to set up a global quota, i.e., aggregate limits on the amount of textile/apparel imports which could come into the U.S. The use of a global quota to determine the maximum imports the U.S. would allow from any country would be far more restrictive than the current policy. The U.S. has not explicitly taken into account the aggregate level of imports in setting quotas for individual exporting countries because under this policy, in order to make room for new suppliers, existing quotas would have to be cut.

The second major change in U.S. policy implicit in this statement was the tying of the growth in quotas to the growth in the U.S. market. This would involve a reduction in quota growth from the six percent per year required by the MFA to about two percent, the rate of growth of the U.S. market. This change in American textile/apparel policy would take away from the exporter's guaranteed access to the U.S. market.

The industry further requested that unused quotas also be reduced, thereby preventing foreign suppliers from regaining their original position in the U.S. market. The initial draft statement stated that to eliminate harmful fluctuations in shipments from countries where quotas were undershipped in the previous year, shipments were to be limited to the previous year's shipments plus one-half of the unfilled portion of the previous year's quotas as a matter of prin-

Exhibit 3. Textile Industry White Paper

	Industry Demand	Previous U.S. Policy	U.S. Policy as Stated in White Paper
Global quotas	The government should set an overall aggregate limit on textile/apparel imports to the U.S.	Only focused on setting limit for individual suppliers. Never explicitly consider aggregate imports in setting individual quotas.	Agreement to conduct a global import evaluation. No implication that this would lead to establishing a global quota.
Quota growth tied to U.S. market growth	Reduce yearly quota growth from 6% per year to 2% per year, the growth in the U.S. market.	Consistent with MFA—6% quota growth per year.	No commitment to tying increased quota grow to rate of growth of U.S. market.
Flexibility provisions	Promote orderly growth by limiting shipments in categories which the quota was not used entirely to previous year's shipments plus ½ unfilled portion of previous year's shipment as a matter of principle.	Allow exporters to: 1) move yardage from one category to another, 2) allow shortfalls to be transferred to the next year, and 3) allow exporters to borrow from the next year's quota.	The suggestion that yearly increases in unusual quotas should not exceed previous year's shipment plus one-half of the unused portion of the previous year's quota was made in very ambiguous language.
Reduce surges from major exporters (Korea, Hong Kong, Taiwan)	Hold imports for Korea, Taiwan, Hong Kong, to 1978 trade levels or 1979 base levels, whichever is lower.	Allow quota growth consistent with MFA—6% per year.	Bilateral negotiations with Hong Kong, Korea, Taiwan did tighten flexibility provisions to reduce the probability of rapid increases in imports. The changes came within the bounds of the MFA.

ciple. If implemented, this statement would have the effect of reversing post-war U.S. trade policy which allowed for the orderly but positive growth in textile imports.

The industry's final major request, which would have forced the U.S. to violate the terms of the MFA, provided that imports from Hong Kong, Korea, and Taiwan be held at 1978 trade levels or 1979 base levels, whichever were lower. This involved a clear abrogation of our bilateral agreements with all exporting countries, which permit a six percent increase in quotas per year. Ultimately, the primary tangible benefit the industry obtained from the White Paper was a commitment to tighten the flexibility provisions in the bilateral agreements which covered imports from Korea, Hong Kong, and Taiwan. These changes, however, were negotiated within the parameters of MFA and did not include tying the growth of imports from these countries to the rate of growth of the U.S. market.

The major changes in the draft version of the White Paper were made during meetings of the interagency Trade Policy Committee. This committee included representatives from the Office of the Special Trade Representative, the Council of Economic Advisors, and from the Departments of State, Commerce, the Treasury, and Labor. The CEA and the Treasury were the most active opponents of any major changes in U.S. policy implicit in the initial version of the White Paper. The modifications of the initial document primarily involved increasing the ambiguity of the language to the extent that the government did not obligate itself to any changes in policy. The negotiators from the office of the Special Trade Representative were convinced, and they ultimately persuaded the Trade Policy Committee, that the key to the success of the White Paper was the ambiguity of the language.

In addition to a tightening of the flexibility provisions with Hong Kong, Korea, and Taiwan, the industry received a very weak commitment from the government to reduce quota growth in the event that filling unused quotas combined with the quota increase required by the MFA could create a surge of imports thereby disrupting the U.S. market. The industry, however, did not get a firm commitment that a global quota would be imposed or that the rate of increase in quotas would be limited to the rate of growth of the U.S. market.

The failure of the U.S. textile/apparel industry to persuade the government to adopt a trade policy which would insulate the industry almost entirely from import competition can in part be attributed to the willingness of the United States to adhere to the Multifiber Arrangement as a part of the broader GATT framework. Although the political power of the industry will probably prevent any significant liberalization of trade in the textile/apparel industry in the near future, the international political framework within which textile/apparel trade is regulated does appear to provide constraints on the ability of the industry to insulate itself completely from foreign competition and hence from all pressures for adjustment.

AUTOS: THE POLITICS OF ESCAPE

The focus of the auto industry case is on the petition brought by the United Auto Workers Union and the Ford Motor Company before the United States International Trade Commission June 12, 1980, for temporary relief from import competition. The International Trade Commission (ITC) is an independent agency set up by the Congress to determine whether an industry has been injured by imports. The Congress established the ITC in part to act as a buffer from industry requests for import protection. If the ITC finds that the industry has been injured the Commission then recommends to the President that the industry receive some relief from import competition. This relief can involve tariff increases, the imposition of quotas or a combination of both these remedies.

In the 1974 Trade Act, Congress mandated that the following conditions had to be met for the Commission to find injury.

1. There must be increased imports—either actual or relative to domestic production—of an article into the United States.
2. The domestic industry producing an article like or directly competitive with the imported one must be seriously injured or threatened with serious injury.
3. The increased imports must be a substantial cause of serious injury, or the threat thereof, to the domestic industry making the article (U.S. International Trade Commission, 1980, p. 93).

The House and Senate report on the escape clause further specified that for an import to be a substantial cause of injury the following two criteria must be met in all cases:

1. Imports must be an important cause of serious injury and;
2. imports must be no less important than any other single cause (U.S. International Trade Commission, 1980, p. 93).

Congress left to the discretion of the ITC commissioners the specification and weight of the factors which are determined to be a source of injury to the industry. As there are no established objective criteria with respect to how to determine the causes of injury or how to weigh them once they are isolated, to some extent the injury determination is left to the subjective judgement of the individual commissioners.

The International Trade Commission's injury determination legitimates any actions the United States may take under Article 19 (the escape clause) of the GATT. Article 19 allows member-states to withdraw tariff concessions on a temporary basis "that as a result of changed circumstances are causing or threatening serious injury of like or competitive products as a result of unforeseen developments'' (Dam. p. 99). The rationale for including this clause in the GATT was that if countries had the assurance that they could temporarily suspend a tariff concession under certain conditons, they would be more likely to take risks in negotiating tariff reductions.

The imposition of trade restraints in response to an injury petition is, however, not automatic on the part of GATT members. The success of the auto industry in obtaining a positive ruling from the Commission depended on their ability to demonstrate a causal relationship between increase in imports to the United States and injury to the industry. Ultimately, the auto industry was unable to do this. The Commission by a 3-2 vote found that imports were not a major cause of injury to the industry. In order to explain this vote I will briefly review the changes in the U.S. automobile market which led to a decline in the competitive advantage of U.S. producers in the U.S. market, the major arguments put forth by the UAW and the Ford Motor Company in support of their petition, and the rationale for the commissioners' decision.

Automobile Industry Policies

After World War II, U.S. automobile producers concentrated primarily on the production of large cars because the sales margins were significantly larger than they were on smaller cars. A House staff report on the auto industry argued that (in the 1960's) "Detroit didn't mind losing 15 percent of the total U.S. market because this segment represented mostly small cars which have a low profit margin" (U.S. Congress, House, p. 53). The specialization in the production of large cars did not pose problems for the industry until the Arab Oil boycott in 1973 led to rapid increases in the price of gasoline. This price increase triggered a sudden increase in the demand for small cars which was unexpected by both the foreign and domestic producers. Foreign producers, however, were better positioned to respond to this shift in demand because in most markets outside the United States fuel efficiency had always been an important factor in automobile design.

After the Arab oil boycott, the U.S. retained a policy of price controls which kept the domestic price of gasoline below world market prices. Once the price stabilized, consumers returned to their preference for larger automobiles. In order to encourage the auto producers to increase the fuel efficiency of American cars without decontrol of the price of gasoline, Congress passed the Energy Policy Conservation Act in 1975. This act set the minimum standards for gasoline mileage for autos produced in the U.S., between 1978 and 1985. By 1985 the law required that passengers cars average 27.5 miles per gallon.

Even prior to this the automobile companies began to implement their own downsizing program to increase fuel efficiency. In downsizing, fuel economy is improved through weight reduction and aerodynamic improvements rather than through fundamental changes in technology. In addition, Ford, GM, and Chrysler also formulated plans to phase in front-wheel-drive cars which required new engines and other components; this program was significantly more expensive than downsizing.

Although the U.S. auto producers' strategies to develop a fuel-efficient car varied, they all revealed an underlying belief that the auto firms had sufficient control over the market to "walk it down" at their own pace. This belief, however, was shattered by the Iranian revolution in the fall of 1978 which resulted in yet another sudden increase in U.S. gasoline prices. These price increases translated into a sudden rise in the demand for small cars. The Department of Transportation (DOT) analysis of the impact of this increase in imports on the industry suggests that despite the efforts of the auto producers to downsize and come up with plans to produce front-wheel-drive automobiles, again they were not prepared to meet this sudden shift in demand (U.S. Department of Transportation, p. iv).

The U.S. auto industry was especially vulnerable to the decline in demand for large cars when the Iranian oil crisis hit, because it was in the middle of the most massive conversion process it had ever attempted—to retool for the production of front-wheel-drive cars. Industry analysts estimated that the cost of this conversion process during the period between 1979 and 1985 would be more than $70 billion in 1980 dollars. The ITC study of the auto industry found that in January-June 1980 the industry reported losses of $2.9 billion, compared with a net operating profit of $2.7 billion in the corresponding period in 1979. (U.S. International Trade Commission, 1980, p. A-43). As Table 1 indicates, U.S. production declined in 1979 to 8.5 million units from 9.2 million units in 1978.

Table 1.   U.S. Imports, Production, and Sales of Autos

Year	Total Imports	$\%^1$	Japan Imports	$\%^2$	$\%^3$	U.S. Production	U.S. Sales
1972	2,485.9	23	697.8	6	*	8,828.2	10.950
1973	2,437.3	21	624.8	5	−1	9,667.2	11,439
1974	2,572.6	29	791.8	9	+27	7,324.5	8,867
1975	2,074.7	24	695.6	8	−12	6,717.0	8,640
1976	2,536.7	25	1,128.9	11	+62	8,497.9	10,110
1977	2,790.1	25	1,341.5	12	+19	9,213.7	11,185
1978	3,024.9	27	1,563.0	14	+17	9,176.6	11,312
1979	3,005.5	28	1,617.3	15	+3	8,433.7	10,671
1980	3,248.3	36	1,991.5	22	+23	6,375.5	8,979

Notes:

All units are thousands of automobiles.

[1]Import sales as a percent of total U.S. sales

[2]Japanese sales as a percent of total U.S. sales

[3]Percent change of Japanese sales over previous year

Source:

"MVMA—Motor Vehicles Facts & Figures 1981 (Detroit, MI: Motor Vehicles Manufacturers Association, 1981), pp. 7, 69, and 71.

By 1980 U.S. production was down to 6.4 million units. This decline in production and sales of American cars was accompanied by a rapid increase in the sales of imports. Total automotible imports to the U.S. increased from 27 percent of sales in 1978 to 36 percent of the U.S. market during 1980.

The International Trade Commission Petition

In response to this decline in sales by U.S. producers and the increase in market penetration by imports, the United Auto Workers Union and the Ford Motor Company turned first to Congress and then to the International Trade Commission to petition the government to provide temporary relief from import competition. The remedy suggested by the Ford Motor Company involved "a five-year quota with the overall limit established at 1976 representative levels of 1.7 million units" (Ford Motor Company, p. IV-3). Of this overall quota 930,000 units would be allocated to Japan with the remainder of the quota assigned to European producers. This proposed remedy would involve a 50 percent reduction of Japanese imports from 1980 sales levels. In support of this petition, the UAW and Ford argued before the Commission that the decline in sales, employment and profitability was a direct result of the increase in imports. Ultimately, however, the Commission determined that the shift in consumer demand from large to small cars (as distinct from imports) and the recession were more significant causes of injury to the industry than the increase in imports.

The UAW petition begins by establishing that while in the first quarter of 1980 imports were 50 percent higher than in the comparable period in 1979, U.S. production of the first four months of 1980 dropped 26.6 percent in units as compared with the same period in 1979 (United Auto Workers Union, p. 116). To link this decline in U.S. production to the increase in imports, the UAW argued that fuel efficiency could not be used to differentiate American-made automobiles from imports. This contention was based on the argument that post-war U.S. trade policy, i.e., low taxes on gasoline and automobiles and government funding of the highway system, created disincentives for U.S. producers to emphasize fuel efficiency as an important characteristic of American cars. The UAW petition emphasized that the rationale used by the auto companies in determining the type of cars to produce should be the relevant criteria for deciding the appropriate attributes of American-made cars. The emphasis of their argument was on the constraints inherent in the decision with respect to the kind of automobile to produce rather than on the factors which the consumer considers in deciding upon what kind of automobile to purchase. The petition then concludes that imports were a close, if not direct substitute for American automobiles and that "the dramatic sales increase by the foreign manufacturers in the United States has directly affected the level of sales which could be achieved by domestic manufacturers" (p. 201).

The Ford Motor company petition makes essentially the same arguments as

the UAW petition with respect to the impact of imports on domestic auto producers. The Ford petition also provides a response to the contention that the
major problems the automobile industry has had to confront were due primarily
to the recession and the inability of U.S. producers to meet the demand for small
cars in the U.S. The petition states that the recession was not the major cause
of injury to the industry because industry profitability began to decline in 1977
due to the increased sales of imports, two years before the recession began. In
addition, Ford argued that the recession could not be a more important cause of
injury to the industry than imports because even during the recession sales of
imported cars increased while aggregate new car sales were down.

In response to the argument that the general shift in demand from large to
small cars was an important cause of injury, Ford contended that the shift in
demand in the U.S. was from large cars to small imports and not to small cars
in general. The Ford prehearing brief suggested that "the significant question is
whether there has been an increase in imports. . . and a decline in the proportion
of the domestic market supplied by domestic producers" (Ford, p. 29). Ford
concluded that "consumer preference for imports is precisely the problem" (p.
31). In this line of reasoning, Ford, like the UAW, attempted to convince the
Commission that all cars are essentially similar and that the underlying factors
which may have had an effect on consumer demand were irrelevant as causes
of injury.

The Commission, however, rejected the arguments presented by the UAW
and Ford. The two commissioners who voted to accept the Ford petition argued,
"No single adverse economic factor has plagued our domestic economy during
the past several years which even approaches the disastrous effect caused by
imports of passenger automobiles on this domestic industry" (International Trade
Commission, 1980, p. 117). The majority of the Commission, however, decided
that imports were not the most significant cause of injury to the industry. Instead
they found that the recession, the shift in demand from large to small cars in
general (not specifically to imports), and the fact that the industry representatives
did not make a convincing case that import relief would really benefit the automobile manufactuers provided reasonable justification to reject the petition.

The Japanese Voluntary Restraint Agreement

In the wake of this defeat, both Ford and the UAW attempted again to persuade
Congress to pass legislation which would impose quotas on Japanese imports to
the U.S. Senators Danforth (R.-MO) and Bentsen (D.-TX) introduced legislation
which would impose a quota of 1.6 million cars a year on Japan for three years.
(In 1980, 1.9 million Japanese cars were sold in the U.S.) The Reagan Administration used this proposed legislation as leverage with which to persuade the
Japanese government to "voluntarily" impose export restraints. On May 1, 1981,

Exhibit 4. Proposed Remedies for the Auto Industry

	Overall Import Limitations	Japanese Import Restraints
Ford Petition	1.7 million units for 5 years	930,000 units (50% reduction)
Danforth Bill	NONE	1.6 million for 3 years
VRA with Japan	NONE	1.68 million units; 16.5% growth of U.S. car sales per year for 3 years.

the Japanese government agreed to restrict exports to the U.S. to 1.68 million units for the fiscal year April 1, 1980, to March 31, 1982. The following year's shipments would be 1.68 million units plus 16.5 percent of the growth of the U.S. automobile market. The government of Japan also agreed to monitor exports in the third year to prevent a rapid increase in exports to the United States.

The Japanese voluntary restraint agreement (VRA) diffused the movement in Congress to legislate import quotas. The agreement, however, was not stringent enough to ensure that domestic producers could increase significantly their sales of large and intermediate-sized cars. Assuming that without export restraints, the Japanese would have sold 2.1 million units in 1981 in the U.S., the first-year limit involved a reduction of 420,000 units. As the industry would probably pick up only about half of these sales due to the shortage of small car production in the U.S., the domestic producers as a group would sell only an additonal 210,000 units. Although most of the producers saw this as a step in the right direction, industry analysts did not consider the increase in domestic sales big enough to make a substantial difference in their profitability.

Thus, the ability of the industry to obtain the protection necessary to force consumers to shift back to cars that were not fuel-efficient, i.e., the majority of those produced by American manufacturers, was limited by the GATT escape clause procedures. These procedures enabled Congress to deflect direct political pressure from the industry which was aimed at persuading Congress to legislate quotas. While the VRA with Japan was negotiated outside of the GATT framework, legislated quotas would have been in direct violation of the GATT agreement and could have seriously threatened the stability of the international trading system.

TELECOMMUNICATIONS: THE POLITICS OF EXPANSION

The telecommunications case differs from the previous two in that it does not involve an overt move on the part of the industry to protect the American telecommunications market. Instead, the U.S. used the GATT negotiations over the government procurement code to gain access for U.S. telecommunications producers to the Japanese market as a way of diffusing potential political pressure from the industry to restrict access to the U.S. market in telecommunications products.

The government procurement code was negotiated during the Tokyo Round of the GATT in order to provide that state agencies would not discriminate in their procurement practices in favor of national suppliers. The general rationale for negotiating the code was to reduce domestic political pressure on governments to buy only locally produced goods by requiring code signatories to entertain bids from foreign suppliers on an equal basis as those from domestic firms. The agreement states its goal is "to secure greater international competition and thus more effective use of tax revenues and other public funds through the application of commercial considerations when governments purchase for their own use" (General Agreement on Tariffs and Trade, p. 137). Prior to the government code, the GATT allowed local sourcing by government agencies. As the Japanese telecommunications firm Nippon Telephone and Telegraph (NTT) was state-owned, prior to its inclusion under the government procurement code it was not required to treat bids from foreign firms on an equal basis with those submitted by Japanese firms.

The American telecommunications industry had also been protected from foreign competition as long as the Federal Communciations Commission (FCC) supported the Bell system's argument that, to retain the integrity of the system, foreign (non-Bell) equipment could not be "plugged into" the Bell system. However, once the FCC began to deregulate the interconnect market in the mid 1960's and allowed consumers to buy their telephones and telephone systems, imports of telecommunications equipment into the United States increased. A report made by the International Trade Commission on the interconnect market found that between 1976 and 1977 imports increased from $87 to $127.6 million (International Trade Commission, 1979, p. 21). Table 2 shows that while imports to the U.S. in telecommunciations equipment increased dramatically as a result of changing U.S. regulatory policy, U.S. producers found limited opportunity to increase their exports as the state-owned Japanese and European telecommunications firms continued to discriminate against foreign suppliers. During this period U.S. exports to Japan were negligible.

The Network of Interests

This imbalance in trade prompted several U.S. firms to pressure the negotiators in the Office of the Special Trade Representative to use the negotiations over the government procurement code as a means to obtain access to the Japanese telecommunications equipment market. The negotiations over whether to include

Table 2. U.S. Imports and Exports of Telecommunications Equipment
(1960-1980)*

Year	Imports	Exports	Balance
1960	124.0**	271.2	147.2
1961	158.0	329.2	171.2
1962	212.4	438.8	226.4
1963	211.5	472.6	261.1
1964	224.4	404.4	180.0
1965	314.0	345.7	31.7
1966	486.3	381.1	(105.2)
1967	536.3	474.8	(61.2)
1968	736.6	532.3	(204.6)
1969	1,005.9	617.9	(388.0)
1970	1,102.5	674.5	(428.0)
1971	1,381.8	692.7	(689.1)
1972	1,671.5	852.8	(818.7)
1973	2,057.0	1.059.7	(997.3)
1974	2,315.2	1,395.3	(919.9)
1975	2,098.3	1,629.6	(468.7)
1976	3,676.2	2,061.3	(1,614.9)
1977	3,748.8	2,196.5	(1,551.3)
1978	5,074.0	2,542.4	(2,531.6)
1979	5,098.0	2,800.7	(2,297.3)
1980	5,460.9	3,296.5	(2,164.4)

Notes:
*Before 1960 statistics on telecommunications equipment were not reported.
**In millions of dollars.
Source: UN Yearbook of International Trade Statistics, 1960-1980.
SITC = 724.0

NTT under the code were perhaps among the most difficult of those held during the Tokyo Round.

They were complicated by the fact that even after the Japanese government agreed that NTT would accept bids from U.S. firms, it was politically unacceptable to extend these bidding opportunities to the European Community. The EC, like Japan, has state-owned telecommunications companies. The U.S., however, accepted an offer from the EC specifing those government agencies to be included under the government procurement code which did not include telecommunications because it opened between $8 and $10 billion in procurement contracts. (Only those agencies covered by the code were required not to discriminate against foreign suppliers.) In contrast to the EC, U.S. negotiators did not believe that the magnitude of bidding opportunities Japan was willing to open up to be adequate without the inclusion of NTT. The initial Japanese offer which was rejected by the U.S. included $5 billion in procurement opportunities. The U.S. had hoped that the Japanese offer would be closer to $7.5 billion and that it would include bidding opportunities in central phone and switching equipment.

The EC offer posed a political problem for the Japanese government because if it would agree to include NTT as one of the entities covered by the government procurement code, the multilateral framework of the code would require that this access be generalized to the European Community. Given, however, the initial reluctance of NTT to accept bids from any foreign suppliers, it was not politically viable for the government of Japan to force NTT to accept bids from European producers while the EC continued to discriminate against foreign producers. In response to these domestic political constraints, the Japanese government suggested that the U.S. and Japan negotiate a bilateral agreement which would be "equivalent to the code" but not a part of the formal agreement covered by the code.

When this offer was made by the Japanese, the negotiators in the Office of the Special Trade Representative perceived that they had two viable negotiating options. The first was that the U.S. could obtain a weak agreement in which only nonsensitive telecommunications equipment items were included but which was covered entirely by the code. Alternatively, the U.S. could push for a more comprehensive bilateral agreement negotiated outside of the code to cover high technology products in addition to including a part of NTT's nonsensitive procurement under the code. The STR decided that the latter was a feasible compromise as it would open up NTT for the U.S. firms, which was more important to the United States than demanding that NTT liberalize its procurement practices on a multilateral basis.

The U.S.-Japan Bilateral Agreement

When the proposal for a bilateral agreement was first presented to the industry representatives who met with STR negotiators in an advisory capacity during the Tokyo Round, it was strongly opposed. Many of these industry officials indicated that they would prefer no agreement to a bilateral agreement because they believed that a bilateral would not really force the Japanese to change anything. This opposition reflected a general belief within the industry that without stronger international sanctions provided by the code, Japan would not live up to the agreement. The industry was also uncertain about the nature of the sanctions to which the U.S. could resort under the bilateral if NTT placed new barriers in the way of telecommunications trade. Others opposed the negotiation of a code equivalent bilateral because they believed that the negotiations to include NTT under the government procurement code would fail thereby providing them with justification for asking Congress to restrict Japanese telecommunications imports to the United States.

In spite of this opposition to the bilateral agreement on the part of the industry the STR continued to hold negotiations with the Japanese over the procedures

Exhibit 5. Telecommunications: Negotiating Positions

NTT	Strongly resisted opening its procurement procedures to foreign firms.
Japanese Government	Willing to negotiate a bilateral due to intense U.S. pressure. Unwilling to include NTT's high technology purchases under the government procurement code.
Office of the STR	Willing to negotiate a bilateral with Japan to cover high technology procurement. Accepted a code consistent agreement as sufficient.
U.S. Industry	Wanted full code coverage because firms believed either 1) it was the only type of agreement which would actually get results; or 2) the negotiations would fail providing a rationale for protecting the U.S. market.

U.S. firms would use to submit bids to NTT. U.S. negotiators remained convinced that the Japanese Diet would never agree to include sensitive items, e.g. digital switches, under the code. To accommodate business criticisms, however, the STR did incorporate into the agreement a provision which would create a monitoring mechanism to ensure that the terms of the agreement were met. If there was evidence that NTT continued to discriminate against U.S. firms, the agreement provided that Japanese firms would be excluded from all U.S. government procurement contracts.

Once the government of Japan had agreed to accept the principle of code-consistent procedures, the Office of the STR believed that it had come upon the best possible agreement given domestic Japanese political constraints. This enthusiasm for the bilateral agreement was strengthened by a determination on the part of the Carter administration to negotiate the agreement before leaving office. At this point, industry and labor groups could no longer influence the shape of the agreement. Instead the STR began to lobby individual firms which remained critical of the absence of full code coverage in an effort to solicit their support for the agreement. Once the negotiations reached this stage an industry representative from the Electronic Industries Association commented that even strong industry opposition to the bilateral could not have stopped the U.S. and Japan from reaching an agreement. He added, however, that if industry had not originally taken a hard line, the STR would have settled for a much weaker agreement.

The United States and Japan signed an agreement December 19, 1980. In this agreement NTT's procurement was divided into three tracks:

1. Non-telecommunications equipment;
2. off-the-shelf public telecommunciations which only needs minor modifications to adapt to Japan's network; and
3 state-of-the-art telecommunications equipment developed specifically for NTT. (This would also include R&D.)

In addition to these three tracks there was a separate agreement in which Japan agreed to facilitate the sales of U.S. equipment in the interconnect market.

The first track which includes mainframe office computers, utility poles, and coaxial cables is included under the government procurement code. This bilateral agreement covers tracks two and three. The creation of these tracks reflects a compromise on the part of the U.S. government because although they contain the same obligations as the government procurement code, they are not subject to an international dispute settlement mechanism. The agreement did, however, provide for its own dispute settlement mechanism which consists of a panel of three arbitrators, one from each country and a third who is not a national of either the U.S. or Japan. Both the U.S. and Japan also agreed that they would use "their best efforts" to implement the findings of this panel. In the event that the recommendations are not implemented, the agreement states that "each Party may take appropriate measures to reestablish reciprocity in the field of government procurement", i.e., withdraw trade concessions. (NTT Procurement Procedures, Attachment II, "Procedures on Non-binding Arbitration). As a further safety valve, the U.S. and Japan also agreed to review the progress of the agreement after three years to determine if it should be expanded or abandoned.

This dispute settlement mechanism in conjunction with the provisions in which NTT agreed both to inform U.S. firms of prospective purchases and to treat their bids on an equal par with those submitted by Japanese firms were the crucial aspects of the agreement from the perspective of the STR. The primary objective of the STR was to give U.S. firms an opportunity to compete in the Japanese market, while not coercing Japan into buying U.S. products. The STR also saw this agreement as a potential first step in the progressive liberalization of trade in telecommunications.

CONCLUSION

Two alternative explanations were suggested at the outset of this paper to indicate why interest group political pressures did not prevail in the formulation of U.S. international trade policy. The first, based on pluralist political analysis, assumed that countervailing interest group pressures played a role in the policy process thus reducing the influence any one group is able to have on the ultimate policy outcome. The second explanation was based on the asymmetric distribution of costs and benefits of trade restrictions. Since the benefits of trade protection are concentrated on the specific industry requesting relief from import competition, while the benefits are widely diffused to all consumers, interest group political pressures in a trade dispute are biased in favor of trade protection. Here, it was suggested that the weakness of actual trade restraints relative to the demands made by the industry for protection could be explained by the reluctance of the

United States to abrogate the GATT agreements which regulate international trade.

In each of the three cases, at the outset the industry perceived that its political strength would be sufficient to allow it to play a determinant role in the final decision. The textile/apparel industry believed that it could exact policy changes from the Carter administration because it posed a credible threat to the congressional ratification of the Tokyo Round Agreements. Prior to the ITC hearings Ford's president, Philip Caldwell, said in a news conference that "it seemed inconceivable to him that the ITC might conclude that imports aren't injuring the domestic industry." He further commented that "the ITC doesn't even have to look into the reasons why U.S. imports of cars and light trucks are approaching three million units this year" (*Wall Street Journal*, October 8, 1980). A representative of the Electronic Industries Association, a major telecommunications industry trade association, suggested that at the outset of the U.S.-Japan negotiations over the government procurement code that the probable failure of these negotiations would provide sufficient rationale for Congress to restrict access of Japanese firms to the U.S. market.

In each of these three cases, however, the industry interests did not prevail, although there was little evidence of strong countervailing interest group pressures in any of them. Instead, leverage against the industry pressure for protection came from the norms and rules of the GATT Charter as they are embedded in the U.S. trade policy. In the textile/apparel case, the demands put forth by the industry representatives were opposed by the CEA and the Department of the Treasury in the interagency committee meetings on the White Paper. These agencies suggested that to implement the policy changes advocated by the industry would involve a break with the previous U.S. policy of adhering to the growth and flexibility provisions specified in the Multifiber Arrangement. In the auto case, the ITC determined on the basis of criteria determined by Congress to implement the GATT escape clause that the primary cause of injury to the industry was not imports. In the telecommunications case, once the STR negotiators determined that a code-consistent bilateral agreement was the most that Japan could offer given domestic political constraints, the industry support of full code coverage did not prevail.

Analysis of the three cases indicates that a significant source of constraints on the ability of interest groups within the three sectors to influence the determination of policy, i.e., their power, comes from the commitment on the part of the United States to sustain a liberal trading order through adhering to GATT norms, rules, and procedures. Underlying this commitment is the belief that an open international trading system reflects the national interest of the United States although it creates the need for specific sectors to adjust to foreign competition and can intensify the process of industrial decline in sectors of the economy which are not competitive internationally.

The international dimension to trade policy differentiates the policy outcomes from other cases of economic regulation characterized by concentrated costs and diffuse benefits. Typically in these cases business has been able to capture a regulatory agency and help formulate policies intended to reduce the competitive pressures in a specific sector. In contrast, U.S. international trade policy tends to increase the competitive pressures to which an industry must adapt. While the conclusions with respect to the constraints on the ability of interest groups to influence policy outcomes may be applicable to those sets of issues which have an international dimension, the same constraints may not be present in issue areas which are purely domestic in scope, e.g., transportation regulation, public utility regulation, etc.

As international economic interdependence continues to increase, it is likely that more and more issues which come within the scope of research in business and society will take on an international dimension. Future research in the field may benefit from exploring possible international dimensions to policy issues to determine the impact international factors may have on domestic political decisions and the ability of economic actors, especially business organizations, to influence these decisions.

ACKNOWLEDGMENT

The author would like to thank all the members of the Business and Public Policy group at U.C. Berkeley for their support for this project. Edwin M. Epstein offered continual encouragement as well as helpful criticism during all phases of this research. Jeanne Logsdon and David Palmer made very helpful comments on drafts of this paper. Conversations with Robert Harris, David Vogel, and Dow Votaw also helped to sharpen the focus of the argument presented here.

NOTES

1. The General Agreement on Tariffs and Trade (GATT) was created in 1947 to provide a legal framework within which the first post-war multilateral tariff negotiations were conducted. The charter for the GATT was based on the commercial policy chapter of the International Trade Organization (ITO). The GATT was to become a part of this more comprehensive international organization after the ITO had been ratified by member states. When the ITO failed to receive congressional ratification, the GATT emerged as the primary organizational and legal framework within which trade is regulated on an international basis. Currently, 88 states are members of the GATT.

2. The Tokyo Round Negotiations of the GATT began in 1973 and were concluded in 1979. These meetings included negotiations over non-tariff barriers in addition to agreements on the reduction of tariff levels. In general terms, non-tariff barriers (NTB's) refer to those policies of national governments which impose costs on foreign producers in order to protect domestic industries from foreign competition, e.g., government procurement practices which discriminate in favor of domestic producers. Those agreements reached at the Tokyo Round which required changes in U.S. trade law had to be ratified by Congress.

3. The Multifiber Arrangement (MFA) was first negotiated in 1973. It was preceded by the Short-Term Arrangement (1961) and the Long-Term Arrangement (1962). Both these agreements

provided a multilateral framework within which importing and exporting countries could negotiate bilateral agreements restricting trade in cotton textile and apparel products. The bilateral agreements set overall quantiative limits on terxtile/apparel imports as well as limits on narrower groups of products. The MFA extended these restrictions to include wool and manmade-fiber products. It came into force January 1, 1974, and has been renewed with some modifications in 1977 and again in 1981.

4.   Article 19 of the GATT states that if a government can demonstrate that imports are entering the country in sufficient quantities to cause or threaten to cause serious injury to domestic producers of like or directly competitive products, it can impose temporary import restraints on a nondiscriminatory basis. The Charter also provides for prior notification and consultation as well as for retaliatory action by the country whose exports are being restricted.

5.   Negotiations over the government procurement code began in 1976 when a Sub Group was formed at the Tokyo Round negotiations. Multilateral negotiations over the substance of the code were concluded April 1979. The bilateral discussions between the United States and Japan over which government agencies to include under the code continued through December 1980.

6.   Several studies (Schattschneider; Bauer, Pool and Dexter; Lowi; and Hayes) have analyzed the impact of interest groups on U.S. international trade policy. Schnattschneider found in his analysis of the Smoot-Hawley Tariff Act of 1930 that the Congress was predisposed toward protectionism and extremely responsive to interest group requests for tariff increases. Schattschneider's analysis illustrates the ability of interest groups to influence U.S. trade policy prior to the creation of the GATT. The other studies, written after the GATT was established, offer alternative explanations to account for why trade policy outcomes do not correspond with interest group demands. Bauer, Pool, and Dexter argue that interest groups in general are not very powerful and that congressional representatives act autonomously. Lowi, in a review of Bauer, Pool, and Dexter's study suggests that the trade policy outcomes result from conflict among interest groups which neutralize the impact each has on the Congress. Michael Hayes, in a rejoinder to Lowi, offers yet a third explanation. He argues that the crucial question analysts of interest group pressure need to ask is not whether interest groups are powerful, but when. These arguments all share the assumption that U.S. international trade policy can be explained within the framework of domestic politics. A discussion of these works is not included here because it would not relate directly to the question of countervailing interest groups. For a critique of these studies see Lenway.

7.   Olson defines a privileged group to be one in which at least one member has an incentive to provide the collective good. In an intermediate-sized group, no single member has sufficient incentive to provide the good, but the group is small enough so that the public good can be provided through a minimum of group coordination or organization.

REFERENCES

Bauer, Raymond A., Ithiel de Sola Pool, and Lewis Anthony Dexter. *American Business and Public Policy: The Politics of Foreign Trade*. Chicago: Aldine, Atherton, 1963, 1972.

Dam, Kenneth W. *The GATT: Law and International Economic Organization*. Chicago: The University of Chicago Press, 1970.

Epstein, Edwin M. *The Corporation in American Politics*. Englewood Cliffs, NJ: Prentice-Hall, 1969.

Ford Motor Company. "Prehearing Brief of the Ford Motor Company," U.S. International Trade Commission Investigation TA-201-44, 1 October 1980.

General Agreement on Tariffs and Trade. *Report by the Director General of the GATT: The Tokyo Round of the Multilateral Trade Negotiation*. Geneva: The General Agreement on Tariffs and Trade, 1979.

Haas, Ernst B. "Why Collaborate? Issue Linkage and International Regimes." *World Politics* 32(April 1980):357-405.

Hayes, Michael T. *Lobbyists and Legislators: A Theory of Political Markets*. New Brunswick, N.J.: Rutgers University Press, 1981.

Kurth, James R. "The Political Consequences of the Product Cycle Industrial History and Political Outcomes." *International Organization* 33(Winter 1979):1-34.

Lenway, Stefanie. "The Politics of Protection, Expansion, and Escape: International Collaboration and Business Power in U.S. Foreign Trade Policy." Dissertation, University of California, Berkeley, 1982.

Lindblom, Charles. *Politics and Markets: The World's Political Economic Systems*. New York: Basic Books, 1977.

Lowi, Theodore. "American Business and Public Policy: Case Studies and Political Theory." *World Politics* (July 1964):677-693.

Olson, Mancur. *The Logic of Collective Action: Public Goods and the Theory of Groups*. Cambridge, MA: Harvard University Press, 1965.

Post, James E., and Patti N. Andrews. "Case Research in Corporation and Society Studies." *Research in Corporate Social Performance and Policy* Vol. 4. Greenwich, CT: JAI Press, 1982.

Schattschneider, E. E. *Politics, Pressures, and the Tariff: A Study of Free Private Enterprise in Pressure Politics as Shown in the 1929-1930 Revision of the Tariff*. Hamden, CT: Archon Books, 1935, 1963.

Truman, David. *The Governmental Process: Political Interests and Public Opinion*. New York: Alfred A. Knopf, 1951.

United Auto Workers Union. "Petition for Relief under Section 201 of the Trade Act of 1974 from Import Competition from Imported Passenger Cars, Light Trucks, and Utility Vehicles before the United States International Trade Commission." Washington, D.C., 12 June 1980.

U.S. Congress, House. Subcommittee on Trade Policy of the House Committee on Ways and Means. *Auto Situation: 1980*. Washington, D.C.: Government Printing Office, 1980.

U.S. Department of Transportation. *The U.S. Auto Industry 1980: Report to the President of the Secretary of Transportation*. DOT-P-10-81-02. Washington, D.C., 1981.

U.S. International Trade Commission. "A Baseline Study of the Telephone Terminal and Switching Equipment Industry." USITC Publication #946. Washington, D.C., January 1978.

———. "Certain Motor Vehicles and Certain Chassis and Bodies Therefor." USITC Publication #1110, Washington, D.C., 1980.

———. "The History and Current Status of the Multifiber Arrangement." USITC Publication #850. Washington, D.C., 1980.

———. "The Multifiber Arrangement, 1973-1980, USITC Publication #1131. Washington, D.C. 1981.

PUBLIC POLICY ADVERTISING AND THE 1980 PRESIDENTIAL ELECTION

William C. Frederick and Mildred S. Myers

During the summer and early autumn of 1980, as voters prepared to turn President Jimmy Carter out of office and replace him with Ronald Reagan, magazine readers were bombarded with dozens of politically oriented advertisements sponsored by large corporations and business trade associations, such as the following:

OVER-REGULATION COULD COST YOU THE SHIRT OFF YOUR BACK
You might never get to wear cotton again.

IF YOU DON'T VOTE, DON'T PUT ALL THE BLAME FOR INFLATION ON WASHINGTON
If you want. . .a president committed. . .efforts to balance the budget, increase productivity, eliminate unnecessary regulation, create responsible monetary policy. . .then. . .vote accordingly.

INSTEAD OF ASKING DAD FOR THE CAR, WILL WE SOON BE ASKING BIG BROTHER?
Let the government decide when, where, and if we drive, and you can bet we'll be grounded from more than a Saturday night date.

Research in Corporate Social Performance and Policy, volume 5, pages 59-86
Copyright © 1983 by JAI Press Inc.
All rights of reproduction in any form reserved.
ISBN: 0-89232-412-0

BY THE TIME YOU'VE READ THIS MAGAZINE [an average reading time of 108 minutes],
THE U.S. GOVERNMENT WILL HAVE SPENT $117,678,081.96

THE CRISIS OF LEADERSHIP
Can we and our leaders bear the burdens of democracy. . .or will the cup of freedom slip
from our trembling hands?. . .lack of good leadership. . .may be the only true crisis among
our many great problems.

These alarming messages appeared at a time when the general public was
troubled by the climbing cost of living, historically high interest rates, and
unsettled international conditions such as those in Iran and the Middle East
generally. By 1980 the electorate had also been witness for some years to a
spirited onslaught by the private sector on government regulation and government
intrusion into the lives of individuals.

It would have been easy, under the circumstances, to see the advertisements
as an attempt by the moneyed interests to saturate the print media in an effort
to insure the election of candidate Reagan who was, indeed, playing upon similar
themes in his run for the presidency. Since political action committee contributions were restricted in amount, and direct corporate contributions were forbidden by law, money could be used instead to bend the will of the electorate
if employed skillfully through sponsorship of public policy advertisements. Such
ads, though forbidden on television, could be displayed in the print media as
another tool in the hands of the Establishment to secure its position of dominance
and affluence in the political economy. This was indeed the general perspective
with which we began our inquiry into the use of public policy advertising by
business during the 1980 presidential election.

The actual story turned out to be considerably more interesting and complex,
an outcome frequently observed when empirical evidence replaces political bias.
Without abandoning our initial views entirely, our subsequent study revealed
that public policy advertising by business during the 1980 presidential election
was multifaceted and often politically neutral or innocuous. Many ad messages
could be interpreted as being as favorable to the Democrats as to the Republicans.
The "Establishment threat" appeared considerably muted. One could even fault
business for being so lacking in advertising skills as to have muffed a great
opportunity to wield significant electoral influence in behalf of its favored
candidate.

Given these (to us surprising) findings, a question is raised about the function
of this type of advertising by business. One must wonder why so much money
and effort are expended on this costly undertaking, what motives are at work in
the business mind, and what final effects are achieved. These matters we discuss
toward the end of the paper.

The initial task, however, is to seek answers to three general questions about
the relationship of public policy advertising and electoral politics:

- To what extent does business try to influence presidential elections by means of mass media advertisements?
- In the 1980 presidential election, did business advertisements favor Reagan over Carter?
- Who sponsored the ads and what issues were uppermost?

HYPOTHESES

To answer these questions, two hypotheses were developed, as follows:

Hypothesis 1. If business wanted to influence the public's choice of presidential candidates by means of public policy advertisements, then one would expect:

a. to observe a larger number of such advertisements prior to the election than following it, and

b. that these advertisements would be concentrated in the period between the nominating conventions and election day, with their frequency increasing as election day approached.

Hypothesis 2. If business favored one presidential candidate over another, then one would expect to observe a larger number of public policy advertisements whose themes were consistent with the avowed views of the favored candidate than with the views of the other candidate(s).

With respect to Hypothesis 1b, it should be noted that the actual campaign for the presidency was underway long before the Democratic and Republican party nominating conventions actually selected their nominees. Few doubted that Jimmy Carter would be renominated by the Democrats, and Ronald Reagan was clearly the Republican front runner by the early summer of 1980. Therefore, political advertising in behalf of the pro-business candidate might well have been expected to appear prior to the nominating conventions, and indeed we discovered that to be the case, as discussed below. In general, though, we preferred to focus on the narrower period of the "official" campaign from July-August to the first week in November.

With respect to Hypothesis 1a, another observation is in order. Initially, we did not foresee the significance of public policy advertisements in the post-election period as a possible influence on public opinion concerning the newly-elected President's legislative proposals. Hence the number of ads appearing after the election might be larger than one would expect if looking only at electoral, as contrasted with post-electoral legislative, activities. This post-election aspect of public policy advertising did become manifest and is discussed later in the paper.

METHODOLOGY

In order to test Hypotheses 1a and 1b, we chose the six months prior to the November election (May 1980 to November 4, 1980) and the six months following it (November 5, 1980 through April 1981). This twelve-month period was sufficiently long to observe frequency trends in public policy ads and, being centered on election day, could be expected to reveal any changes directly associated with the electoral campaign period.

Three magazines were identified as sources of public policy advertisements: *Business Week*, published for an audience interested in and presumed to be generally supportive of business; *Newsweek*, reaching a large general audience with varied points of view; and *Atlantic*, oriented toward an intellectual/professional audience not always sympathetic to business views and values.

All full-page advertisements appearing in these three magazines during the twelve-month period were examined and counted. From this sample, public policy advertisements were identified and counted. We define a public policy advertisement (PPA) as one that, directly or by implication, advocates a position on some matter of national or public concern. We prefer the term "public policy advertising" to the more commonly-used "advocacy advertising" to emphasize the public policy aspects of such ads and because all ads in one way or another advocate something, whether purchase of a product or service or the acceptance of a specific approach to a public policy problem.[1]

Each PPA was examined for its public policy content. Generally speaking, an ad focused on one general, overriding theme, such as control of inflation, or the costs of government regulation, or the need for energy conservation. In addition, most PPA's had something to say about a number of other somewhat subsidiary but related issues, such as the desirability of offshore oil drilling or the need to control government deficits. Each PPA can therefore be identified with one major theme and often with one or more subsidiary issues. A theme or issue might appear as the main focus of one ad but be handled only as a subsidiary theme in another ad. Because of the large number and dispersion of all ad issues—both major and subsidiary—this paper discusses only those appearing as major themes.

The sample of public policy advertisements seemed to divide into three broad categories and one subcategory.

Category I ads were those intended to "sell" a public policy or a point of view, rather than an advertiser's product or service. In addition to those quoted at the beginning of this paper, examples include

- Pullman, Inc., calling for "a change of signals" on government regulation;

- a series of ads from the American Council on Life Insurance urging Americans to "support all reasonable and equitable steps" to control inflation and to mail in to the Council a "ballot" stating their willingness to restrict their use of credit, to oppose government regulation, deficit spending, and other inflation-inducing practices;
- a series of ads from the Chemical Manufacturers Association detailing the steps that member companies are taking to control water pollution, manage chemical wastes safely, and ensure worker safety and health, steps that "meet or exceed" federal requirements.

Category I ads make little or no reference to the sponsor's product or service and do not contain sales appeals. These ads are the "purest" of all public policy ads, appealing directly and obviously to the reader's interest in a public policy issue.

Category II ads sold an advertiser's product or services along with, or by means of, public policy issues. They might well be called "piggyback ads," as advertisers hitched a public policy issue onto a standard sales format, combining the two purposes into a single advertisement. Many of these ads covered energy-related issues such as advocacy of public lands exploration and drilling or national energy independence. Examples include

- a Tenneco series describing their exploration ventures throughout the country (and implying the company's ability and willingness to use that expertise to plumb for public-lands minerals);
- an American Gas Association series promoting natural gas as a clean, efficient, economical, and abundantly available fuel (and implying its superiority over other energy sources);
- Association of American Railroads ads debunking the "myth" that rail transport is more costly than truck or barge transport (and decrying public subsidies to those forms);
- the famous Warner and Swasey ads, with their ideological messages so bald that they would belong in *Category I* were it not for the inset in each ad describing a particular Warner & Swasey machine.

Some of the energy-related ads fell into a subcategory, which we have labeled *Category IIA*, that had implications for national energy supplies or usage but made no direct political statement. Ads that seemed merely to be riding a bandwagon or capitalizing on the notion of energy conservation as a good selling point fell into this group. An example is seen in Alcoa's ads touting their energy-saving windows, not just as good products but as making a contribution to the nation's general need to conserve energy. Of all the PPA's in our sample, *Category IIA* ads were the most neutral politically, and they were included only because the ad's public policy message, though bland, helped justify the product's sales appeal.

Category III consisted of public relations ads that were meant to promote a company's image as a good corporate citizen by demonstrating its commitment or responsiveness to current public concerns or values. Others have called such ads "institutional advertising" or "corporate image advertising." Representatives of this type of ad include

- Control Data's descriptions of various social projects it has developed and funded;
- Champion International's informational pieces on the technological future and the choices people will be making then;
- Philip Morris's and MacDonald's announcements of art exhibitions and public television shows they have supported.

Although innocuous politically, *Category III* ads in general have as one purpose the instilling of faith in the general beneficence of private enterprises. Their appearance at a time (such as the 1980 presidential election campaign) when national debate raged about the purported superiority of private sector institutions over public sector initiatives would tend to exert some influence on public opinion favorable to the proponents of private enterprise.

In order to test Hypothesis 2 concerning political favoritism shown by public policy advertisements, we needed some standard against which to judge an ad's political content. For this purpose, each of the two major parties' platforms were analyzed, and a list was compiled of those issues of greatest interest to the business community and on which they might expend some advertising dollars. Additionally, we made use of a summary of such issues prepared by *Business Week*, and we drew on our own memory of the campaign (Campaign Issues References).

The respective positions of candidates Reagan and Carter were then identified and matched against a master list of salient business-related campaign issues. Table 1 singles out a few of the more prominent ones to illustrate the process. A comprehensive list of the criteria used to classify public policy ads as *Pro-Reagan* and *Pro-Carter* appears in Appendix I.

All public policy ads were then examined and classified as exhibiting a particular public policy posture: *Pro-Reagan, Pro-Carter, Neutral* (neither pro-Reagan nor pro-Carter but referring to a public policy issue), and *Shared Views* (Reagan and Carter shared a general viewpoint regarding the ad's major public policy issue). Following the election of Reagan to the presidency, the name of the pro-Carter ad posture was switched to *Pro-Democratic* for the six-month period after the election when legislative struggles replaced electoral ones.

A special cautionary note is in order at this point. The compilation of business-related campaign issues, the identification of a candidate's position on any one

Table 1. Positions of Reagan and Carter on Selected Campaign Issues, 1980

Reagan	Issue	Carter
Private development	• Synfuels development	Federal support
Through market pricing	• Energy conservation	Of key importance; with government aid
Through private research	• New energy sources	Favor, if environmentally safe
Favor private action	• Exploration and drilling on public lands and offshore	Restrain, with environmental safeguards
Increase	• Nuclear plants	Retire
Abolish	• Department of Energy	Retain
More free market, less government	• Free market vs. government controls	Government programs, controls, and guidance where needed
Broad-based reduction	• Taxes	Targeted, specific reductions
Through free market; no CPA	• Consumer protection	Through government action; favor CPA
Protection against government intrusion	• Freedom and privacy (personal)	Protect against government and business intrusion
Preserve and strengthen family traditions; no ERA endorsement	• Women's rights	Favor ERA

Source: 1980 Republican Platform Text and 1980 Democratic Platform Text as reported in *Congressional Quarterly*, July 19, 1980 and August 16, 1980.

issue, and particularly the classification of public policy advertisements as pro-Reagan or pro-Carter is hardly a precise or objective exercise. Judgment and interpretation, along with the biases and perspectives of the investigators, are involved. Other investigators might have reached different conclusions about the salience of some campaign issues or whether a particular ad leaned more toward one candidate's view than another's. In our case, where doubt existed we tended to put the ad into the neutral category. Although we are as confident about our own objectivity as most investigators appear to be, we acknowledge that other interpretations and ad classifications might have been made by others.

A final methodological note concerns analysis of the data. An SPSS program was used to tabulate and classify the data, and Chi-square tests of statistical significance were undertaken at relevant points. Much of the data is reported in the tables and charts in following sections of the paper, and significance tests are noted where appropriate.

RESULTS AND ANALYSIS

The Hypotheses

Hypothesis 1a, positing that the number of public policy ads would be larger prior to the election than following it, was not confirmed. Although there were 254 such ads before the election and 208 after it, the difference between the two periods is not statistically significant.[2]

Furthermore, our 462 public policy ads represented only a modest proportion of total full-page ads of all kinds: 8.4 percent prior to the election and 7.7 percent following election day. These very low percentages created the first twinge of doubt in our minds about the alleged saturation of the media with business viewpoints, and this is a matter to which we return at a later point in the paper.

Hypothesis 1b posited a concentration of public policy advertisements in the post-convention and pre-election day period, with their frequency increasing as election day approached. This hypothesis was generally confirmed.

Public policy ads were indeed concentrated during the critical September/ October/pre-election November period, numbering 132 (or 50 percent) out of a total of 264 for the entire six-month pre-election part of the year. In other words, half of all public policy ads in the six months preceding election day appeared in less than half that period. Additionally, as revealed in Figure 1, the month of September represented the highest monthly totals for each of the three publications in the pre-election period, and October almost matched this performance. Ad volume remained relatively high for *Business Week* during the pre-election segment of November but dropped off for both *Newsweek* and *Atlantic*.

With respect to the frequency rate increasing as election day approached, the Figure 1 data seem to indicate that this part of Hypothesis 1b is not confirmed, since the ad totals actually declined during October and in the pre-election segment of November. (The period prior to the election covered the November 1980 issue of *Atlantic*, the November 3, 1980, issue of *Newsweek*, and the November 3 and November 10, 1980, issues of *Business Week*, all of which were on the newsstands and delivered to subscribers prior to election day. This distinction between pre-election and post-election November is shown in Figure 1 and later in Figure 2.) However, another way of examining ad frequency is on a month-by-month basis. During the politically critical months of September and October when undecided voters were making up their minds, public policy ads ran at an average rate of 54.5 each month, while during the May-August period the average rate was only 33 ads per month. And in the pre-election part of November, the average rate was approximately 46 per month.

For these reasons, we conclude that Hypothesis 1b was generally confirmed, both as to concentration of ads and their increasing frequency prior to the election. It should be noted, however, that whether the figures on concentration and ad rates per month are statistically significant depends upon their variance from the number of public policy ads placed during these same months in other years, and our study did not attempt to ascertain this information.

Hypothesis 2 posited that there would be a larger number of public policy ads expressing views consistent with those of the favored business candidate than with the views of the other candidate(s).

This hypothesis was confirmed, as revealed in Table 2: 46.5 percent of all pre-election ads were pro-Reagan, while only 4.7 percent favored Carter positions. It is noteworthy that ads in the neutral category constituted 40.9 percent of pre-election totals, and this is another commentary on the question of media saturation to which we return at a later point. By dropping the neutral ads, we found the pre-election ads favoring Reagan views were 78.6 percent, with Carter-leaning ads making up only 8 percent, and shared viewpoints coming in at 13.3 percent. Either computation gives pro-Reagan ads an advantage of 10 to 1 over pro-Carter ads. Business was indeed sending a one-sided political message to the electorate.

The Advertisers

If the business community was intent on influencing public opinion in the public policy realm, as this study indicates, one wonders just who was doing the advertising and what major issues were thought to be the most important.

The total number of advertisers who sponsored public policy ads during the twelve-month period was 106; 88 of these were individual companies, 14 were trade associations, and 4 were governments. The ten most frequent advertisers,

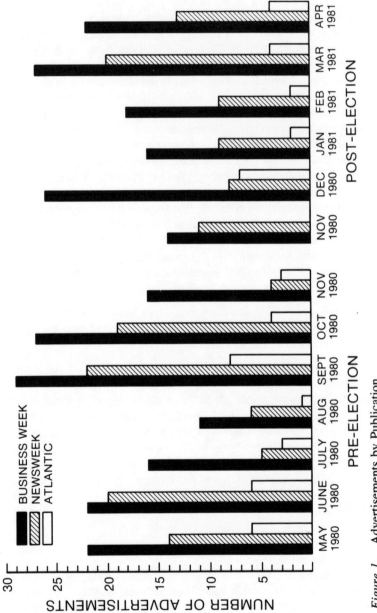

Figure 1. Advertisements by Publication

68

Table 2. Pro-Reagan vs. Pro-Carter (Pro-Democratic) Ads:
Pre- and Post-Election

Posture of the ad	Pre-election		Post-election		Total	
Pro-Reagan	118	(46.5)	89	(42.8)	207	(44.8)
Pro-Carter	12	(4.7)	16	(7.7)	28	(6.1)
Shared Views	20	(7.9)	16	(7.7)	36	(7.8)
Neutral	104	(40.9)	87	(41.8)	191	(41.3)
TOTAL	254	(100.0)	208	(100.0)	462	(100.0)

Note Figures in parentheses are percentages.
$X^2 = 2.03182$ (3df) (non-significant)

before and after the election, are shown in Table 3. Note that the first five are trade associations; they account for 63.8 percent of the ads from this top group before the election, 56.4 percent after it.

This predominance of trade association sponsors has been confirmed by other sources, including a public affairs executive of a Fortune-1000 corporation who told us that his and other companies often band together and use their trade associations for "message" advertising. In addition, a survey by *Industrial Marketing* reported that companies often "pool funds behind an organization or association" for two reasons: "One, the expense needed to even dent public

Table 3. Most Frequent Advertisers: Pre- and Post-Election

Advertiser	Frequency of ads					
	Pre-election		Post-election		Overall	
	Freq.	Rank	Freq.	Rank*	Freq.	Rank
American Gas Association	14	1	9	2	23	1
American Council on Life Insurance	14	1	6	5	20	2
Chemical Manufacturers Association	14	1	5	8	19	3
American Insurance Association	12	2	5	8	17	4
Association of American Railroads	6	5	10	1	16	5
ARCO	7	4	8	3	15	6
ALCOA	8	3	4	9	12	7
Warner & Swasey	6	5	6	7	12	7
Control Data Corporation	7	4	4	11	11	8
Insurance Company of North America	6	5	5	8	11	8
TOTAL	94[1]		62[2]		156[3]	

Notes:
[1]This figure is 37.0% of all pre-election ads.
[2]This figure is 29.8% of all post-election ads.
[3]This figure is 33.1% of all ads.
*Advertisers ranking 4 and 6 in post-election frequency do not appear here because their overall rank was lower than 10 advertisers listed here.

opinion is staggering. Two, more than a few. . .companies have some serious credibility problems because of. . .years of bad press'' ("IM's Survey''). In other words, by having trade associations promote the industry's point of view, companies can get, as one executive put it, "more bang for the buck." They also can protect themselves from the skepticism or incredulity that might arise from, for example, a Hooker Chemical Company ad on responsible chemical waste disposal. Given this rationale, it is not surprising that 82.1 percent of all *Category I* ads—those intended to promote a public policy or a point of view—were placed by trade associations, not individual companies.

Of all the ads sponsored by trade associations, 62.9 percent of those placed before the election and 53.1 percent of those after it were pro-Reagan. On the other hand, the largest percentage of ads by companies (50.2 percent before and 44.7 percent after the election) were neutral. The correlation between trade associations and numbers of pro-Reagan ads, as well as between companies and numbers of neutral ads, is significant at the .001 level. One might therefore infer that the trade association as ad sponsor can be used by individual companies to get across a political message deemed to be too sensitive for direct linkage to a given corporation's name.

Concerning the political posture of ads placed by the ten most frequent advertisers, we found that 45.7 percent prior to the election were pro-Reagan, as opposed to only 7.4 percent that could be called pro-Carter. Neutral ads accounted for 38.5 percent and shared views for 8.5 percent. Following the election, the pro-Reagan figure dropped dramatically to 29 percent of the top ten's ads, while neutral ads jumped to 46.8 percent.

Although our list of most frequent advertisers shows a varied group of industries, the total sample gives a more concentrated picture. There were three insurance associations and two insurance companies among the advertisers with five or more ads, for the highest industry concentration. They were followed by the oil industry, with four companies leading the petroleum charge. The oil companies, coupled with the energy industry's trade associations (such as the American Gas Association and the Edison Electric Institute), accounted for a huge preponderance of ads on energy-related issues. Although insurance, oil, and gas dominated the overall industry standings, the chemical industry's trade association tied for first place before the election and ranked third overall, a not surprising finding in view of the public's concern about the disposal of chemical wastes and the potential threat to workers and consumers of various chemical compounds used in production.

The Issues

An impressively large number of issues were called to the attention of the ad-reading public by the advertisers. Major issues—that is, the central theme of any ad—numbered 91; and subsidiary issues—that is, any additional accom-

Table 4. Most Frequently Occurring Major Issues
Pre- and Post-Election

Issue	Pre-election		Post-election		Total	
	Freq.	Rank	Freq.	Rank	Freq.	Rank
Energy conservation	34	1	22	1	56	1
Coal usage	9	5	18	2	27	2
New energy sources	14	2	10	3	24	3
Inflation control	14	2	7	5	21	4
Energy supplies (national)	10	4	7	5	17	5
Gas usage	7	7	8	4	15	6
Health care delivery	8	6	6	6	14	7
Government regulation, anti- or costs of	11	3	2	8	13	8
Tax incentives for business	5	8	8	4	13	8
National defense	8	6	3	7	11	9
Free/private enterprise, pro-	2	9	8	4	10	10
Product liability	8	6	2	8	10	10
Truck and barge public subsidies, anti-	2	9	7	5	9	11
Auto safety, improving and promoting	7	7	2	8	9	11
TOTAL	139[1]		110[2]		249[3]	

Notes:
[1]This figure was 54.7% of all pre-election ads.
[2]This figure was 52.9% of all post-election ads.
[3]This figure was 53.4% of all ads.

panying theme in any ad—totalled 70. Eliminating overlap between these two lists gives a grand total of 116 different issues that were included in the 462 ads in the sample. The entire list appears in Appendix II, and the most popular issues are contained in Table 4.

While energy and inflation dominate the Table 4 list of the most frequently appearing issues, a whole host of other controversial matters got their share of attention: health care delivery, government regulation, business tax incentives, national defense, and free enterprise. All of these issues were a central part of the campaign's political rhetoric. But energy accounted for over half (55.8 percent) of the public policy issues we found; and although we are reporting only figures on major issues here, energy loomed very large among the subsidiary issues as well.

The public policy advertisements in our sample carried different amounts of political weight. Some (*Category I*) were strong and direct in their appeal. Others (*Categories IIa and III*) offered politically bland or innocuous messages. Advertisers therefore were faced with questions of strategy in both the choice of media and the timing of PPA's for maximum intended impact. The choices made, as well as the allocation of ad budgets among the different types of PPA's,

Table 5. Category Distributions: Pre- and Post-Election

Category	Pre-election		Post-election		Total	
I	59	(23.2)	52	(25.0)	111	(24.0)
II	135	(53.1)	101	(48.6)	236	(51.1)
IIa	35	(13.8)	33	(15.9)	68	(14.7)
III	25	(9.8)	22	(10.6)	47	(10.2)
Total	254	(100.0)	208	(100.0)	462	(100.0)

Note:
Figures in parentheses are percentages. They may not add to 100 due to rounding.
$X^2 = 1.020$ (3df) (non-significant)

reveal a good deal about the motives embedded in public policy advertising by business.

A somewhat surprising finding, as revealed in Table 5, is that Category I ads (those intended to promote a public policy or a point of view, rather than an advertiser's product or service) numbered less than one fourth of all PPA's. The pre-election and post-election differences were minimal and statistically nonsignificant.

Media Placement Strategy

Remembering that *Category I* ads contained the most direct and unqualified public policy messages, where would business be most likely to place them for the largest political impact? A logical answer is in a mass circulation magazine of diverse readership, and indeed this is what we found. Both before and after the election, a higher percentage of ads in this category appeared in *Newsweek* (with a goodly sampling in *Atlantic* as well) than in *Business Week*, with the correlation between *Category I* ads and their appearance in *Newsweek* significant at the .001 level. Assuming that there is little need to preach to those who share your beliefs, it is understandable that ads of this sort would be concentrated in the magazines whose readership and political views were more scattered across the ideological spectrum.

The largest number of PPA's (51.1 percent of the total sample) fell into *Category II*, those ads intended to promote an advertiser's product or service along with, or by means of, public policy issues. Of these, 53.1 percent came prior to the election and 48.6 percent following it. The two-to-one disparity between *Category I* and *Category II* ads is striking. The motives and intents at work here are not entirely clear, but it is possible to infer that even those advertisers who advertise primarily to sell products or services are not averse to promoting a point of view or to raising public consciousness about a particular issue at the same time. In fact, given the preponderance of *Category II* ads, we have concluded that the major motivation underlying our entire sample of PPAs is commercial rather than primarily or solely ideological or political.

This conclusion has been reinforced by other studies. An *Industrial Marketing* survey of "corporate" or institutional advertising practices (Maher) reported the most important objectives of such advertising as follows:

	Objectives	
	Primary	*Secondary*
• To improve the level of awareness of the company	61%	53%
• To provide unified marketing support for products, services, and capabilities	58%	47%
• To enhance or maintain the company's reputation and good will [our *Category III*]	24%	77%
• To advocate specific actions—or counter the advocacy of others—on issues of importance to the company, its industry or business in general [our *Category I*]	5%	22%
• To communicate the company's concern and record of achievement on social and environmental issues [our *Category I* and/or *II*]	3%	8%

These figures indicate that public policy advertising ranks quite low in comparison with other objectives held by those in charge of ad budgets. Estimates range from *Industrial Marketing's* 37 percent of a company's ad budget to a 10 percent figure given to us by a high-ranking officer in a Fortune-1000 corporation. A related bit of confirming information comes from a study of public affairs practices of large U.S. corporations: Of the various techniques employed by public affairs departments, "issues advertising" is used by only 23 percent of the companies and ranks last in a list of seven or eight such techniques (*Public Affairs Offices*).

Yet another aspect of *Category II* ads reinforces the notion that the primary intention of these ads is to promote the advertiser's product or services and only secondarily to promulgate a political viewpoint. Sixty-nine percent of these ads appeared in *Business Week* (67.4 percent before the election and 71.3 percent afterwards) whose readership is more likely to include the primary marketing audience of those industrial advertisers than either *Newsweek* (where only 26.7 percent of *Category II* ads appeared) or *Atlantic* (4.2 percent). The correlation between *Category II* ads and their appearance in *Business Week* is significant at the .001 level.

Those ads (*Category IIA*) that made no direct political or policy statement but used the notion of energy conservation to promote their product were small in number and represented only 14.7 percent of all PPAs (13.8 percent before election and 15.9 percent after). They were divided almost equally between *Business Week* and *Newsweek*, with only a few in *Atlantic*. Energy conservation is a topic deemed equally well-suited for an industrial or a general-reader audience, as these figures seem to suggest.

Category III was the smallest at 10.2 percent of the total. This group of ads intended to promote an image of good corporate citizenship accounted for 9.8 percent of the sample prior to the election and 10.6 percent following it. During the pre-election period, just over half (52 percent) of these ads appeared in *Newsweek*, dropping to 36.4 percent after the election. Although the numbers of ads involved here are too small to compute statistical significance, one might normally expect corporate image advertising to be beamed at a general audience rather than a predominantly business one. In the post-election period, however, half of these *Category III* ads were in *Business Week*, perhaps a self-congratulatory response to or affirmation of Reagan's avowed faith in the private sector as an important source of support for social and cultural programs. There was little attempt either before or after the election to convince the intellectual/ professional—and perhaps skeptical—readership of *Atlantic* of the virtuous citizenship of corporate America.

Timing Ads for Political Impact

Beyond the matters of advertisers and the issues they chose to target, plus the strategic choice of media vehicle, is the important question of timing the ads so they will have maximum impact on ad readers. Here the pre-election and post-election differences are quite illuminating.

Figure 2 shows pro-Reagan advertisements by publication for the twelve-month period. The ads peaked in all three magazines after the party conventions and before the election. Pro-Reagan ads in *Business Week* reached their highest point in September and their second highest point in October. For *Newsweek* and *Atlantic* the high point of pro-Reagan ads was recorded in October. Also interesting to note were an upsurge of pro-Reagan ads in both *Business Week* and *Newsweek* in June 1980, prior to the party conventions; another jump in December's *Business Week* and January's *Newsweek*, after the election but before the inauguration; and yet another concentration of pro-Reagan ads in all three publications in March 1981, during the period when the new President was building support for his economic program and tax bill. These media peaks illustrate that connections between public policy advertising and the political process were not limited to the choice between Reagan and Carter, and we return to the post-election era later on in the paper.

Some of the more unabashed political and ideological ads appeared only a few times, most of them before the election. For example, the Automobility

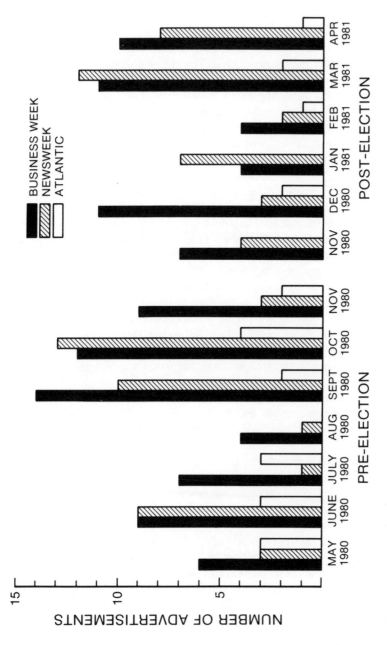

Figure 2. Pro-Reagan Advertisements by Publication

75

Foundation (of the National Automobile Dealers Association—the one that lobbied so hard and so successfully to defeat used-car disclosure rules) ran three ads, all opposing government regulation as expensive and restrictive of personal freedoms. They appeared in *Business Week* in May, October, and November (the week before the election) 1980. The National Cotton Council ran only two ads during the year, both warning of the costs of government regulation to consumers, both appearing before the election. The American Council on Life Insurance's ads on the need to control inflation and reduce government deficits and regulation culminated, in *Newsweek* and *Business Week* issues just prior to the election, with the ad mentioned at the beginning of this paper-the one urging people to vote for "congressmen, senators, and a president committed to effective anti-inflationary efforts." Similarly, SmithKline's "Forum for a Healthier American Society," which ran all year, just "happened" to focus, in September, October, and the first week in November issues of *Newsweek*, on the need for reindustrialization, the need to reduce government growth, and America's crisis in leadership (replete with references to the U.S. embassy hostages in Iran). Warner & Swasey has been advertising on public policy issues since 1936 (Sethi, p. 15), but it is probably safe to say that the timing of their September ad against government spending (also mentioned as an example at the beginning of this paper) and their October ad on the need to clamp down on deficit spending was not accidental. Almost all ads of this sort (with the exception of those from Warner & Swasey, as explained earlier) were *Category I* ads, selling a policy or a point of view rather than a product. By timing as well as by subject matter, they were closely associated with election issues and with the point of view of candidate Reagan and the Republican Party.

A comparison of issue frequencies before and after the election (Table 4) suggests that some issues became less compelling advertising copy once the change in policy or ideology promised by Reagan's election seemed assured. For example, messages about reducing the role of government or the need to control inflation declined after the election, as did those on consumer protection and social problems (not shown in Table 4). This is not surprising, because Reagan's announced views on "big government" and his promises about inflation control via tax cuts, reduced government spending, and tight money policy would seem to make further appeals to public opinion unnecessary.

In the same vein, comparison of the Republican and Democratic platforms shows that consumer protection and social problems were likely to receive less federal attention from Reagan than they had under Carter, who favored establishment of a Consumer Protection Agency (which Reagan opposed) and federal assistance projects (while Reagan urged turning assistance programs back to states and municipalities). Also down after the election were ads promoting energy conservation and environmental protection (the latter not included in Table 4), two more issues on which the Democrats promised a great deal more attention and control than did the Republicans. Both parties favored energy conservation and environmental protection, but the Republicans advocated conservation through higher prices in the marketplace, rather than federal restriction, and also urged redressing the balance between energy needs and environmental protection, favoring the former and downplaying the latter. Somewhat surprisingly, however, ads promoting or extolling the free enterprise system quadrupled after the election; one would have thought that the ideological watchdogs might have relaxed a bit after free enterprise's champion was elected, but not so.

Before leaving the question of timing and intended influence, one other group of ads should be mentioned: those calculated to influence the legislative rather than the elective process. It was their post-election appearance (which through focusing on the election we did not anticipate) that caused so little overall difference in pre-election and post-election ad volumes. To be sure, an elected President is only halfway home; the promised program has to be pushed through Congress. For marshalling public opinion toward these goals, public policy advertising might prove as worthwhile as it had during the campaign itself.

Such ads did increase in frequency following election day (and post-election peaks were recorded in all three magazines, as shown in Figures 1 and 2). For example, there was a considerably larger number of ads advocating tax reform of one sort or another. United States Steel ran an ad three times during March 1981, as Congress was deliberating Reagan's tax proposals. The ad appeared twice in *Business Week* and once in *Newsweek*. The Savings and Loan Foundation sponsored ads in *Newsweek* urging readers to pressure Congress for tax incentives to encourage savings which, in this case, referred to proposed legislation allowing the "all-savers" certificate.

Other issues that bulked larger in numbers in the post-election period included advocacy of particular energy products (especially coal), the need to reindustrialize, and the importance of improving productivity. All of these post-election increases which occurred while the new President was urging passage of his economic programs were to be expected. National security is another issue that appeared more frequently after the election, again understandably, given Reagan's and the Republican Party platform's advocacy of a military buildup requiring Congressional approval.

These ads had no direct connection with the election *per se*, but they do illustrate the attempts by business to use the print media for political (in this case, legislative) purposes. It is also enlightening, and somewhat amusing, to note a slight change in the slogan the Savings and Loan Association used in its ads. The 1980 pre-election ads proclaimed, "If we all speak up, Washington *has* to listen" (emphasis theirs). By January 1981 that was changed to read, "If we all speak up, Washington *will* listen" (emphasis theirs). Does this change suggest that the people in Washington after January 1981, in Congress as well as in the Executive Branch, were thought to be more receptive than those there previously? A devoted ad follower could easily believe so.

SOME CONCLUSIONS ABOUT PUBLIC POLICY ADVERTISING AND THE BUSINESS ESTABLISHMENT

This study has focused on attempts by business to influence the electorate by means of public policy advertising, with special attention to the 1980 presidential election. As interesting and important as this topic may be, other more significant matters are intertwined with it, deserving comment.

Media Balance

It is sometimes, and perhaps even widely, believed that public policy advertising by business, supportive as it is of the system of private enterprise, represents a threat to balanced debate of public policy issues (Sethi, pp. 4, 17-18; and chapter 8). With its ample funds and easy access to the media, some argue, business may well crowd out opposing viewpoints while saturating the media channels with its own vested interest perspectives. In the worst case, elections would be sewed up and public opinion marshalled in favor of business-oriented legislative initiatives not necessarily in the public interest.

We do not find this argument convincing, so far as our study's findings are concerned. In our sample, public policy ads constituted only 8.3 percent of all types of full-page ads, suggesting that business in general does not assign a very high priority to this type of media message when compared with straight commercial selling, a point confirmed by others, as noted earlier. Moreover, those ads devoted almost exclusively to putting across some public policy message (*Category I*) represented only 24 percent of all public policy ads, suggesting that advertising budgets used for direct and exclusively political purposes are relatively modest. Surely if business were truly interested in saturating the print media with its political and ideological views, it would be more generous in funding such efforts. Just as surely, one would expect the occasion of a presidential election campaign to bring forth a maximum effort on the part of business to influence the electorate to choose that candidate perceived to be most favorable to business, but an 8 percent (or even a 24 percent) effort is not impressively large.

Additionally, we suspect that the public interest may well be preserved in these matters, somewhat fortuitously, by the ineffectiveness of the ad campaigns themselves. While many of the ads are attractive, attention-riveting, and emotion-stirring, an even greater number are dull, overly detailed, vapid, and unclear about intent. In some of them, business, while quick on the draw, has obviously shot itself in the foot. Few of the series of ads from any single source last long enough to have an enduring impact, the most obvious exception being Warner & Swasey's 41-year campaign to save America from socialism by promoting free enterprise. While extreme, their ads have at least gotten the message across.

The most that might be said about the inherent dangers of print media saturation, so far as our study is concerned, is that we acknowledge a *potential* lack of balance. After all, pro-Reagan ads greatly outnumbered pro-Carter ads. Even here, though, checks exist. Internal Revenue Service rules concerning business expense deductibility act as a curb on an ad's political content by encouraging a mixed message of product promotion along with public policy views (Sethi, chapter 6).

Also, the natural cynicism many feel toward business advertising of any kind will tend to assert itself in these cases and will water down the effectiveness of an ad's public policy appeal. The skeptical and amused reactions we heard to United States Steel's "We're Involved" campaign some years ago, and to Mobil's more recent efforts, are two cases in point.

Some public affairs and advertising executives are aware of these limitations. One experienced corporate executive told us that he thinks threatening ads—the ones that predict dire consequences, such as Big Brother taking away your driving rights, or losing your cotton shirt due to government-induced inflation—are poorly received. Private surveys by corporations have shown that readers do not believe them and do not want to be bullied. The same surveys also found that what he called "overkill" ads, such as US Steel's and Mobil's, create skepticism.

Information-content ads, like those of the Chemical Manufacturers Association, have been found to be most effective, *given that*, according to this executive, part of the purpose of this advertising is to create a climate in which these public policy issues of concern to the company are thought about, to raise public consciousness that they *are* issues. This kind of consciousness-raising *could* lead to influencing the public policy process itself but is not the specific intent of the ad. Similarly, John Johnson, vice president of advertising at LTV, says, "I think strident advocacy advertising has peaked out. You've got to use a lot of restraint in this sort of thing. I don't think stridency is in a company's best interest. The public is really scared of that" (Maher, p. 59).

Our study's findings imply that there is an economic limit (although admittedly a high one in some cases) to the amount of money a firm or trade association is willing or able to devote to these public policy purposes, as well as some point of diminishing returns when the ad-reading public tires of messages of any kind. Moreover, if one imagines that magazine readers read nothing but the public policy advertisements, then it would be possible to see that a problem exists; but all three magazines we surveyed carry pro and con views on many topics of current public interest. As advertising executives well know (sob!), people do not buy magazines just for the ads.

For all these reasons, we think the dangers of print media saturation have been overplayed. One must look deeper into the culture for the significance that public policy advertising has for both business and society.

Sustaining the System

We turn now to the ideological significance of public policy advertisements and the probable role they play in sustaining the basic framework of the business system. To the extent that *any* promotional ad aids a firm's profit-seeking goals, the general ends and structure of a private enterprise system are enhanced, though not always completely secured. It could be argued from this standpoint that all advertisements, whether purely commercial or intended to influence public policy, have ideological import and function. They help cement the system together, validating its declared purposes and higher ends. This is not to overlook the undoubted reality, though, that while all ads may share this common outcome or purpose, some public policy ads are clearly "more equal than others" in this regard. After all, a clarion call to confront, in the words of one ad, "the [national] crisis of leadership" stirs more political hackles than an appeal to use natural gas more efficiently. But each message, issued by a private firm operating within a capitalist order, contributes its small bit to legitimizing that system and its overarching values.

This latent or covert (and frequently overlooked) function of public policy advertising is considerably more important in fortifying the business system than is normally realized. Acting as it does at a lower, somewhat submerged layer of public consciousness than the media messages themselves, its cement binds the public mind more firmly to acceptance of things as they are. As long as this covert function is performed well, there is little need for a blatant media campaign that might squeeze out the opposition's viewpoints. Charles Lindblom has developed a similar line of thought, arguing that both commercial and political advertising form part of an overarching institutional system that safeguards the corporate and governmental *status quo* (Lindblom, chapter 15).

The Real Danger

In our view, the real damage from business's public policy advertisements occurs when an overly optimistic impression about the nation's problems is conveyed. The entire list of issues we culled from a year's supply of three major magazines' public policy ads identifies important—and sometimes critically important—problems that call for serious attention by both private and public sector leaders. A naive or otherwise ill-informed reader—and their numbers must be legion—could with little difficulty acquire from these ads a soothing picture of the social scene, national problems, and the role of business in it all.

The real lesson business apparently wants the ad-reading public to learn is: "We're doing our part concerning [some national problem], and we will do more—and probably solve the problem—if given a chance by government." This view, if widely adopted, would reinforce general acceptance of the business order while overlooking the negative impacts of business on society. It also projects an unbalanced picture of social and national reality. Few of our truly compelling national problems—including those identified in our ad sample— lend themselves to simplistic approaches or one-dimensional ideological solutions. Causing or even encouraging the public to believe so is a gross disservice rendered by these ads. Therein lies the real danger of public policy advertising by business.

Again, Lindbolm's observations are pertinent.

> To succeed in its purposes, which are perhaps only half understood by businessmen themselves, corporate molding of citizen volitions on grand issues does not need to accomplish tyranny over the mind, nor even a uniformity of opinion on the grand issues. Far short of either, we have already noted, it need only persuade citizens not to raise certain issues, not to make demands in politics on those issues (pp. 210-211)."

And:

> Although sales promotion and manipulation of political volitions alike obstruct popular control by creating some degree of circularity in it, they may obstruct it again—hence doubly—through a more diffuse disservice to the populace. The messages confuse and deceive the public. The result is that, although people do not always do what leadership wants, they are incapable of knowing and protecting their own interests (p. 219).

We conclude by adverting to our initial belief that business made a strong effort through public policy advertising to influence voters to elect Ronald Reagan. The hypothesis was only partially supported by our study. Pro-Reagan ads did indeed peak before the election in the three magazines. More ads favored Reagan's position than Carter's. A few ads were obviously and enthusiastically pro-Reagan, constituting a direct attempt to influence voters and, later on, the legislative process. The overwhelming number and proportion of public policy ads, though, were devoted to selling products or services by linking their usage with one or more public policy issues, and we have concluded that the major motive operating in the sponsorship of those ads was commercial, not political.

Even more encouraging is the lack of confirmation that business saturates the print media with pro-business political messages to the exclusion of other points of view. Certainly, we found no concerted or sinister Establishment plot to influence public policy in this way. What did emerge was only a to-be-expected (and almost mild) preference for a conservative Republican presidential candidate over a moderately liberal Democratic candidate.

APPENDIX I

CRITERIA FOR CLASSIFYING PUBLIC
POLICY ADVERTISEMENTS

Anything that directly advocated, or indirectly suggested or implied, or from which could be reasonably inferred a need for, any of the following public policies, policy directions, programs, or corrective action in prevailing policies and programs was considered to be:

Pro-Reagan

- Reduce the role of government, government costs, deficit spending, and taxes
- Control inflation (through fiscal and monetary policy, reducing government spending, etc.)
- Greater reliance on private, free market decisions
- Improve productivity and support reindustrialization
- Strengthen national security and national defense
- Protect freedom and privacy from government intrusion
- Control crime (too much permissiveness)
- Preserve family traditions
- Promote private transportation (automobiles)
- Protect consumers through free market
- Promote private health care, voluntary cost control, and deregulation of health care industry
- Base national energy policy on free-market decision making:
    Rapid oil and gas decontrol
    Deregulate coal mining and coal usage
    Conserve energy through market pricing
    Private synthetic fuels development (no government aid)
    Energy independence through increased market supplies
    New energy sources and technologies through private research
    Private exploration and drilling on public lands and offshore
    Increase nuclear power
    Redress balance of energy needs and environmental protection
    Abolish Department of Energy
- Strong, firm national leadership

Pro-Carter

- Restrain government spending and deficit spending
- Control inflation by monetary and fiscal restraint
- Deregulate anticompetitive industries (railroads and trucks)
- Reduce taxes selectively (not broad-based), and liberalize depreciation rates to stimulate industry
- Protect consumers by government actions, including a Consumer Protection Agency
- Favor a national health insurance program and comprehensive care
- Promote mass transit, deregulate trucks, provide railroad rate flexibility, and aid the automobile industry
- Protect privacy from government and business intrusion

- Favor passage of the Equal Rights Amendment (for women)
- Base national energy policy on energy conservation and environmental concern, aided by government:
    Gradual oil and gas decontrol
    Increase coal usage
    Federal support for synthetic fuels development
    Energy independence
    Favor new and environmentally safe energy sources
    Restrain private exploration and drilling on public lands, with environmental safeguards
    Retire nuclear plants
    Develop solar energy
    More controls on oil companies
    Retain Department of Energy

The pro-Reagan and pro-Carter criteria were derived from the respective platforms of the Republican and Democratic parties.

APPENDIX II

PUBLIC POLICY ISSUES AND THEMES APPEARING IN BUSINESS-SPONSORED ADVERTISEMENTS IN ALL ISSUES OF *ATLANTIC, BUSINESS WEEK*, AND *NEWSWEEK* FROM MAY 1980 THROUGH APRIL 1981

A major issue or theme is defined as the dominant message of a public policy advertisement. Less prominently featured but related issues and themes in an advertisement are defined as subsidiary issues and themes. Major issues totaled 91 and subsidiary issues 72. Eliminating overlap and duplication produces a grand total of 120 separate issues and themes that were featured in the ad sample.

Issue or theme	*Major*	*Subsidiary*
Air pollution control	X	X
Alaskan gas pipeline	X	X
Alcoholism, control of	X	
Aluminum can recycling	X	
Antitrust (revamp)		X
Arms control		X
Arson control	X	
Arts, support of	X	
Auto safety, improving and promoting	X	X
Balance of trade (international)		X
Carpooling, pro-	X	X
Chemical waste disposal, managing	X	

Coal gasification	X	X
Coal usage	X	X
Competition, market		X
Conservation of resources	X	X
Consumer protection	X	
Credit use, limit		X
Crime control	X	X
Defense spending, pro-	X	
Depreciation allowances for business	X	X
Deregulation	X	
Economic growth, pro-	X	X
Education, higher, support for	X	
Employing/training the disadvantaged/hard core	X	
Energy conservation	X	X
Energy independence	X	X
Energy supplies, national	X	X
Environmental protection	X	X
Export trade, increase/pro-	X	X
Family life, pro-	X	X
Fifty-five mile-per-hour speed limit, pro-		X
Food additives		X
Foreign policy, restoring/improving		X
Forest management, public interest	X	X
Free/private enterprise, pro-	X	X
Free speech	X	X
Freedom, pro-		X
Genetic engineering, future implications	X	
Global food supplies	X	
Government-business cooperation		X
Government-business-labor cooperation	X	X
Government-business-labor-education cooperation		X
Government growth, anti-/reduce	X	X
Government regulation, anti-/costs of	X	X
Government/deficit spending, anti-	X	X
Health care delivery	X	X
Hispanic rights	X	
Home buying and selling	X	
Home mortgage money	X	
Industrial minerals policy	X	
Inflation control	X	X
Innovation		X
Insurance rate discrimination		X
(by age, sex, marital status)		
International crises (Iran)		X
Leadership, reasserting America's in the world		X
Leadership crisis, national	X	
Liability claims against government	X	
Lifelong learning and career development	X	
Limit pollution controls	X	
Liquified natural gas		X
Literacy, improving	X	

Mass transit	X	
Media bias against business	X	
Medical (hospital) malpractice claims/costs	X	
Minority enterprise, aid to	X	
Monetary policy, improve		X
Municipal tax savings (city budget)	X	
National defense	X	X
Natural gas usage	X	X
New energy sources	X	X
Noise pollution	X	
Nuclear energy, pro-	X	X
Nuclear licensing procedure		X
Ocean resources, future policies	X	
Occupational safety and health	X	
Offshore drilling	X	X
Oil and gas exploration	X	
Oil usage	X	X
Pioneering spirit		X
Political risk of multinational corporations	X	
Prisoner education	X	
Privacy, personal, protection of	X	X
Product liability	X	
Productivity, improvement of	X	X
Profits, pro-	X	X
Public lands drilling/exploration, usage	X	X
Public television, support of (for children)	X	
Recovering domestic oil	X	
Red-lining		X
Reducing consumer (household) costs		X
Reindustrialization	X	X
Retirement/pensions	X	
Safe chemical products	X	
Scientific discovery, lag in		X
Shale oil recovery and mining	X	X
Shareholder ownership	X	
Single-issue politics, anti-	X	
Social experimentation, slowing		X
Social goals, strengthening		X
Social problems, solving		X
Solar energy	X	X
Space program, pro-	X	
Strip mining		X
Support new President (Reagan)	X	
Synthetic fuels	X	X
Tar sands oil recovery	X	X
Tax-free savings	X	
Tax incentives for business	X	X
Tax reduction for business		X
Technological future	X	
Technological innovation		X
Technological progress	X	

Transporting hazardous chemicals	X	
Truck and barge public subsidies, anti-	X	
Urban neighborhood renewal	X	X
Water pollution control	X	
Wildlife conservation	X	
Youth voting, pro-	X	

ACKNOWLEDGMENTS

This study was partially supported by the Business, Government, and Society Research Institute of the Graduate School of Business at the University of Pittsburgh through a grant from the General Electric Foundation. The authors are especially grateful to Norma Walde for initial identification and classification of the public policy advertisements, to Sandra Kerbel for technical advice and helpful suggestions concerning analytical design, to Vasudevan Ramanujam for data analysis and construction of tables, and to others who made constructive comments on earlier versions of this paper.

NOTES

1. For other, more comprehensive definitions, see Sethi, pp. 7-14 and 53-55.
2. The period prior to the election covered the November 1980 issue of *Atlantic*, the November 3, 1980, issue of *Newsweek*, and the November 3 and November 10, 1980, issues of *Business Week*, all of which were on the newsstands and delivered to subscribers prior to election day.

REFERENCES

Campaign Issues References: "1980 Republican Platform Text, "*Congressional Quarterly*, July 19, 1980, pp. 2030-2056; "1980 Democratic Platform Text," *Congressional Quarterly*, August 16, 1980, pp. 2390-2420; "Behind the Campaign Rhetoric: What the Candidates Really Believe About Economic Policy," *Business Week*, November 3, 1980, pp. 74-78; "The Deep Division on the Big Issues," *Business Week*, November 3, 1980, pp. 78-88.

"IM's Survey of Corporate Advertising." *Industrial Marketing* (February 1982):12.

Lindblom, Charles E. *Politics and Markets: The World's Political-Economic System*. New York: Basic Books, 1977.

Maher, Philip. "Advocacy Advertisers Shift to the Soft Touch." *Industrial Marketing* (February 1982):58-69.

Public Affairs Offices and Their Functions: Summary of Survey Responses. Public Affairs Research Group, School of Management, Boston University, 1981.

Sethi, S. Prakash. *Advocacy Advertising and Large Corporations: Social Conflict, Big Business Image, the News Media, and Public Policy*. Lexington, MA: Lexington Books, 1977.

THE MANAGEMENT OF
CORPORATE CONTRIBUTIONS

John J. Siegfried, Katherine Maddox McElroy
and Diane Biernot-Fawkes

American corporations contributed $2.9 billion to charities in 1981. Through the decade of the 1970s, corporate donations increased almost 13 percent annually, growing from about $800 million to $2.7 billion. Today more and more corporations view their contributions as a form of investment rather than as classic philanthropy (i.e., pure gifts). As contributions budgets grow there is increasing concern over the efficiency of these expenditures, and the growth in contributions frequently requires the employment of professional contributions managers. It is rare today to find the CEO of a major corporation managing contributions out of his "hip pocket." The formal management of the contributions function in large corporations is the subject of this report.

RESEARCH APPROACH AND METHOD

In order to improve our understanding of how corporations administer their charitable contributions, we undertook an interview survey of 240 large cor-

Research in Corporate Social Performance and Policy, volume 5, pages 87-102
Copyright © 1983 by JAI Press Inc.
All rights of reproduction in any form reserved.
ISBN: 0-89232-412-0

porations in 14 metropolitan areas between June 1980 and July 1981. Each firm was interviewed for about one hour, 202 by personal visits and 38 by telephone. Eleven of the firms were found to have little discretion over their contributions because they were closely-controlled subsidiaries; since these firms did not really "manage" their donations, they were deleted from the sample, leaving the 229 firms that constitute the basis of this report.

Two of the authors did all of the interviewing personally, thereby insuring consistency of the interviews and interpretations of the responses. Eighty-six percent of the visits (196) were to the national headquarters of a firm, while 14 percent (33) were to subsidiaries that were operated autonomously, at least in the contributions area. Since the 33 firms denoted as autonomous subsidiaries made their contribution decisions largely independent of their parent company, they are treated as headquarters units with regard to interpretation of responses to the survey questions. Financial data were rarely obtained for the subsidiaries, and the financial data we report apply generally to large, publicly-held firms whose headquarters personnel were interviewed.

The sample consists of large firms in eight major industries: food products, textiles and apparel, chemicals, metals, machinery, public utilities, retailing, and banking. Their average number of employees is 14,210 and average annual pre-tax net income is $91 million. All but 10 of the firms had 500 or more employees. Fifty-one of the 135 industrial firms in the sample were on the 1980 Fortune 500 list.

The 14 metropolitan areas covered (Atlanta, Baltimore, Cincinnati, Cleveland, Dallas, Denver, Louisville, Memphis, Milwaukee, Minneapolis, Nashville, Pittsburgh, St. Louis, and Seattle) represent the various regions of the country and house the headquarters offices of numerous large firms in the eight selected industries. They rank between tenth and fiftieth in Standard Metropolitan Statistical Area population, and all together account for 10.6 percent of the 1980 U.S. population. The industries were chosen to afford the opportunity for a reasonable sample size and to represent various sectors of the economy.

In each case an initial telephone call to the firm attempted to identify the person most familiar with the firm's contributions policy. In about 90 percent of the cases, we were able to interview the most knowledgeable person (regarding contributions) in the firm. The firms in the sample were not chosen randomly. Rather, they were the firms that agreed to be interviewed from a list of large firms in each metropolitan area, classified in the sample industries.[1] About 80 percent of the firms we contacted agreed to an interview. The bias generated by refusal to talk with us is unknown.[2] Our sample firms generally seem to be slightly higher contributors than the national average of large firms, which could be due to the metropolitan areas and industries we chose or could be caused by the reporting bias.

Most of the data reported in this study pertain to fiscal 1980. Some of the firms interviewed in mid-1981 had only fiscal 1981 data available by the time we reached them. We have made no adjustment for this problem. Since almost all of our statistics are ratios, the aggregation of two fiscal years should be innocuous.

In general, we interviewed the individual with final authority for normal philanthropy decisions. The organization location of the philanthropy function in our sample of 229 firms is reported in Table 1. It is evident that reponsibility for corporate contributions is dispersed through many departments, but located primarily in the public affairs department or with one of the general executives. In fact, 15 of our interviews were with either the chairman of the board or the president of the firm.

The trustees of most corporate foundations were also officers or members of the board of the corporation. Thus, about one third of the firms assigned responsibility for contributions decisions to the public affairs department, one third kept responsibility within the general executive officers, and the remainder of the firms scattered the responsibility among the finance, administration, personnel, accounting, and marketing departments.

DESCRIPTIVE RESULTS

The sample firms are described in Table 2. In general, we interviewed large firms (employment average of 14,210 and annual pre-tax net income average of $91 million). They had from one to 7000 geographic locations (average 105) and operated in an average of nine states.

The firms in our sample contributed 0.84 percent of their pre-tax net income (PTNI) to charities. This is a slightly greater fraction of PTNI than has been reported in other surveys. For example, the Conference Board's 1981 survey of

Table 1. Department of Interviewee

Department	No. of Firms	Percentage of Firms
Public affairs*	74	32.3%
General executive**	52	22.7
Finance	38	16.6
Administration	19	8.3
Foundation	19	8.3
Personnel	12	5.2
Accounting	8	3.5
Marketing	7	3.1
Totals	229	100.0

Notes:

*Includes vice-presidents and directors for public affairs, community relations, corporate communications, social policy, and other similar titles.

**Includes chairman of the board, president, CEO, secretary, treasurer, vice-chairman, executive vice-president, assistant to the president, vice-president (with no special designation).

Table 2.   Characteristics of Sample Firms

	Mean	Minimum	Maximum	No. of Responding Firms
Total employees	14,210	40	171,650	224
Employees in headquarters (HQ) city	3,320	10	79,000	222
Pre-tax net income (PTNI) (in thousands)	$90,850	40	1,083,270	184
Contributions as percent of PTNI per firm	1.79%*	0.01%	25.00%	181
Percent of decisions made at HQ (on $ basis)	86.90%	0.01%	100.00%	211
Percent of total contributions made to HQ city charities (on $ basis)	69.40%	0.01%	100.00%	205

Note:
*Simple mean of all percentages; weighted mean (total contributions/total PTNI) is 0.84%.

about 500 large firms (Troy) found a contributions to pre-tax net income ratio of 0.6 percent for firms of similar size. The ratio of contributions to PTNI for all corporations with assets greater than or equal to $10 million in the *1976 Statistics of Income, Corporation Income Tax Returns* is 0.7 percent, although these firms average only $21 million in annual profits. It appears that the firms in our sample are more generous vis-a-vis the firms in other, more comprehensive sets of data on large firms.

The firms made an average of 221 separate gifts per year (counting all United Way contributions as one contribution and counting all educational matching contributions as a single contribution) for a total annual value of $770,359. This and other statistics on gifts are reported in Table 3. Thus, the average amount per gift was about $3,500. This number overstates the typical gift, since United Way contributions are usually a firm's largest single gift, which inflates the average. Single contributions generally range from about $100 to $100,000.

We performed a simple analysis of the relationship between the average gift size and the amount of total contributions. The elasticity of gift size with respect to total contributions is .537. This indicates that the typical contribution of the firm increases in size by about five percent when total contributions grow by ten percent.

Over half the firms were able to give us estimates of the amount of time donated to charitable activities. Valuing this time at a conservative $18,000 per year, donated employee time constitutes 2.7 percent of cash contributions. The most common donation of employee time was the loaning of executives to local United Way campaigns, typically for six-week to two-month periods annually. Of the interviewed firms, 153 donated blocks of employee time to United Way campaigns.

Table 3. Annual Contributions (1979-80) by Firms Providing Data

| Type of Contribution | Average Annual Value | Range | | Median Annual Value | No. of Reporting Firms |
		Minimum	Maximum		
Cash contributions	$770,339	1,000	10,000,000	275,000	184
No. of cash gifts*	221	3	1,800	100	207
Smallest cash gift	$133	5	1,000	50	208
Largest cash gift**	$101,804	200	2,500,000	25,000	207
Employee time***	$20,753	0	500,000	500	158
In-kind contributions	$100,750	0	8,000,000	1,000	160

Notes:

  *Counts matching gifts to educational institutions as one gift.

  **Excludes United Way Campaign

  ***Monetary values were computed from person year estimates and our estimate of average annual incomes according to the employee positions.

In-kind contributions varied widely, from nothing to an estimated $8 million annually. They averaged $100,000, which is 13 percent of cash contributions. When pro-bono work and in-kind gifts are included, we find that cash contributions understate total contributions by about 13.5 percent, a considerable amount.

THE MANAGEMENT OF CORPORATE CONTRIBUTIONS

Headquarters Decisions

Most of the decisions regarding contributions are made at corporate headquarters (see Table 2). Based on the dollar amount of contributions controlled, 87 percent of the decisions are made at headquarters. Because a good deal of the money allocated at headquarters flows to other geographic locations, however, only 69 percent of the dollars go to charities in the headquarters city.

Twenty-nine percent of the firms restrict all corporate contributions decisions to their headquarters personnel. Although 28 percent of the firms offer considerable autonomy to their plants or divisions in making contributions, over half of these still exercise budget review from headquarters. The remaining 43 percent of the firms permit limited contributions from their plants or divisions, the most common limitation being a maximum allowable amount per contribution. Other frequent limitations include an absolute annual limit on total contributions from the plant or division, and a limitation based on a percentage of operating profits generated by the plant or division.

Contributions Policy

The contributions policy of the firm requires two basic decisions: how much to contribute and to which organizations the funds should be contributed. Eighty-two percent of the firms have a corporate policy on contributions, and 60 percent of those have a formal written policy statement or guidelines. Thus, almost half (111) of the interviewed firms have a formal contributions policy.

In general, the corporate board of directors, chief operating officer, or a committee of high-level executives sets the broad policy, specifying the total amount of contributions, guidelines for eligible recipients, and areas of emphasis. They then usually assign responsibility for administering the program to a designated officer. Table 4 indicates the locus of the general policy-setting in our sample firms. In almost every case very high level executives or the board of directors are directly involved. This is somewhat surprising, given the relatively small dollar value of corporate contributions but may be explained by the importance of corporate philanthropy to the firm's external image.

Almost all of the firms (92 percent) reported that the relationship of corporate executives to individual charities affects the allocation of funds. Sixty-eight percent answered with an unqualified yes, 24 percent said executive interests influenced contributions slightly, and eight percent said they have no effect. Some of the latter group have taken elaborate procedural steps to insulate contributions decisions from executive influence. For example, 19 firms reported that a major purpose of their corporate foundation is to foster autonomous decisions in allocating contributions.

Comparisons reported in Table 5 suggest that the position of the primary policy-setter sometimes influences the substance of the firm's contributions policy. Firms appear to make significantly more contributions (the difference is statistically significant) when the staff or trustees of a corporate foundation set the policy than when the president or CEO establishes it. When foundation

Table 4.   **Primary** Policy-Setter for Corporate Contributions

Primary Policy Setter	Number of Firms	Percentage of Firms
Committee of executives	63	27.5%
President or CEO	52	22.7
Board of directors	41	17.9
Chairman of board	25	10.9
Trustees of foundation	212	9.2
Designated corporate officer	18	7.9
Committee of foundation executives	8	3.5
Plant committee	1	0.4
total	229	100.0

Table 5. Corporate Contribution Statistics Classified by Primary Policy-Setter

| | | Primary Policy-Setter | | | | |
	Total	Chairman or Board of Directors	President or CEO	Committee of Executives	Foundation Staff or Trustees	Designated Officer
Approximate sample size*	175	50	40	48	23	13
Contributions/ PTNI—simple mean	1.82%	1.61	1.20	1.80	2.18	3.75
Contributions PTNI—weighted mean	0.84%	0.90	0.68	0.74	1.09	0.69
Percentage of decisions made at HQ (on $ basis)	85.8%	88.1	79.8	87.5	91.1	77.3
Percentage of total contributions made to HQ city charities (on $ basis)	67.8%	66.0	72.0	68.6	59.5	72.5
PTNI ($000)	90,250	78,827	55,266	79,727	229,298	40,279
Employees	16,410	15,378	9,175	13,862	40,709	10,182
Avg. gift size	3,523	2,957	2,933	3,621	6,316	2,493

Note:
*The number of respondents varies slightly by type of information. One firm reported a plant committee as the primary policy-setter.

personnel set policy, firms seem to maintain greater control of contributions at their headquarters (where the foundation people are normally located) and appear to allocate significantly less of their budget to charities in their headquarters city. When operating personnel set contributions policy, it appears that more control over contributions is delegated to non-headquarters (usually operating) personnel.

Budgeting Total Contributions

Contributions are part of the annual budget in 89 percent of the firms. Most use a formula to determine the dollar amount of contributions in their budget. Of the 184 firms that budget contributions, 109 (59 percent) figure it as a percentage of PTNI, 45 (29 percent) base it on the previous year's contributions (incremental budgeting), and 13 (7 percent) specify an absolute amount.

The process of determining how much of the corporation budget to allocate to contributions was evaluated by asking the respondents to rate the influence of different factors, which are listed in Table 6. Respondents were asked to rate each factor as very important, somewhat important, or completely irrelevant with respect to its role in determining the overall quantity of contributions by the firm. The strong influence of the chief executive officer is obvious. In only 11 percent of the cases was his influence irrelevant in determining the amount of contributions.

It appears that contributions are budgeted incrementally, depending heavily on previous year's contributions, and depend critically on earnings. Firms seem to respond to changes in earnings very quickly, adjusting contributions as soon as it is apparent that current year's earnings deviate from their forecast level. A

Table 6.   Factors Influencing Size of Total Corporate Contributions

Factor	Percent Very Important	Percent Slightly Important	Percent Irrelevant	Number of Responding Firms
Discretion of CEO	67.7%	21.4	10.9	229
Size of previous year's contributions	64.6	19.7	15.7	229
Earnings in current year	48.0	18.8	33.2	229
Size of firm relative to community	36.7	32.8	30.6	229
"Fair Share" obligation	33.8	33.3	32.9	228
Earnings in previous year	30.1	12.2	57.6	229
State of the economy	27.1	24.9	48.1	229
Number of employees	8.7	323.3	59.0	229
Volume of requests	8.3	22.7	69.0	229
Number of customers	5.7	14.8	79.5	229
Marginal tax rates	1.7	15.3	83.0	229
Stockholder relations	1.3	3.6	95.1	225

third of the firms indicated that their size relative to their community influenced giving, although the direction of the impact was mixed. Some firms felt a responsibility to shoulder a greater share of the costs of the philanthropic activities in smaller communities, since in many cases they dominated those communities. At the same time they reported that because there are considerably fewer demands on firms located in smaller communities, which tend to have fewer social problems, their giving in those locations might be less than in larger cities. A third of the firms also expressed the view that the "fair share" idea, promoted heavily by United Way, influences their giving. Although some reacted negatively to this concept, they generally conceded that this approach was effective in eliciting contributions.

Twenty-seven percent of the firms noted the state of the economy as an important determinant of total contributions. Three quarters of these firms said it had a positive effect because contributions increase with profits, which rise during expansions. A quarter of the firms, however, indicated that, all else being equal, their giving rises during contractions, since social service agencies are usually under greater pressures in recessions. Of little importance to the budgeted amount of contributions were the number of employees, the volume of requests, the number of customers, or stockholder initiatives.

The "price of giving," that is, the marginal tax rate, was almost never mentioned as a determinant of the amount of contributions, at least within a range of modest tax rate changes. Even though only four firms considered it very important, and only 35 firms considered it even slightly important, the marginal tax rate has been shown to influence total corporate giving in aggregate time series analyses (Nelson). This apparently conflicting evidence might be reconciled if firms actually do respond to changes in tax rates (relative prices) but do not do so consciously. Moreover, many of the officers we interviewed did not hold responsibility for corporate contributions during periods of widely-fluctuating corporate tax rates, e.g., World War II and the Korean War, periods that were included in the time series studies. Our interviewees, therefore, had little experience with which to assess their firms' reactions to tax rate changes.

The data from 157 of the firms permit a more detailed examination of the impact of the budgeting process on contributions. The 109 firms that established a contributions budget as a percent of their pre-tax net income contributed, on average, 2.2 percent of PTNI. The 48 firms that budgeted contributions by making marginal changes from the previous year's budget gave to charities, on average, 1.1 percent of PTNI. Some of this disparity can be analyzed with a multiple linear regression that measures the impact of the budgeting process and other differences on the contribution percentage of PTNI. The regression variables included firm size (measured by employment) and a binary variable for the type of budgetary process. The results indicated a statistically significantly higher giving rate for firms using a percentage of PTNI to budget contributions (vis-a-vis incremental budgeting), holding size constant.

There is a logical reason to expect that the budgeting process may influence the amount of actual contributions. To a large degree, annual contributions develop into "implicit contracts" between the contributing firm and the charitable organizations receiving the gifts. In many cases expectations develop that the gifts will be continued in the future. Budgeting on the basis of PTNI will lead to fluctuations in contributions proportional to fluctuations in earnings. However, this process may be assymetrical if implicit contracts develop. When PTNI grows rapidly, the firm initiates new contributions, which it is then more or less obligated to continue independent of future fluctuations in PTNI. If profits subsequently decline, the *fraction* of PTNI may rachet upward in order to honor these implicit contracts. The net result is that the average fraction of PTNI donated to charities by firms using this budgeting system creeps upward. A noticeable difference in contributions consequently develops between such firms and those using alternative budgetary systems.

Allocating Contributions

Most of the actual administration of corporate contributions is done by a corporate officer designated to allocate the funds (see Table 7). Half of the firms in the sample delegate this authority to one individual, or to a committee that largely follows the recommendations of one individual.[3] About a quarter of the firms had allocation committees that were active in making decisions. In very closely held firms, the president or CEO frequently made the allocation decisions personally. Only two firms used plant committees consisting of employees of all levels to allocate the contributions.

The ratio of contributions to profits was approximately the same for all firms except those in which the president or CEO primarily allocated the contributions, in which case contributions/PTNI was less than half that of other firms. We believe this suggests that as contributions grow (relative to firm size, here meas-

Table 7.   **Primary Responsibility** for Allocation of Contributions

Primary Allocator	Number of Firms	Percentage of Firms
Designated officer	114	49.8%
Committee of executives	58	25.3
President or CEO	221	9.2
Trustees of foundation	16	7.0
Committee of foundation officers	7	3.1
Board of directors	6	2.6
Chairman of board	5	2.2
Plant committee	2	0.9
	229	100.0

ured by profits), there is less likelihood the chief operating officer will maintain day-to-day control of the eleemosynary functions of the firm. As contributions grow, responsibility for allocating them is usually passed on to a committee of executives, given to a designated officer, or assigned to a corporate foundation staff.

The individual responsible for administering corporate philanthropy screens requests, researches philanthropic organizations, makes initial allocation decisions (and talks with curious academics). He or she usually has other major responsibilities as well. We visited firms that had as many as 15 full-time employees assigned to the administration of corporate contributions and others where it was literally handled "out of the back pocket of the CEO," occupying so little of his time as to be unmeasurable. On average the firms had about three quarters of a full-time person working on contributions, commonly consisting of an executive spending about a quarter of his time on the activity, a secretary spending a little less than half-time, with the remainder occupied by committee meeting time.

In deciding what organizations are to receive charitable contributions, some firms relied on other organizations that evaluate charities. Thirty percent of the firms used their local Better Business Bureau, 28 percent used special local organizations set up for the purpose of evaluating charities, and 15 percent used the National Information Bureau to check out potential donees.

Most firms also tried to collect information on the giving behavior of other firms. Seventy-nine percent said they knew something about the policies of other firms. Thirty-five percent claimed some general knowledge of corporate contributions policies of other firms, 33 percent said they got information specifically from other firms, 19 percent obtained information from publications, seven percent asked the charities themselves about what other donors were doing, and five percent exchanged information at meetings of contributions officers. One firm in our sample even hired a special consultant just to obtain information about the policies of other firms.

We asked the firms what specific characteristics of charities they try to assess when considering requests for donations. The most important factor was the effectiveness of the charity in delivering its services, which was mentioned by 53 percent of the firms. Thirty-five percent of the firms specifically examined the ratio of the charity's budget to services delivered. Also very important to the contributors were the administration of the charity's budget (48 percent), in particular, the ratio of fund-raising costs to service expenses; the reputation of the charity (29 percent); and the rationale for the organization's charitable services (18 percent). About 10 percent of the firms examined the people running the charity, which other firms had made commitments to contribute, and whether the charity was providing redundant services. About five percent of the contributors looked for complementarities between the charity's services and the employees and activities of the firm, and how well the charity had defined its goals.

In setting the broad policy guidelines, most firms identified types of organizations that would not qualify for charitable support rather than attempt an inclusive list of those that would qualify. The most common prohibition was on direct giving to religious organizations for sectarian purposes. Fifty-nine percent of the firms prohibited such giving, although most permitted contributions to church-affiliated organizations that have other non-sectarian purposes, such as hospitals and schools. While most firms also said that they would not contribute to political organizations, we did not consider these to be charitable organizations. The only other categories that were prohibited by a considerable number of firms were controversial organizations (e.g., those providing abortion services), gifts to individuals, elementary and secondary schools, and public institutions of higher education, each of which was excluded from eligibility for contributions by about 10 percent of the interviewed firms. Eight percent of the firms do not allow contributions to organizations that receive some funds from government (which is also the reason many public colleges failed to gain support), and five percent of the firms barred gifts to organizations focusing on national issues, to fraternal organizations, as well as gifts for medical purposes or operating funds. In contrast, two percent of the firms prohibited contributions toward endowments. Obviously, the preferences of the donors varied widely. Twenty-five percent of the interviewed firms said they had no general prohibitions on recipients of their contributions.

CORPORATE CONTRIBUTION PATTERNS

The results of the allocation decisions are revealed in Table 8. In a nutshell, slightly under half of the corporate contributions dollars go to health and welfare (including all of the United Way donations), about a quarter go to educational

Table 8.   Allocation of Contributions by Purposes of Recipient and Geographic Scope of Organization

	Average Percentate	Lowest Percentage	Highest Percentage	No. of Reporting Firms
Health and welfare	45.3	0	98.0	195
Education	24.3	0	63.0	195
Civic	12.7	0	60.0	195
Culture and art	12.0	0	50.0	195
Other	5.7	0	70.0	195
Local causes	90.8	9.0	100.0	196
National causes	9.2	0	91.0	196

institutions, and about an eighth each are devoted to the arts and civic organizations. The remainder we classify in a miscellaneous category.

The health and welfare category encompasses United Way agencies, social service agencies, hospitals, medical clinics, and disease-oriented societies such as the Heart Fund, March of Dimes, and the National Cancer Society.

Gifts to higher education, particularly private universities, constitute the majority of funds contributed to education. The education category also includes donations to elementary and secondary schools and to vocational trade schools.

Civic causes are those that address urban problems, primarily legal and economic problems of citizens. These programs' goals are to rehabilitate criminals, to train and find jobs for convicts and unemployed minorities, to provide legal services for low-income citizens, and to develop values among youth and adults. Examples include halfway houses, the Boy Scouts and Girl Scouts, boys clubs, the League of Women Voters Education Fund, the Urban Coalition, YMCA, YWCA, the Salvation Army, Junior Achievement, and the various police and firemen's benevolent associations.

Corporate support of culture and the arts includes sponsorship of art exhibits, symphony fund drives, local theaters, and the construction of new arts centers. The miscellaneous category includes, for example, donations to individuals (several firms ran their own "welfare" programs, usually restricted to retired employees), religious, political, and not-for-profit fraternal organizations, the Humane Society, and the support of public television.

Most of the contributions were allocated to organizations whose fund-raising and target audience were centered on local or state areas, both headquarters and plant locations. Only about 10 percent of total contributions went to national organizations, including the United Negro College Fund, the Public Broadcasting System, the Brookings Institution, and the American Enterprise Institute. Local fund-raising efforts by nationally affiliated agencies, e.g., March of Dimes, Heart Fund, etc., are treated as local contributions in this accounting. Executives indicated that they are predominantly interested in the communities in which they operate and, therefore, give to national associations almost exclusively through local chapters. An average of 70 percent of all contributions (to both local and national causes) remains in the headquarters city. Since, however, this average includes 23 firms that have no operations outside their headquarters city, it is apparent that multiple plant firms give considerable attention to their non-headquarters' community responsibilities.

The primary allocator of contributions appears to have a moderate impact on the distribution of contributions. Distribution patterns are reported in Table 9. Foundations appear to emphasize education and national organizations. The president or CEO seems to give more to health and welfare organizations and civic organizations, where the benefits to the firm might be more direct. Operating officers show a preference toward local eleemosynary organizations.

Table 9. Allocation of Contributions Classified by Primary Allocator

	Number of Firms	Type of Charitable Organization					Geographic Scope of Charitable Organizations	
		Health and Welfare	Education	Arts	Civic	Other	Local	National
Total	195*	45.3%	24.3%	12.0%	12.7%	5.3%	90.3%	9.7%
Foundations with autonomy	20	42.8	31.6	10.4	10.2	4.9	88.8	11.2
Total less foundations with autonomy	175	45.6	23.5	12.2	13.0	5.4	91.0	9.0
Committee of executives	49	39.8	24.7	13.9	15.5	5.4	89.5	10.5
President or CEO	15	50.0	20.7	9.5	15.5	3.8	91.1	8.9
Chairman or Board of Directors	9	41.1	26.1	10.8	18.8	3.3	85.1	14.9
Foundations without autonomy	18	43.9	31.1	11.2	8.9	4.9	87.2	12.8
Designated officer	102	48.3	23.6	11.6	10.7	5.6	91.5	8.5

Note:
*Categories do not add to total because two firms used primarily plant committees to allocate contributions, and they are not reported due to small sample size.

SUMMARY

Our interview data reveal a wide variety of ways in which firms manage their corporate philanthropy function. Most commonly the public relations department or general executive officers administer charitable contributions. The vast majority (87 percent) of the contributions decisions are made at corporate headquarters, although as much as 30 percent of the donations are to organizations located outside the corporate headquarters community.

Large firms, which form our sample, typically have a formal policy on corporate contributions. Two budgetary methods predominate: incremental budgeting, and budgeting a specified fraction of pre-tax net income for contributions. The discretion of the CEO, inertia (the size of last year's budget), earnings, and the method of budgeting all appear to exert considerable influence on the degree of corporate generosity.

Typically about half the contributions go to health and welfare organizations and a quarter to educational institutions, with the remaining quarter divided between civic groups and arts organizations. When the allocation is made by operating officers, there appears to be an emphasis on local organizations providing health and welfare or civic services. Foundations, on the other hand, seem to place a greater emphasis on educational giving and contributions to organizations with a national scope.

The rapid increase in contributions (a rate of about 13 percent annually over the last decade) means that many firms are, for the first time, recognizing a large area of expenditure that is frequently not monitored, evaluated, or controlled. The wide variety of methods firms have adopted to manage their contributions implies that considerable experimentation with management techniques is underway, but no consensus about how to deal with these problems has yet developed.[4]

ACKNOWLEDGMENTS

The authors are Professor of Economics at Vanderbilt University, Economist at TCS Management Group, Inc., and Junior Economist at TCS Management Group, Inc., respectively. This study was made possible by the financial assistance of a group of large corporations which generously supported the Columbia Center for Law and Economic Studies' project on the Impact of the Modern Corporation, and by the invaluable access to information provided by the 240 firms that donated their time by granting us personal interviews.

NOTES

1. We initially identified firms, their size and industrial classification from information obtained from local chambers of commerce, supplemented by Dun and Bradstreet's *Million Dollar Directory, 1980.*

2. The firms that declined to be interviewed were generally either privately owned or closely held publicly-owned companies.

3. While a committee of executives was involved in allocating contributions in 41 percent of the firms, it had primary responsibility for this activity in only 25 percent of the cases. And while 50 percent of the firms designated primary authority to a specific officer, 68 percent had a designated officer responsible for implementing either his own, a committee's, or some other officer's decision.

4. For more analysis of corporate contributions based on the 229 firm survey, see McElroy and Siegfried (1982).

REFERENCES

McElroy, Katherine Maddox, and John J. Siegfried. "The Effect of Firm Size on Corporate Philanthropy," unpublished manuscript, Vanderbilt University, 1983.

McElroy, Katherine Maddox, and John J. Siegfried. "The Effect of Firm Size and Mergers on Corporate Philanthropy." Working Paper 82-W20, Vanderbilt University, August 1982.

Nelson, Ralph L. *Economic Factors in the Growth of Corporate Giving*. New York: National Bureau of Economic Research, 1970.

Troy, Kathryn. *Annual Survey of Corporate Contributions*, 1982 edition. New York: The Conference Board, 1982.

OCCUPATIONAL SAFETY AND HEALTH:

SOCIAL PERFORMANCE,

INFORMATION ASYMMETRY AND

GOVERNMENT REGULATION

James L. Chan

Occupational injuries and illnesses result in enormous human and economic costs. Firms have legal, contractual and social obligations to protect employee occupational safety and health (OSH), and both firms and employees have self interests in reducing OSH risks and costs. For this purpose, both management and labor need information about OSH risks, but have asymmetric access to it. This inhibits the proper valuation of OSH risk premium in the labor market and the reduction of non-obvious risks. The corporate social responsibility doctrine requires that workers be fully informed about their exposure to OSH risks. Its implementation

Research in Corporate Social Performance and Policy, volume 5, pages 103-119
Copyright © 1983 by JAI Press Inc.
All rights of reproduction in any form reserved.
ISBN: 0-89232-412-0

is, however, often hampered by economic and political barriers. This paper therefore argues that to carry out the intent of the 1970 OSH Act, the Federal government should adopt an information strategy—requiring full disclosure of OSH risks by firms and public funding of OSH research and information dissemination.

Since occupational injuries and diseases cost workers' lives and limbs, stockholders' profits, and citizens' tax dollars, OSH is an appropriate focus of research in corporate social performance and accounting. The technological and medical aspects are researched by engineers and health professionals. The social and economic dimensions have been studied by legal scholars (Calabresi), labor economists (Smith; Chelius; Viscusi, 1979a, 1979b, 1980), political scientists and public policy analysts (Kelman, 1980, 1981; Nichols and Zeckhauser). In the real world, occupational safety and health problems do not exist in disciplinary compartments. Solving them requires the integration of technological/medical, legal, political and economic considerations (Ashford).

Given its significant social and economic consequences, OSH should be an attractive area of social accounting research. Unfortunately, the literature is sparse. Chan's analysis of OSH disclosures in corporate annual reports appears to be the only paper focused on this topic. Brief references exist in AICPA and Jensen. Preston offered a description of disclosures in a special report. By and large the literature is descriptive. Descriptive studies are useful in a discipline's early development. However, as Preston has pointed out, criteria for evaluating disclosure practices cannot be developed unless the underlying purpose of social accounting and reporting is ascertained. In view of this need, this paper analyzes the usefulness of OSH information to decision-making of management and labor. Management needs OSH information to discharge its many responsibilities. Labor demands OSH information to determine wage premium, prevent accidents, and seek government intervention. Problems arise when relevant information is not available, disseminated, or used. Occupational health problems are particularly vexing. Due to the often adversary relations between management and labor on OSH matters, the objectives of management and social (labor) reporting are not always compatible (Hopwood, Burchell and Clubb). OSH information economics and politics become important issues. Why? Information is not costless; possessing it gives power. Analysis of these issues leads to the consideration of the role of government.

SOCIAL AND ECONOMIC COSTS OF ACCIDENTS

The social and economic costs of work-related accidents are enormous.[1] Partly due to the information problems discussed shortly, accident cost data are inadequate. Available suggestive evidence, presented in Table 1, should be interpreted with caution.

Table 1. Occupational Injuries and Illnesses

Year	Cases	Deaths Rate*	Private Sector Incidence Rates			
			TRC	LWC	NFC/NLWD	LWD
72	14100	17	10.9	3.3	7.6	50.0
73	14200	17	11.0	3.4	7.5	53.3
74	13400	15	10.4	3.5	6.9	54.6
75	12600	15	9.1	3.3	5.8	56.1
76	12500	14	9.2	3.5	5.7	60.5
77	13000	14	9.3	3.8	5.5	61.6
78	13000	14	9.4	4.1	5.3	63.5
79	13200	13	9.5	4.3	5.2	67.7
80	13000	13	8.7	4.0	4.7	65.2

Notes: Data Source: *Accident Facts* for the years indicated.
*Per 100,000 workers.
OSHA Definitions:

> Incidence Rate = [(No. of injuries & illnesses × 200,000)
> OR (No. of lost workdays × 200,000)] / [(Total hours worked by all employees during period covered)];
> 200,000 = base for 100 full-time equivalent employees working 40 hours per week for 50 weeks annually.
> TRC = Total recordable cases
>   = (Fatal cases) + (Lost workdays cases) + (Nonfatal cases without lost workdays)
> LWC = Lost workday cases
> NFC/NLWD = Nonfatal cases without lost workdays
> LWD = Lost workdays

According to the National Safety Council, the annual number of deaths due to work-related accidents in the U.S. ranged from 12,500 to 14,200 during the last 10 years. The death rate per 100,000 workers has declined during the same period. Table 1 also shows the various "incidence rates" of occupational injuries and illnesses, developed by OSHA for recordable cases, lost workday cases, nonfatal cases without lost workdays, and the number of lost workdays. Note that death, which is certainly the worst case, is not separately recognized in OSHA's incidence rates. Furthermore, an unknown number of occupational illnesses go unrecorded. Despite these problems, OSHA statistics are among the most consistent and comparable data sources available.

A rigorous evaluation of the OSH social performance should relate the incidence rates to such explanatory variables as the level of economic activities, age and experience level of the workforce, and the intensity of public regulation (Smith; Viscusi, 1979b). A quick perusal of Table 1 suggests that the incidence rates have remained fairly stable over the last 10 years. This suggests that, on the whole, OSH efforts have not been very successful. Only nation-wide statistics are presented in Table 1. Since incidence rates differ among industries and occupational categories, the evaluation of individual firms' performance should be related to their respective industry norms (Chan).

Table 2. Costs of Work Accidents
(Billions of Dollars)

Year	Workers' Comp. Payments	NSC Cost Estimates			
		Visible Costs	Other Costs	Fire Losses	Total
72	4.0	5.2	5.2	1.1	11.5
73	5.1	6.4	6.4	1.2	14.0
74	5.7	6.8	6.8	1.7	15.3
75	6.5	7.0	7.0	2.0	16.0
76	7.5	7.9	7.9	2.0	17.8
77	8.6	9.3	9.3	2.1	20.7
78	9.7	10.6	10.6	1.8	23.0
79	11.9	12.6	12.6	2.1	27.3
80	13.4	14.0	14.0	2.2	30.2

Note: Data Source: Accident Facts for the years indicated.

How much do accidents cost in monetary terms? Table 2 summarizes available statistics. Workers' Compensation payments increased from $4 billion in 1972 to $10 billion in 1980. These are internalized social costs financed by firms' insurance premium payments. The National Safety Council estimates that "visible costs" of work accidents—wage losses, insurance administrative costs, and medical costs—have also doubled to $10 billion in 1980. "Other costs," including the money value lost by other workers and accident investigation costs, are believed to be equal to the visible costs. All these costs and fire losses totaled $11.5 billion in 1972 and about $30 billion in 1980. These figures should be adjusted for inflation. Even though these figures are rough estimates, they are the best available.

In addition to the above private-sector costs, expenditures for OSHA programs increased from $70 million in Fiscal Year 1973 to the current level of $200 million (Table 3). Additional research costs have more than doubled from $25 million to about $80 million during the same period. Costs of complying with specific OSHA standards are estimated to be huge. For example, the chemical label requirement proposed by OSHA would allegedly cost industries $14 billion.

OBJECTIVES OF OSH MEASUREMENT AND REPORTING

In the absence of explicit accounting standards and auditing, one should view the cost figures cited above with skepticism. Two types of efforts are needed to improve the quality of OSH cost data. The first is the development of cost accounting concepts and standards. These will increase the reliability and credi-

Table 3. Public Expenditure for OSH
(Millions of Dollars)

| | OSHA | | | NIOSH | | | |
FY	EC&I	Stat.	Total	Research	Train.	Total	Source
73	6.5	4.8	69.3	21.2	3.9	25.1	75
	(9%)	(7%)					
74	4.5	5.1	70.0	23.6	3.5	26.1	76
	(6%)	(7%)					
75	8.9	5.6	95.8	25.0	7.2	32.2	77
	(9%)	(6%)					
76	4.8	5.4	114.9	32.5	4.5	37.0	78
	(4%)	(5%)					
77	17.6	6.0	130.2	33.3	1.5	37.6	79
	(14%)	(5%)					
78	26.6	6.7	150.7	42.1	3.5	50.9	80
	(17.7%)	(4.4%)					
79	34.3	6.4	161.0	43.7	8.5	56.8	81
	(21.3%)	(4.0%)					
80	37.9	7.1	185.6	52.5	9.4	65.6	82
	(20.4%)	(3.8%)					
81*	57.3	7.1	213.6	63.9	14.3	82.9	82
	(26.8%)	(3.3%)					
81	49.8	6.5	200.8	76.2	20.9	102.3	83
	(24.9%)	(3.3%)					
82*	80.0	9.0	242.6	64.3	12.3	81.4	82
	(33.0%)	(3.7%)					
82*	50.1	8.8	192.5	51.8	5.8	60.2	83
	(26.0%)	(4.6%)					
83*	56.9	9.0	206.3	48.4	N.A.	N.A.	83
	(27.6%)	(4.4%)					

Note:
* Budgetary estimates

EC&I = Education, consulting and information
Stat. = OSH statistics
Train. = Training
Source = Appendix to the Budget of the United States Government for the fiscal year (FY) indicated in the
last column.

bility of figures, which are often used in the heated arguments over the "economic feasibility" of OSHA standards. The second are industry-wide and eventually nation-wide information networks for aggregating firm-level cost data.

The underlying purpose of OSH measurement and reporting is to motivate management, labor, and government to reduce occupational injuries and illnesses. Their awareness and actions will be facilitated by such information as

- the monetary and nonmonetary costs of accidents,
- the distribution of accident costs, and
- efforts made by all parties to increase OSH.

The complexity of OSH creates great difficulties for measurement systems. First, the concept requires that causality be established between employment and the occurrence of an injury or illness. While the severing of a hand by a machine in a factory is undoubtedly job-related, it is far more difficult to relate ill health, e.g. cancer and mental stress, directly to employment. Furthermore, the toxicity of some chemicals is latent. Symptoms of some occupational diseases do not manifest themselves until years later, perhaps after the worker is no longer employed by the firm exposing him. Causality is a factual question. Scientific evidence unfortunately is often equivocal. Who carries the burden of proof, and how heavy should it be? Resolutions of these questions are important in allocating responsibility and ultimately in the costs of compensating and caring for the victims.

Second, threats to employee safety and health in the workplace are so numerous that they are very costly to identify and evaluate exhaustively. Common safety threats include fires, explosions, electrocution, dangerous machines, noise, heat stress, and vibration. Health hazards include noise, harmful dusts (such as silica, asbestos, beryllium and cotton dusts), carcinogens, heat stress, vibration, and radiations. There are at least 12,000 known toxic substances in workplaces, and more chemicals are being introduced at a very fast rate. There are disagreements on hazard threshold levels, and scientific research has not yet documented all of them (Ashford).

Third, it is more difficult for workers to recognize health than safety hazards. They may not be told what toxic materials they are handling. Scientific data concerning exposure levels and toxicity are often protected by patents and licenses. Furthermore, the hazards may be detected only with scientific instruments, which workers may not have or be allowed to use.

The above concerns suggest the need for social reports on OSH. Such reports should recognize that management and labor may have quite different perspectives on OSH problems. The next two sections deal with these.

MANAGEMENT PERSPECTIVE

Employers have traditionally been held responsible for employees' OSH. This "social responsibility" has over time evolved into explicit legal and financial responsibilities.

Legal Responsibilities[2]

Disputes over who should bear how much of what costs, related to illness and accidents, often results in lawsuits. Under common law, employers are required to exercise due care for employee safety. They should provide safe tools and equipment, require customary and safe procedures, and use only qualified personnel. Employers not meeting these requirements may be found negligent and held liable for damages. Three lines of defense are, however, available against charges of negligence: the accident was caused by a co-worker; besides assuming ordinary risks of a particular trade, the employee knew and accepted extraordinary risks; and the employee contributed to the accident. Posner has argued that the common law provides an efficient mix of accident prevention by both employers and employees. That may be the case, however, only when both sides have equal access to OSH risk information. Delays under the common law system aggravated the victim's pain, suffering, and economic hardship, as well as prolonged the employer's financial uncertainty. These considerations provided impetus for a system of "no fault" insurance—State Workers' Compensation laws.

State Workers' Compensation laws provide for defined payments for compensable injuries and illness. While it is unnecessary to assign fault, the occupational origin of an injury or illness remains to be demonstrated. Unpredictable and possibly large damage awards and uncompensated costs borne by the worker are "internalized" by the firm in the form of Workers' Compensation insurance premium. Experience rating—relating premium to accident records—also to some extent provides economic incentive for accident prevention. Currently close to 90 percent of American workers are covered under some form of Workers' Compensation.

Evidently, Workers' Compensation laws did not achieve all social goals with respect to employment-related accidents and illnesses. The Federal Coal Mine Health and Safety Act was passed in 1969, after 78 coal miners died in a coal mine explosion in Farmington, West Virginia. The Occupational Safety and Health Act (OSHAct) quickly followed in 1970. In contrast to the economic incentive approach of Workers' Compensation, OSHAct mandates direct government regulation of the workplace. The Occupational Safety and Health Administration (OSHA) was created to promulgate standards and enforce the law, whose intent was "to assure so far as possible every working man and woman in the Nation safe and healthful working conditions." Employers were charged with the duty of complying with specific OSHA standards, and the catch-all "general duty" to protect employees' OSH. The legislation, however, did not address the questions of "How much OSH?" and "At what costs?" Fortunately for employers, the Act's economic feasibility provision serves as a safety valve. To labor, it provides an excuse for management inaction.

The passage of the OSHAct has encouraged the inclusion of OSH in labor contract bargaining. Unions seek to reinforce employers' legal responsibilities with additional contractual obligations, such as contributions to OSH research, coverage beyond OSHAct, arbitration over OSH disputes, unlimited union inspection rights and firm's funding of union's use of OSH experts, training union OSH personnel, periodic medical examinations for employees, and the establishment of joint OSH committees (Ashford). The provisions are mixed blessings to management. They increase employee participation and responsibility for their own safety and health. Unfortunately, they also erode management control.

In sum, management's OSH responsibilities are numerous and substantial. Methods for measuring management performance in discharging them are clearly needed.

OSH Performance Measurement

Both effort and outcome information is necessary for evaluating firms' OSH performance. The former tells how hard firms try, the latter how well they succeed. Chan's study provides some examples of OSH efforts described in firms' annual reports.

- Launching safety campaigns, giving awards and prizes
- Compliance with OSHA regulations
- Establishing corporate level OSH committees
- Creating OSH positions, departments or programs
- Increasing employee information access, training and providing medical examinations
- Incorporating OSH considerations in capital investment and operating decisions
- OSH research and development
- Increasing OSH-related expenditures

Many of these accident prevention efforts are amenable to financial measurement. In general, reducing more OSH risks requires greater accident prevention costs. (See Figure 1). The costs increase exponentially because complex problems tend to be solved last.

Capital investments in employee OSH are one kind of accident prevention costs. McGraw-Hill Publications Company has been conducting annual surveys of these efforts. Table 4 shows actual OSH-related capital expenditures from 1972-1981, and planned capital expenditures for 1982-1985. The data are valuable in providing a sense of the magnitudes. For example, a total of about $7 billion in OSH-related capital investments are planned for 1983-1985. As always, careful interpretation is necessary. First, what qualifies as an OSH-related investment? It is easy to cost out separate safety equipment, but as OSH considerations are integrated into plant and equipment designs and operating procedures, distinctiveness diminishes. Ironically, reported OSH investments may consequently decline. Second, operating costs should not be overlooked. Some industries are more capital intensive than others. Thus more capital investment does not necessarily mean being more socially responsible. Finally, these efforts,

Table 4. Capital Investment in OSH
(Millions of Dollars

| Year | Manufacturing | | Non-manufacturing |
	Durables	Non-Durables	
72	627	418	2234
73	787	526	2303
74	1143	712	2548
75	888	820	2134
76	603	783	2029
77	941	939	2411
78	1185	1271	4189
79	1328	1045	1944
80	1091	1247	1789
81	1095	1625	2393
82**	1053	1549	2596
83-85*	1533	1914	3245

Notes:
** Planned
* Planned annual average
Source:Tenth Annual McGraw-Hill Survey of Investment in Employee Safety and Health.

laudable as they are, should not be equated with success in actually reducing the frequency and severity of accidents.

In addition to the above accident prevention costs, management performance may be judged in terms of minimizing accident costs of the kinds described in Table 2. In general, the higher the OSH risk, the more numerous and severe will be the accidents, and thus the greater the accident costs. An analytic framework for relating both accident prevention costs and accident costs to OSH risks is presented in Figure 1. The optimal level of OSH risks for the firm is where the sum of these two types of costs is minimized.[3]

For a given level of OSH to be achieved, managers should choose the least costly method of implementation. Alternatively, for a given budget, managers should maximize OSH. The utility of OSH information, as with social accounting information in general, lies in helping management to achieve social objectives.

Outcome measures are needed to evaluate the success of accident prevention efforts. Firms are required to follow standard OSHA definitions in recording accidents. Chan found that most firms had not used the resulting information in social reporting for annual reports. Even if the data were available, there are several pitfalls in regarding these as indicators of managerial effectiveness.

First, since improving OSH involves avoiding occupational injuries and illnesses, measuring OSH directly is difficult. Consequently, inputs rather than outputs are found to be emphasized in measurement systems. Chan has found this to be the case in OSH social reporting. Second, there is a tendency to

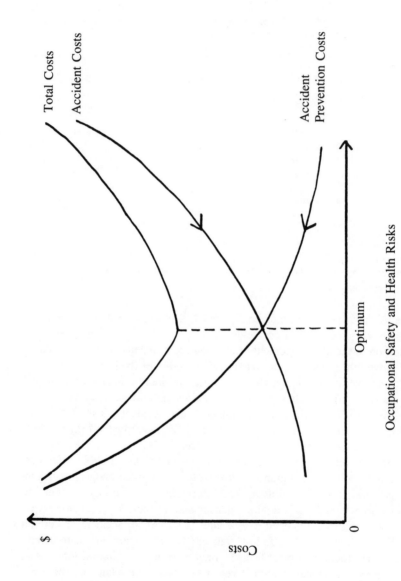

Figure 1. Optimum Level of OSH.

interpret changes in reporting statistics as clear evidence of managerial performance, when they result from joint actions of management, labor, and government.
Some changes are due to the reporting system itself. Recall the earlier discussion
on measuring firms' capital investments in OSH. The third pitfall is "the almost
irresistible tendency to suppress 'unfavorable' data" (Preston). This tendency is
greater when management has superior private knowledge of OSH risks.

This section has presented a management perspective of OSH in the belief
that an objective of social accounting and reporting is to increase management
awareness and control of OSH problems. Management has to reconcile OSH
objectives with other objectives, such as saving costs and maintaining management control. Some (e.g. Jensen and Meckling) assume that management is the
agent of owners. If so, management represents a partisan interest in the economic
system. Labor is the other economic interest to be reckoned with.

LABOR PERSPECTIVE

In this discussion, the relevant factors in employees' job satisfaction are economic
compensation and occupational safety and health. OSH information is useful as
supporting evidence for demanding OSH risk premium and post-accident compensation, and helps to prevent accidents. For the first purpose, the following
information is relevant: likely economic loss due to injuries and illnesses, com-
pensations to cover part or all of the loss, wage premium for bearing extraordinary
OSH risks. Information relevant for accident prevention includes the existence
and identity of OSH hazards, the extent of worker exposure to them, and the
consequences of exposure and preventive measures.[4]

Bearing OSH risks is a part of an employment contract whose terms may be
regarded as mutually advantageous (Simon). For this reason, it has been argued
that "since employment with a particular company is not compulsory, financial
rewards encompass *all* aspects of the employment relationship and that there is
no such thing as social—or at least 'uncompensated social'—elements in that
relationship" (AICPA Committee on Social Measurement). The validity of this
assertion depends on the extent to which wage rates reflect the underlying OSH
information.

Distinguish the following two situations. In the first, the OSH risks of a
particular occupation (e.g. construction, coal mining) are known to current or
prospective employees. These individuals can then make informed choices, and
in the aggregate there should be a reasonably good match between jobs of varying
OSH risks and individuals of differing risk preferences (Cropper; Viscusi, 1979a).
In this situation, labor, particularly if unionized, often succeeds in obtaining an
explicit OSH risk premium, an addition to the basic wage rate. For example,
the contract between the Mechanical Contractors Council of Central California
and Plumbers specifies a $.50 wage premium for every two hours working at a

height of 30 feet or more from structure level. In the contract between the National Steel and Shipbuilding Co. in San Diego, California, and Iron Workers, employees are paid an additional $.15 for every additional hour spent welding in an environment with air pressure over 600 p.s.i. or being sealed in a tank for testing purposes (U.S. Bureau of Labor Statistics). These and several other examples of the OSH provisions in labor contracts illustrate the general proposition that, when employees are well-informed about OSH and have bargaining power, they may be at least partially compensated for the OSH risks they voluntarily assume. The actual wage rate consists of a basic component and a "risk premium," which is an increasing function of measurable OSH risks. This is shown in Case A in Figure 2.

Note that it is unnecessary for *every* worker to be fully informed about OSH risks. So long as the bargaining agent is aware of the risks, even uninformed or partially informed workers belonging to the union receive the economic benefit. Unorganized labor therefore faces the double jeopardy of being under-informed about OSH risks and in a weak bargaining position for obtaining risk premium.

In the second situation, Case B in Figure 2, typically involving OSH hazards posed by new toxic substances, an employee is *not* well-informed about the risks, and actual exposure is greater than perceived exposure. Consequently, not only is the employee unable to protect him/herself or to demand corrective action by management or OSHA, he/she will also fail to demand an OSH-related risk premium. Since actual wage rate is based on perceived exposure, the employee incurs an opportunity cost—the wage premium he might be able to bargain for, had he known the actual level of exposure. In other words, his nominal rate should be discounted for uncompensated risk-bearing to arrive at the true and lower effective rate.

This situation occurs for several reasons. First, management itself may not be aware of the risks. Even if it is, it may conceal them, minimize their significance or use equivocal scientific information to avoid positive action. When will management inform itself and communicate the information to employees? The answer may boil down to economics—large and profitable firms can better afford the costs of producing or obtaining the information; small and marginal firms typically have worse OSH records and often face the dilemma of tolerating OSH problems or going out of business. Second, even if the scientific community has objectively determined the health effects of various levels of exposure, "acceptable" levels of exposure are socially determined. In the final analysis, the cost-benefit criterion is invoked, with labor and management often disagreeing. Third, technical and health data for certain chemicals may be protected by the "property rights" of the firm in the form of patents and licenses.

Besides seeking compensation or finding a job with acceptable OSH risks, labor can also take various actions to prevent accidents. Workers suspecting violations may also file anonymous complaints to OSHA to trigger OSHA inspections.

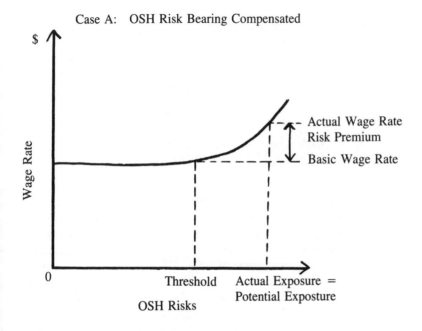

Case A: OSH Risk Bearing Compensated

$

Wage Rate

Actual Wage Rate
Risk Premium
Basic Wage Rate

0   Threshold   Actual Exposure =
                      Potential Exposture

OSH Risks

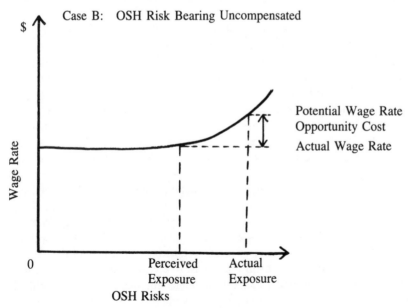

Case B: OSH Risk Bearing Uncompensated

$

Wage Rate

Potential Wage Rate
Opportunity Cost
Actual Wage Rate

0   Perceived   Actual
         Exposure   Exposure

OSH Risks

Figure 2. Effect of OSH Information on Compensation for Risk Bearing.

115

In short, while labor and management may share the same basic goal of OSH, they are interested in minimizing their own costs. The market system under conditions of perfect information will efficiently allocate risks. As must be clear by now, imperfect information is characteristic of OSH. When firms are unable or unwilling to produce and share information, a role for government may arise.

TOWARD A PUBLIC POLICY
ON OSH INFORMATION

Currently OSHA relies heavily on on-site inspections and penalties to enforce its standards. However, due to manpower shortage, OSHA inspections are infrequent. Penalties are also modest. Result: lack of substantial economic incentives to comply with OSHA standards (Viscusi, 1979b; Nichols and Zeckhauser). Many in the business community oppose OSHA. They feel that its standards are at best costly, and at worst trivial and unnecessary (U.S. Senate). Even managers in a socially aware business are more mindful of the firm's costs than of OSHA criteria. Ten years' experience has shown that the procedural approach adopted by OSHA has not been effective in reducing occupational injuries and illnesses in the U.S.

Alternative regulatory strategies should be considered. An analogy may be drawn between OSHA and another regulatory agency, the Securities and Exchange Commission (SEC), which is charged with protecting investors in the securities of publicly held corporations. Instead of getting involved in the day-to-day operations of firms under its jurisdiction, the SEC tries to make sure that information, including "bad news," reaches the capital market. It is then up to the investors to make their decisions on the basis of the available information. Full disclosure of information serves as a deterrent to illegal acts. Similarly, if OSHA can make sure that OSH risk information is disseminated in the labor market, employees can make informed trade-offs between economic benefits and OSH. If the labor market functions efficiently, there will be less need and justification for government intervention.

To some extent, OSHA is already pursuing the information strategy. With the exception of small firms, most employers are required by OSHA to keep accurate and timely records of the occurrence of occupational injuries and illnesses on OSHA Form 200 and retain them for at least five years. They are also required to post at each establishment of the firm annual summary totals of recordable cases and the number of lost workdays. Furthermore, OSHA's own information activities—education, consulting, and statistics—increased. Expenditures for these activities increased from about $11 million (or 26 percent of total OSHA program costs) in FY73 to $89 million (or 37 percent of OSHA's budget of $243) for FY82 (Table 3). Note that FY81 actual spending was less than budgeted. Furthermore, OSHA's FY82 budget was revised downward by $50 million, as consistent with the Reagan Administration's deregulation philosophy.

The information strategy is critically important in combating occupational health problems, where an essential problem is the substantial lack of relevant information. Firms may be unwilling or unable to deal with these issues. Research is costly. Unless the firm can appropriate the benefits of research, it tends to under-invest in it. Furthermore, dissemination of research results may be restricted by patents or other barriers. A public agency, such as the National Institute of Occupational Safety and Health (NIOSH), is needed to conduct the research and disseminate findings. The budget of NIOSH has more than tripled over the last 10 years, from $25 million to $81 million. Again, note that NIOSH's FY82 budget was reduced by $21 million by the Reagan Administration.

Evidence suggests that the Federal government has in recent years allocated proportionately more resources to information programs. This is consistent with a deregulation philosophy, which advocates minimizing the government's intrusions in the private sector. Providing information is an integral part of any other regulatory strategy. OSHA has spent its first ten years largely on relatively visible safety problems. Its next great challenge will be occupational health issues, where information may be the critical element.

ACKNOWLEDGMENTS

I am grateful for the helpful comments of Ahmed Belkaoui, James C. McKeown, and Lee E. Preston on previous drafts of this paper. Thanks are also due to my former colleagues at the Health Studies Program at Syracuse University, William Johnson, Nicholas Karatjas and Stephen Strand, with whom I began my research on occupational safety and health issues. I also appreciate the able assistance of Vikram Sharma, Lisa Virella and Lois Yee. This paper is No. 42 of Studies in Governmental and Social Accounting. Its completion was partly supported by released time granted by the Department of Accounting, College of Business Administration, University of Illinois at Chicago.

NOTES

1. The term "accidents" is used throughout this paper to refer to events giving rise to employment-related injuries or illnesses.
2. This section relies heavily on Chelius, Smith, and Ashford.
3. Idea adapted from Ashford.
4. Synthesized from the OSH literature.

REFERENCES

Accident Facts. National Safety Council. Chicago: various years.

American Institute of Certified Public Accountants, Committee on Social Measurement. *The Measurement of Corporate Social Performance*. New York: CPA, 1977.

Ashford, Nicholas A. *Crisis in the Workplace: Occupational Disease and Injury*. Cambridge, MA: MIT Press, 1976.

Budget of the United States Government—Appendix. U.S. Office of Management and Budget. Washington: 1973-1982.

Calabresi, G. *The Costs of Accidents: A Legal and Economic Analysis*. New Haven, CT: Yale University Press, 1970.

Chan, James L. "Corporate Disclosure in Occupational Safety and Health: Some Empirical Evidence." *Accounting, Organizations and Society* 4, No. 4 (1979): 273-281.

Chelius, J. R. *Workplace Safety and Health: The Role of Workers' Compensation*. Washington: American Enterprise Institute, 1977.

Cropper, M. L. "Health, Investment in Health, and Occupational Choice." *Journal of Political Economy* (December 1977):1273-1294.

Hopwood, A. G., Stuart Burchell, and Colin Clubb. "The Development of Accounting in Its International Context: Past Concerns and Emerging Issues." Paper presented at the Third Charles Waldo Haskins Seminar on Accounting History, Georgia State University, Atlanta, April 20, 1979.

Jensen, Michael C., and William Meckling. "Theory of the Firm: Management Behavior, Agency Costs and Ownership Structure." *Journal of Financial Economics* 3 (1976):305-360.

Jensen, R. E. *Phantasmagoric Accounting: Research and Analysis of Economic, Social and Environmental Impact of Corporate Business*. Sarasota, FL: American Accounting Association, 1976.

Kelman, Steve. "Occupational Safety and Health Administration," in James Q. Wilson (ed.), *The Politics of Regulation*. New York: Basic Books, 1980.

————. *Regulating America, Regulating Sweden: A Comparative Study of Occupational Safety and Health Policy*. Cambridge, MA: The MIT Press, 1981.

Major Collective Bargaining Agreements: Safety and Health Provisions. U.S. Bureau of Labor Statistics. Washington: 1976.

The Measurement of Corporate Social Performance. American Institute on Certified Public Accountants, Committee on Social Measurement. New York: 1977.

McGraw-Hill Publications Company, *Survey of Investment in Employee Occupational Safety and Health*. New York: McGraw-Hill, 1982.

National Safety Council. *Accident Facts*. Chicago: National Safety Council, various years.

Nichols, A. L., and R. Zeckhauser. "Government Comes to the Workplace: An Assessment of OSHA." *The Public Interest* (Fall 1977):39-69.

Posner, Richard. "A Theory of Negligence." *The Journal of Legal Studies* 1, No. 1 (1972).

Preston, Lee E. "Research on Corporate Social Reporting: Directions for Development." *Accounting, Organizations and Society* 6, No. 3 (1981):255-261.

Simon, Herbert A. "A Formal Theory of Employment Relation," in *Models of Man*. New York: Wiley, 1957.

Smith, R. S. *The Occupational Safety and Health Act: Its Goals and Its Achievement*. Washington: American Enterprise Institute, 1976.

U.S. Bureau of Labor Statistics. *Major Collective Bargaining Agreements: Safety and Health Provisions*. Washington: U.S. Bureau of Labor Statistics, 1976.

U.S. Office of Management and Budget. *Budget of the United States Government—Appendix*. Washington: U.S. Government Printing Office, 1973-1982.

U.S. Senate, Subcommittee on Labor of the Committee on Labor and Public Welfare. *Occupational Safety and Health Act Review, 1974*. Washington: U.S. Government Printing Office, 1974.

Viscusi, W.K. *Employment Hazards: An Investigation of Market Performance*. Cambridge, MA: Harvard University Press, 1979a.

———. "The Impact of Occupational Safety and Health Regulation." *Bell Journal of Economics* 10 (1979b):117-140.

———. "Imperfect Job Risk Information and Optimal Workmen's Compensation Benefits." *Journal of Public Economics* 14 (1980): 319-337.

A PRELIMINARY THEORY OF COMPLIANCE WITH OSHA REGULATION

Barbara Gray Gricar

Extensive government regulation of the traditional domains of management has greatly complicated corporate decision-making in recent years, and assessing corporate social performance under the host of regulatory pressures created during the 1970s offers a relatively untapped area for organizational research. Despite the attention to organizations as open systems and to environmental influences on organizations, much of the organization theory literature has ignored the imperative created by government regulation.

This paper examines organizational response to federal regulation by analyzing the responses of 34 foundries to the Occupational Safety and Health Administration. The research demonstrates that firms exhibited different patterns of response to OSHA regulation and that several organizational variables accounted for the differences. In particular, responses were a function of the ideological views of the top management of the firms; responses were also related to the

Research in Corporate Social Performance and Policy, volume 5, pages 121-141 size and boundary-spanning activities undertaken by the organization. The expectation that environmental uncertainty would influence responses was not supported.

BACKGROUND

Early contingency theorists, Lawrence and Lorsch for example, focused on market and technological aspects of the organization's environment, and more recent refinements of contingency models (Duncan, Osborne and Hunt, Downey and Slocum, Tung) failed to specify the regulatory environment as a distinct domain worthy of consideration. Yet government control over American business has increased substantially during the 1970s (MacAvoy) and indications are that regulatory pressures on business will not subside in the 1980s (O'Toole). Perhaps more than any environmental domain, government regulation constitutes a true environmental imperative for businesses.

Environmental contingency theory would predict similar responses among firms facing the same regulatory imperative, but there is evidence to the contrary. Business response to regulation varies from compliance—about 22 percent of inspected firms met OSHA standards in 1974 (Nichols and Zeckhauser)—to outright resistance. (In *Marshall v. Barlow's Inc.*, a firm's refusal to admit OSHA inspectors without a warrant was upheld by the Supreme Court.) The possibility that response to regulation varies across firms under similar regulatory conditions raises an important research question: What accounts for differences in response to approximately identical regulatory pressures? A few recent studies have sought to answer this question. Miles offers a rich description of how the tobacco industry responded to the Surgeon General's Report, and Sonnenfeld provides detailed cases of the forestry industry's response to regulation. Connor and Siebler report on the effects of regulatory responses on the future of long-term care facilities.

This paper offers an empirical analysis of the implications of one regulatory imperative—the Occupational Safety and Health Act (OSHAct). Specifically, the study investigates the responses of 34 manufacturing firms to enforcement activities of the Occupational Safety and Health Administration (OSHA). The research examines the influence of key organizational variables on compliance responses made by the firms to OSHA enforcement activities. The analysis offers a preliminary explanation for differences in corporate social performance regarding compliance with OSHA regulation.

THEORETICAL FRAMEWORK

A review of the organizational literature on regulation identified five variables which might account for differences in responses to OSHA by otherwise similar firms. The following paragraphs describe each of these variables and develop rationale for the inclusion of each of them in this study.

Ideology. Bourgeous, McAllister and Mitchell have suggested that business' imperative to organize in a particular way may be determined more by managerial values and inclinations than by technological and environmental contingencies. Indeed, many researchers, including Child and Montanari, have pointed to a relationship between values, or ideology, and strategic response. Pfeffer maintains that organizations plan and select courses of action in light of ideological values and attempt to manage their internal and external resources in ways that are consistent with those values.

The idea that regulation engenders ideological reactions within firms is well supported. Recent arguments by Weaver, Lilley and Miller, and Dunlap et. al. claim that ideology accounts for differences between the government and regulated firms about the existence of regulation as well as about its goals and operational methods. OSHA, for example, "has generated fierce antagonism in the business community and is viewed by many as the quintessential government intrusion" (Nichols and Zeckhauser). As one of the 42 "social" regulatory agencies, born out of a concern that the government intervene to protect various interest groups from the negative externalities associated with unfettered business practices, OSHA illustrates the *"new American ideology"* characterized by communitarian values rather than the traditional ideology of individualism and free enterprise (Lodge).

Evidence that ideological issues influence regulatory response was provided by Downey et. al., who found that individual normative factors (defined as moral, ethical and political beliefs) were significant in explaining compliance with OSHA regulation. Furthermore, Zander proposed that compliance with regulations was a function of organizational acceptance of them. It is expected, then, that the greater a firm's ideological opposition to regulation, the less compliance behavior it will exhibit.

Size. Despite debate among organizational researchers about the influence of size on structure, it has been suggested that size directly affects response to regulation (Currington). It seems intuitively reasonable to expect that larger, more visible firms are likely to be inspected more frequently, and therefore will exhibit more technical, informational, and administrative responses than smaller firms that may never be inspected. Currington reasoned that compliance with OSHA standards may also be affected by the degree to which a firm has knowledge of and understands the law's requirements and that larger firms are more likely to have safety departments to handle such interpretations. Indeed, according to Lilley and Miller, many small firms were not even aware of OSHA standards which applied to their operations.

Specific research by Rinefort on OSHA compliance behavior showed that size did affect the nature and extent of safety activities undertaken by firms. More general support for the prediction was offered by Salancik. In a study of compliance with federal government demands for affirmative action, he found greater compliance among larger than smaller firms, even when both were equally dependent on the federal government for contracts. However, research by Crenson suggested just the opposite effect for size; larger steel companies were less responsive to clean air regulations than small firms. Salancik accounted for these differential effects of size as differences in the social and moral consensus behind regulatory demands.

Pfeffer and Salancik indicate that firms try to manage their dependencies on other organizations in order to control environmental contingencies. However, to the extent that size enhances organizational power to control the environment (Pfeffer), less strategic choice over dependencies is afforded to smaller firms (Aldrich and Pfeffer). Therefore, we anticipated that smaller firms would be less able to manage the regulatory environment than larger firms, and that larger firms would adapt more readily to a regulatory environment that they themselves were more apt to control.

Uncertainty. The late 1960s and early 1970s saw the development of the belief that uncertainty is a major determinant of organizational structure. Uncertainty, according to Galbraith (1973, 1977), refers to the difference between the amount of information an organization has and the amount it needs to accomplish its tasks. Environments which are both dynamic and complex were found to create the most uncertainty (Duncan). Tung added to this the dimension of routineness. Uncertainty, in turn, has been found to influence a host of other organizational variables. In the face of increased uncertainty, organizations adopt different organizational structures (Burns and Stalker; Lawrence and Lorsch; Tung). Uncertainty also requires decision-makers to handle increasing quantitites of information, and to develop better capabilities to plan for changes in the environment (Galbraith, 1973).

As the environment becomes more uncertain, greater differentiation and complexity of environmental scanning becomes necessary (Miles). Executives who engaged in high uncertainty tasks engaged in more information-acquisition activities (Miles) and relied more on external sources of information (Blandin, Brown and Koch) than those in routine activities.

One information-processing strategy in response to uncertainty identified by Galbraith (1977) is that of environmental management, a process of coping "with external forces by ingesting them or acquiring control over them" (Katz and Kahn). Environmental management ranges from coopting (Galbraith, 1977) and managing competition (Perrow) to lobbying and public relations (Pfeffer and Salancik).

While there seems to be widespread agreement about the impact of uncertainty on organizational behavior, there is little consensus about how to measure uncertainty or its consequences. The debate concerns whether uncertainty refers to objective or perceived changes in the environment. Weick has argued that organizational members create or enact the environment to which they then respond. To the extent that decision-makers have difficulty making these interpretations, they experience uncertainty. To account for this "enactment process" researchers developed a variable known as perceived environmental uncertainty (PEU) (Duncan, Downey and Slocum). PEU typically includes managers' perceptions of the unavailability of relevant information, and their inability to assign probabilities to future events and to predict responses to one's actions.

In a study of the impact of several environmental pressures, firms characterized changes in the regulatory area as sudden and often unanticipated (Fahey and King). It is reasonable to expect that OSHA regulation would create considerable uncertainty for industry regarding interpretation of standards, promulgation of new standards, unannounced inspections and lack of uniformity in enforcement. We anticipated that firms that perceived more uncertainty about OSHA regulation would limit their adaptive responses.

Dependence. Dependence occurs when one organization controls the resources of, or otherwise has authority over, another. This control or authority constrains the behavior of the dependent organization. The federal government's use of its legislative, executive, and judicial power to mandate precise behaviors of firms, who have limited ability to change these mandates, creates interorganizational dependence. Industry's vehement complaints of overregulation suggest that businesses experience considerable dependence on the federal government in highly regulated domains. The potential for increased dependence is particularly high for regulatory agencies such as OSHA and the Environmental Protection Agency which have the power to levy fines for noncompliance. MacAvoy claims these regulations exert as much control over industry as price controls (which applied to about 10 percent of the gross national product during the late 1970s). He states:

> These newer controls inherent in health and safety regulation, that have many of the effects easily recognized in a public utility, cover another 20 percent of industry so significantly that for all intents and purposes that sector is also regulated. . . .All of industry now undertakes pollution and safety-related investments, checks price increases, monitors output quality, with a federal agency in mind (MacAvoy, p. 4).

To the extent that firms are dependent on the government for control of their affairs, they will exhibit greater compliance behavior.

Boundary Spanning. Organizational members in boundary positions form the link between the firm and its environment. A firm's adaptability to environmental constraints is hypothesized to vary with the expertise of its boundary personnel to select, transmit, and interpret environmental information (Aldrich and Herker). In rapidly changing environments in particular, boundary personnel must be adept at developing external information sources to keep up with economic, technological, political, social and regulatory changes which affect their operations. Boundary functions include identifying a firm's relevant environment, gathering information from it, assigning meaning to the information, and initiating reaction on the basis of it. Organizations need to gain as much information as possible about unexpected, relevant events which may occur (Adams). In the case of regulation these events include congressional action, promulgation of new regulations, judicial decisions, and introduction of new methods of compliance.

The importance of boundary spanning to organizational adaptability and design has been argued by several researchers. Failure of boundary spanners to glean information about the environment may be more detrimental to an organization than the securing of irrelevant information (Miles) and may directly affect the organization's survival (Pfeffer and Salancik). In a study of R and D groups of a large U.S. firm, Tushman found that boundary spanners connected the internal network to external sources of information and showed that boundary spanning is essential for innovation. Finally, Leifer and Huber linked boundary spanning to changes in organizational structure. They found that boundary spanning was a better predictor of structure than was perceived environmental uncertainty.

This research leads us to hypothesize that boundary spanning will directly influence adaptive responses to OSHA regulation. Those firms with boundary spanners who routinely monitor changes in the regulatory environment, who keep abreast of technological changes, and who engage in inter-industry dialogue are more likely to initiate voluntary compliance responses in anticipation of OSHA enforcement than firms with less active boundary-spanning functions.

Adaptive Response to Regulation

The changes that organizations have had to make because of regulation are well publicized. Regulation means increased paperwork (Weidenbaum) and greater emphasis on information-gathering and external relations to keep abreast of new regulations and methods of compliance. Regulation constrains decision-making, particularly with respect to new investments and innovations. MacAvoy estimates a one-quarter to one-half percent per year reduction in GNP growth because of regulation. Long-range planning for new products, hiring and promotion, expansions and new technology must take into account a host of governmental standards or even be postponed or suspended for lack of capital. Those organizations which have closed because the cost of pollution controls or other safety features has exceeded returns represent the extreme adaptive response.

Gricar has developed four classifications of adaptive responses to regulation—technical, informational, administrative, and environmental management. *Technical* responses are defined as changes in the technology or physical work space required to produce the organization's product(s). They include major changes in equipment or procedures (such as the installation of dust collectors or the undertaking of feeding studies), special maintenance activities (such as monitoring air contaminants), or protection of workers from hazards. Technical responses often require substantial capital investment which may or may not increase productive capacity while promoting compliance with regulations.

Informational responses refer to changes in the way the firm monitors, records, or disseminates information about its own compliance behavior. Specifically, informational responses include training employees in compliance procedures (e.g., forklift truck driver training) and internal monitoring of industrial hygiene (such as air quality) and employee health (e.g., yearly chest x-rays).

A third type of response, *administrative*, refers to changes in organizational design such as structural reorganization or creation or modification of policies and procedures. Jackson and Morgan identified three such structural responses to regulation: (1) the development of regulation-related specialists, (2) an increase in formalization and standardization, and (3) increased centralization of control.

Actions taken to change the nature of environmental demands constitute a fourth type of response, called *environmental* management. Benson has noted that in the face of implicit economic threat, an organization will attempt to refute and discredit ideological claims of the competing group and to establish the superiority of its own perspective. Pfeffer and Salancik have identified a variety of strategies for managing environmental demands. Examples of environmental management include legal contest of citations or sanctions, service on committees to establish new regulatory standards, and lobbying to influence federal administrative policy or legislation.

DATA AND METHOD

The research on regulatory impact is based on a study of OSHA's impact on 34 foundries in the midwest. Foundries are a subset of the primary metal industry, which has had the fourth highest accident rate in the United States in recent years.[1]

The corporations ranged in size from 12 to 439,300 employees and from $0.5 million to $37,841 million in sales. Eighteen had fewer than 500 workers, while 16 employed 500 or more. Eighteen were single businesses; the remainder were subsidiaries of larger firms. The sample included 15 iron, 8 steel, and 11 nonferrous foundries, but these technological differences were considered to be insignificant compared to the similarity of safety and health problems across the industry.

Data were collected through on-site interviews with the safety director and/ or the highest ranking management official responsible for safety and health policy, which included safety engineers, vice-presidents for manufacturing or industrial relations, and company presidents. The two-hour to five-hour interviews covered the individuals' beliefs about and reactions toward regulation and the firms' reactions to specific experiences with OSHA. In addition, interviewees provided archival records including annual reports, records of OSHA inspections, citations and employee complaints, legal documents, training program materials and safety committee minutes.

Validity. One of the strongest arguments for the validity of the data is a carefully executed process of entrée to the sample firms. Since the inquiry probed into areas which were privileged and politically sensitive, the researcher sought entrée to the firms through officials of four trade associations who personally contacted interviewees for 19 of the firms. In subsequent telephone conversations the researcher assured the firms of confidentiality and urged them to respond only to questions which did not jeopardize privileged information. The majority of firms furnished confidential information without hesitation or offered it even before it was solicited.

In addition, information furnished by respondents pertaining to accident rates was verified against independent data provided by the Bureau of Worker's Compensation and a 95 percent reliability was obtained using Pearson's r.[2] This eliminated any lingering doubts about the truthfulness of the interviewees.

Measures of the Variables

Ideology. Ideology was defined here as the degree of espoused acceptance of government regulation. Since none of the existing measures of ideology in the literature took into account the current socio-political environment created by regulation, a scale of four ideological types (Exhibit 1) was designed for this research.

Exhibit 1.   Ideologies about Regulation.

1.   Ideologies *Opposed* to Regulation

Believe only corporate social responsibility is profit-making
View regulation as a corporate tax on profits
Believe the government should not regulate safety and health
Claim that organizations know best what is right for their workers, not the government
Believe in contesting the legality of the law in court
List only deficiencies in the OSHA program
Resent government intrusion into free enterprise
Advocate resistance to government intervention

2.   Ideologies *Mildly Opposed or Indifferent* to Regulation

Oppose regulation in principle, but respect the law of democracy
Believe compliance is a sacrifice of profits, but will do it if forced to

Regulation is okay as long as it doesn't give anyone a competitive edge
Believe the best strategy is to wait and see and do nothing extra
Will substitute words for action whenever possible
See little change needed by management to ensure safety and health

3. Ideologies *Reluctantly Accepting* of Regulation

Don't believe that they have any choice but to comply
See regulation as inevitable
See opportunity in regulation, i.e., the reduction of insurance premiums, less labor problems, greater productivity
Believe compliance pays off in social or community recognition
Admit they have some problems in safety and health, i.e., management assumes some of the responsiblity

4. Ideologies *Supporting* Regulation

See safety and health as goal equal to profit-making
Believe government and OSHA should work together to improve safety and health of workers
Believe corporations have a responsibility to protect (serve) the public good (of the workers and the community)
Believe the government is acting rightfully and that government intervention in safety and health is necessary to protect the public good
See change as necessary

Four raters independently assigned an ideology to each top manager after content-analyzing the responses to six of the interview questions. (See Appendix A for a list of the questions). Final ideology ratings were those selected by a majority of the raters. An interrater reliability of 0.90 was obtained by using mean squares in the Spearman-Brown prophecy formula.

Size. Size was measured in two ways: (1) the number of employees in the company (or in the parent corporation if the foundry was a subsidiary) and (2) the 1978 annual sales. Since the Pearson's correlation between the two measures was 0.99, the first measure of size was used for statistical analysis.

Dependence. Dependence refers to the degree of perceived control OSHA exerts over an organization. Perceived dependence was measured by asking the top managers to rate each of 45 regulatory agencies according to the following scale.

Please assign a rating to each agency according to how much control you feel it exerts on your business: (1) no control at all—does not affect my business; (2) some control—influences occasional decisions; (3) a great deal of control—influences major decisions; and (4) the most control over my firm in the past three years.

A firm's dependence score was calculated from the rating they assigned to OSHA.

Boundary Spanning.   Boundary spanning was measured by a questionnaire which listed 24 information-gathering activities or sources of information pertaining to safety and health in the foundry industry. Respondents were asked to rate the frequency with which they utilized these boundary spanning activities as illustrated by the sample questions:

1	2	3	4	5
Weekly	Monthly	Quarterly	Yearly	Never

Using the scale previously mentioned, please indicate how often you (or someone from your firm)

—attended a trade or technical association meeting about safety and health.
—sought legal information pertaining to OSHA.

A mean boundary-spanning score was calculated for each respondent. Questionnaire reliability, determined by a Pearson's r between odd and even numbered questions, was .90.[3]

Uncertainty.   A measure of perceived environmental uncertainty (PEU) was composed of 12 items patterned after instruments used by Leifer and Huber and Osborne and Hunt, modified to fit the safety and health environment of the study. Questions took the form: "How often do you believe the information you have about OSHA is sufficient for decision-making?" Responses were on a scale anchored at five points ranging from "seldon or never" to "usually or always." PEU for each respondent was calculated as the mean of responses to the 12 items. Internal reliability of the questionnaire was .87.[3]

Adaptive Responses.   Responses were determined by content analysis of the interview data and archives. Frequencies were tabulated for the four categories of adaptive response mentioned earlier— technical, informational, administrative, and environmental management. Examples of the kinds of responses within each category appear in Appendix B.

Data Analysis.   Pearson's product moment correlations were calculated to determine if the expected association between the independent variables and the adaptive responses were found. To further examine the combined contribution of size, ideology, uncertainty, boundary spanning, and dependence on each of the four response types, multiple regression analyses were performed.

RESULTS AND DISCUSSION

Table 1 presents the correlation matrix for all variables in this study. The correlation analysis revealed that three of the five independent variables were associated with adaptive responses. Total responses (the sum of all four types of response) were positively correlated with ideology, size, and boundary spanning. When each type of response was examined as a separate dependent variable, ideology, size, and boundary spanning were each significantly associated with three of the four response types. Ideology correlated positively with technical, informational, and administrative responses, but not with environmental management response. In other words, the more a manager was in favor of government regulation, the more compliance responses of a technical, informational, and administrative nature his/her firm undertook. These findings are consistent with Zander's contention that compliance with regulations is a function of organizational acceptance of them. They also suggest the possibility of voluntary compliance; that is, firms predisposed toward regulation may be more inclined to take steps to comply with OSHA standards on their own initiative rather than responding only when prompted by citation.

Size of the firm was positively correlated with informational, administrative, and environmental management responses. These findings support the idea that increased size may enable firms to engage in more sophisticated internal organizational responses and to support a greater number of externally directed responses as well.

Boundary spanning was positively associated with all four types of response at significant levels.

Neither perceived environmental uncertainty nor dependence displayed any significant effects on adaptive responses. While the mean score for all firms on the dependence scale was 3.36 (1 = low, 4 = high), the correlation coefficients between dependence and each response type were negligible and insignificant. This suggests that, while these firms reported a high degree of dependence on OSHA, their perceived dependence did not influence compliance behavior. Hence no support was found for the hypothesized relationship between dependence and compliance. It is interesting, however, to note the significant negative correlations of dependence with size and ideology. These findings suggest that firms experiencing more dependence tended to be smaller and have managers with ideologies more opposed to regulation.

The correlations between perceived uncertainty and adaptive responses were also negligible or not significant. The negative r for environmental management responses, however, is consistent with our predictions that firms would exhibit fewer responses when faced with uncertainty. Any suspicion that a relationship might exist between boundary spanning and uncertainty is not warranted, since the correlation between them is only .05 and not significant.

Table 1. Correlation Matrix[a]

	Mean	STD	Ideology	Size	Uncertainty	Dependence	Boundary Spanning	Env'l. Mgmt. Response	Admin. Response	Info Response
Technical Response	5.794	2.544	.38**	.11	-.06	.02	.44**	.38***	.44**	.51***
Informational Response	5.794	4.312	.39***	.44**	-.08	.07	.39***	.49***	.66***	
Administrative Response	2.294	1.947	.57***	.29*	-.60	.03	.55***	.57***		
Environmental Management Response	5.676	3.373	.09	.29*	-.22	.04	.52***			
Total Response	18.882	9.673	.40**	.40**	-.14	.07	.56***			
Boundary Spanning	1.809	.436	.28	.18	.05	.02				
Dependence	3.367	.809	-.31*	-.40**	.23					
Uncertainty	2.634	.702	-.19	-.22						
Size	26,901	79,902	.34*							
Ideology	2.265	.963								

Notes:
[a]Pearson's Product Moment Correlations
*p ≤ .05
**p ≤ .01
***p ≤ .001

Regression Analysis. The combined effects of the independent variables on responses were also investigated in continuous multiple regression analyses. Technical, informational, administrative, and environmental management responses were regressed individually on the five independent variables.

Table 2 presents the regression results by type of response. Beta values indicate that both ideology and boundary spanning contributed substantially to technical response, although the results did not reach significant levels. Both ideology and boundary spanning did exhibit significant contributions when regressed alone against technical response. Addition of the other variables into the regression equation depressed the contributions of ideology and boundary spanning to levels slightly below significance; however, their beta values still remained substantial. The contributions of size, PEU, and dependence to technical response were small and well below significance. About 28 percent of the variance in technical responses was explained by the five independent variables. The fact that this contribution to R^2 was not significant, however, suggests two possibilities: (1) the intercorrelations among the independent variables are masking the contributions of ideology and boundary spanning, and (2) variables other than those accounted for in this study have a much greater effect on levels of technical response.

Size was the only variable to contribute significantly to informational response in the regression analysis. Some effects were observed for ideology and dependence but these were not significant, and none were observed for boundary spanning of PEU. Apparently the correlation between boundary spanning and informational responses was overshadowed by the strong effect of size. The combined variance in information response accounted for by all five variables acting together was 41.7 percent, which was statistically significant.

The variation in administrative response was significantly accounted for by ideology and boundary spanning. Size and dependence also had some effect on administrative response although not significant. Perceived environmental uncertainty contributed little to the variance in administrative response. Collectively the independent variables explained 56 percent of the variance in administrative responses, and this combined effect was highly significant.

For environmental management responses, boundary spanning had the expected significant effects. Ideology, size, dependence, and PEU contributed to some extent, although their separate effects were not significant. Together these variables accounted for 40.7 percent of the variance in environmental management responses, a significant result.

Summary

Overall the findings support some, but not all, of the predicted results. Large amounts of the variance in informational, administrative, and environmental management responses were accounted for by the five independent variables

Table 2. Multiple Regression Analysis of Five Independent Variables on Adaptive Responses

Type of Response	R^2	Ideology	Size	Boundary Spanning	Perceived Environmental Uncertainty	Dependence
Technical	.276	.304	-.011	.351	-.052	.128
	(1.528)	(1.931)	(.002)	(2.956)	(0.068)	(.354)
	<n.s.>	<n.s.>	<n.s.>	<n.s.>	<n.s.>	<n.s.>
Informational	.417	.275	.432	.240	-.032	.337
	(2.865)	(1.954)	(4.979)	(1.715)	(0.031)	(3.048)
	<.05>	<n.s.>	<.05>	<n.s.>	<n.s.>	<n.s.>
Administrative	.559	.450	.129	.442	-.005	.197
	(5.078)	(6.941)	(0.591)	(7.677)	(0.001)	(1.381)
	<.01>	<.05>	<n.s.>	<.05>	<n.s.>	<n.s.>
Environmental Management	.407	-.168	.259	.544	-.268	.158
	(2.747)	(0.718)	(1.761)	(8.661)	(2.190)	(.662)
	<.05>	<n.s.>	<n.s.>	<.05>	<n.s.>	<n.s.>

taken collectively. The correlational analysis revealed that three of these independent variables (ideology, size, and boundary spanning) were consistently associated with adaptive responses at significant levels. Some of these individual effects were confirmed in the multiple regression analysis. However, the fact that beta weights for ideology, size, and boundary spanning individually on responses were not always significant is probably explained by two factors. First, because of missing values, some cases are eliminated in the regression, thereby reducing the power associated with sample size. Second, multicollinearity among the independent variables probably obfuscates the contributions of some variables. Nonetheless, the data does provide moderately strong support for the notion that firm size, managerial ideology, and level of boundary-spanning activity are important determinants of OSHA compliance behavior.

For technical responses, the variables examined here were not significant predictors of variance when taken as a whole. It seems likely that the variance in technical responses is linked to some other variable(s). For example, frequency or severity of OSHA inspections may be a better predictor of technical responses, since many technical deficiencies are directly or indirectly implied when a citation is issued following an OSHA inspection.

CONCLUSIONS

The research findings lend support to the theory that the top managers of these foundries hold definite ideological views about regulation and that these views differ across firms despite their common regulatory environment under OSHA. Moreover, the research found that firms exhibited different patterns of adaptive response or modes of compliance to OSHA regulation. The levels of these responses were found to vary with differences in ideological views, with firm size and with the extent of boundary-scanning activity undertaken by the firm.

The influence of ideology on responses is of particular importance since this variable, while treated theoretically in literature on regulation, has received little empirical attention in organization theory. The findings confirm the intuitive observations of current ideological debate over regulation and suggest that ideology should be given serious consideration in explaining regulatory impact. Additionally, Child and Pfeffer have both pointed to the role of ideology in strategic decision making. In the broader context of corporate social performance, decisions regarding regulatory compliance can certainly be construed as strategic in nature. Therefore, the role of managerial ideology in shaping other strategic decisions about the corporation's role in society deserves careful attention in future research.

While the significant associations of size with informational and environmental management responses confirmed the researcher's expectations, the nonsignificant association with technical and administrative responses is puzzling, but may be accounted for by multicolliniarity among the independent variables. It may also be that an intervening variable such as regulatory experience (which may be linked to firm size or technology) is more critical than size in explaining technical and administrative responses to regulation.

The strongest results were obtained for boundary spanning, which suggests that this variable also needs more consideration in organization theory and that boundary spanning should be a central variable in explaining regulatory response. These findings are consistent with those of Leifer and Huber who found that boundary spanning was a better predictor of organizational structure than was uncertainty.

The fact that dependence had little observed effect on responses was puzzling, but may be due to the lack of variance in the dependence measure. The majority of respondents indicated that they felt a great deal of dependence on OSHA.

The most surprising findings were the lack of significant effects by perceived environmental uncertainty on responses. These findings run contrary to the prevailing arguments in the literature on the importance of uncertainty as a predictor of structural and behavioral dimensions of organizations. While the lack of significant effects by PEU was unexpected, a number of explanations are plausible. First, it may be that despite uncertain aspects of the regulatory process (i.e, new standards, unexpected inspections, etc.) firms generally do know what to expect from the regulatory agency (or at least, in this case, from OSHA). In other words, OSHA simply creates little uncertainty for firms, and correspondingly, managers perceive little uncertainty. A second, complementary explanation may lie in the possibility that firms reduce uncertainty through environmental management responses, and therefore, actually perceive less uncertainty because they have taken steps to remove or minimize whatever uncertainty arises. This idea is supported by the negative (although not significant) relationship between PEU and environmental management response, which can be interpreted as the more environmental management undertaken by a firm, the less uncertainty its managers perceive.

A third explanation concerns the relationship between uncertainty and dependence. Pfeffer has noted that uncertainty is only problematic for an organization when it occurs with dependence, that is, when the events can have a consequence for the organization. While most firms in the study indicated they experienced substantial dependence on OSHA relative to other regulatory agencies, this study did not examine the magnitude of this dependence relative to other factors such as dependence on suppliers, customers, leaders, competitors, etc. The firms' perceived dependence on OSHA may have been negligible relative to these other factors and hence the effect of perceived uncertainty would be less as well.

Finally, it is interesting to speculate about the applicability of these findings to corporate social performance in general. For example, others (Ackoff, Sethi and Post) have offered typologies of corporate social response. These findings on the role of ideology can help explain the basis for such typologies. Future work should examine how managerial ideologies and beliefs shape responses to other regulatory and social concerns faced by corporations.

Additionally, what has been referred to as boundary spanning in this study is becoming institutionalized in many firms as the environmental scanning function. If the findings of this study are at all indicative, environmental scanning may be an increasingly important key to explaining and predicting corporate social performance in the future.

APPENDIX A

INTERVIEW QUESTIONS FOR IDEOLOGY MEASURE

1. What are your views about government regulation of business and about OSHA in particular?
2. What areas of business, if any, should be regulated by the government? Why?
3. What do you believe is the long-term goal of OSHA? Do you agree with it?
4. How should the safety and health of workers best be assured?
5. What changes would you make in OSHA?
6. What constitutes corporate social responsibility?

APPENDIX 2

ADAPTIVE RESPONSES

TECHNICAL RESPONSES

Maintenance

Monitoring the effect of engineering controls
Routine maintenance checks

Equipment Change

Retool a machine
Add new engineering controls
Install or adjust ventilation system
Install noise control equipment
Replace offensive materials with less dangerous ones
Eliminate a hazardous operation
Install or purchase air monitoring equipment

Worker Protection

Provide workers with new protective equipment
Re-instruct in or increase use of existing protective equipment

INFORMATIONAL RESPONSES

Training

Stepped up safety and health training (through booklets, films, job training institutes) for workforce
Training of supervisors in safety and health management
Motivation or incentive systems
Policies and procedures manual developed or utilized trade association manual
Training employees in the use of monitoring equipment

Planning

Track costs of OSHA compliance
Develop grievance system for workers' complaints
Establish contingency fund for safety and health or OSHA compliance
Develop own data collection system for loss time accidents
Computer analyze loss time data
Conduct safety and health research and development

ADMINISTRATIVE RESPONSES

Structural

Establish safety committee
Modify safety committee structure
Create new positions: loss control officer, government relations manager, industrial hygienists
Upgrade position of safety engineer
Move safety and health function from one functional area to another
Increase plant security

Procedural

Modify safety committee responsibility
Pay workers for walkaround
"OSHA administrative solutions," i.e., reducing 8-hour day, rotate workers' exposure to hazard

Policy

Add or amend safety and health clauses in union-management contract

ENVIRONMENTAL MANAGEMENT RESPONSES

Political

Gather economic data, argue for deregulation
PR efforts toward employees or the public, image advertising
Solicit employee contributions to PAC
Lobby for changes in standards
Contact congressman or senator regarding safety and health concerns

Legal

Require entry warrant of inspectors
Contest a citation or penalty
Hide an operation, spike a sample

NOTES

1. Bureau of Labor Statistics.
2. Small differences are attributable to two percent administrative costs which some firms did not include in premium rates reported to the researcher.
3. The sums of odd-and even-numbered questions were correlated using Pearson's r and this value was corrected using the Spearman Brown Prophecy Formula.

REFERENCES

Ackoff, Russell L. *Redesigning the Future*. New York: Wiley, 1974.
Adams, J. Stacy. "The Structure and Dynamics of Behavior in Organizational Boundary Roles," in M. Dunette (ed.), *Handbook of Organizational and Industrial Psychology*. Chicago: Rand McNally, 1976.
Aldrich, Howard, and Diane Herker. "Boundary Spanning Roles and Organization Structure." *Academy of Management Review* 22, No. 2 (1977): 217-230.
————, and Jeffrey Pfeffer. "Environments of Organizations." *Annual Review of Sociology* 2 (1976): 79-105.
Benson, J. Kenneth. "The Interorganizational Network as a Political Economy." *Administrative Science Quarterly* 20 (June 1975): 229-249.
Blandin, J.S., W. B. Brown, and J. L. Koch. "Uncertainty and Informational Gathering Behavior: An Empirical Investigation." Paper presented at the National Academy of Management Meeting, 1974.
Bourgeous, L. J. III, D. McAllister, and T. R. Mitchell. "The Effects of Different Organizational Environments Upon Decisions About Organizational Structure." *Academy of Management Journal* 21 (September 1978): 508-514.
Burns, T., and G. M. Stalker. *The Management of Innovation*. London: Tavistock Publications, 1966.
Child, John. "Organizational Structure, Environment and Performance: The Role of Strategic Choice." *Sociology* 6 (1972): 2-22.
Connor, Patrick, and Jane Siebler. "Organizational Impact of Regulation on Long-Term-Care Facilities." Paper No. 80-4, The Center for Business and Government, Willamette University, Willamette, Oregon, May 1981.
Crenson, M. *The Un-Politics of Air Pollution: A Study of Non-Decisionmaking in the City*. Baltimore: Johns Hopkins Press, 1971.
Currington, William P. "The Impact of the Occupational Safety and Health Act on Occupational

Injuries: An Economic Model.'' Paper presented as part of the Symposium on Economic and Behavioral Models of Response to Regulation, Eastern Academy of Management Meeting, Buffalo, 1980.

Downey, H. K., and C. R. Greer. "Compliance with Social Legislation Affecting Industry: A Preliminary Investigation of Decision Criteria." *Proceedings: American Institute for Decision Sciences* (October 1977): 459-461.

Downey, H. K., and J. W. Slocum. "Uncertainty: Measures, Research and Sources of Variation." *Academy of Management Journal* 18 (1975): 562-578.

Duncan, Robert B. "Characteristics of Organizational Environments and Perceived Uncertainty." *Administrative Science Quarterly* 17 (1972): 313-327.

Dunlap, J. T., A. D. Chandler, G. P. Shultz, and I. S. Shapiro. "Business and Public Policy." *Harvard Business Review* (November-December 1979): 85-102.

Fahey, Liam, and William R. King. "Environmental Scanning for Corporate Planning." *Business Horizons* (August 1977): 61-71.

Galbraith, J. R. *Designing Complex Organizations*. Reading, MA: Addison-Wesley Publishing Company, 1973.

——. *Organization Design*. Reading, MA: Addison-Wesley Publishing Co., 1977.

Gricar, Barbara G. "The Environmental Imperative Created by Government Regulation: Predicting Organizational Response." Ph.D. Dissertation, Case Western Reserve University, August 1979.

Jackson, J. H., and C. P. Morgan. *Organization Theory*. Englewood Cliffs, NJ: Prentice-Hall, Inc., 1978.

Katz, R., and H. Kahn. "Common Characteristics of Open Systems," in F. E. Emery (ed.), *Systems Thinking*. Middlesex, England: Penguin Books, Inc., 1969.

Lawrence, Paul, and Jay Lorsch. *Organization and Environment*. Cambridge: Harvard University Press, 1967.

Leifer, R., and G. Huber. "Relations Among Perceived Environmental Uncertainty, Organization Structure and Boundary-Spanning Behavior." *Administrative Science Quarterly* 22 (June 1977): 235-247.

Lilley, William III, and James C. Miller III. "The New 'Social Regulation.' " *The Public Interest* (1977): 49-61.

Lodge, George. *The New American Ideology*. New York: Knopf Publishing Company, 1975.

MacAvoy, Paul. "The Existing Condition of Regulation and Regulatory Reform," in *Regulating Business*. San Francisco: Institute for Contemporary Studies, 1978.

Marshall vs. Barlow's Inc. United States Supreme Court. 46 LW 4483, 1978.

Miles, R. H. *Macro-Organizational Behavior*. Santa Monica, CA: Goodyear Publishing Company, 1980.

——, and Kim Cameron. *Coffin Nails and Corporate Strategies*. Englewood Cliffs, NJ: Prentice-Hall, 1982.

Montanari, John R. "Operationalizing Strategic Choice," in John H. Jackson and Cyril P. Morgan (eds.), *Organization Theory*. Englewood Cliffs, NJ: Prentice-Hall, 1978.

Nichols, Albert L., and Richard Zeckhauser. "Government Comes to the Workplace: An Assessment of OSHA." *The Public Interest* (Fall 1977): 39-69.

Osborn, Richard N., and James G. Hunt. "Environment and Organizational Effectiveness." *Administrative Science Quarterly* 19 (1974): 231-246.

O'Toole, James. "What's Ahead for the Business-Government Relationship." *Harvard Business Review* (March-April 1979): 94-105.

Occupational Safety and Health Act Review. U.S. Senate, Subcommittee on Labor of the Committee on Labor and Public Welfare. Washington: 1974.

Perrow, Charles. *Organizational Analysis: A Sociological View*. Belmont, CA: Wadsworth Publishing, 1970.

Pfeffer, Jeffrey. *Organizational Design*. Arlington Heights, ILL: AHM Publishing Corp., 1978.

————, and Gerald R. Salancik. *The External Control of Organizations*. New York: Harper and Row, 1978.

Post, James. "SMR Forum: The Corporation in the Public Policy Process—A View Toward the 1980's." *Sloan Management Review* (Fall 1979): 45-52.

Rinefort, Foster. "A New Look at Occupational Safety." *Personnel Administrator* (September 1977): 29-36.

Salancik, Gerald R. "Interorganizational Dependence and Responsiveness to Affirmative Action: The Case of Women and Defense Contractors." *Academy of Management Journal* 22, No. 2 (1979): 375-394.

Sethi, S. Prakash. *Up Against the Corporate Wall: Modern Corporations and Social Issues of the Eighties*. Englewood Cliffs, NJ: Prentice-Hall, 1982.

Sonnenfeld, Jeffrey. *Corporate Views of the Public Interest*. Auburn House Publishing Company, 1982.

Tushman, Michael L. "Special Boundary Roles in the Innovation Process." *Administrative Science Quarterly* 22 (December 1977): 587-601.

Weaver, Paul H. "Regulation, Social Policy and Class Conflict." *The Public Interest* (Spring 1978): 45-63.

Weick, Karl. *Social Psychology of Organizing*. Reading, MA: Addison-Wesley, 1969.

Weidenbaum, Murrary. "The Costs of Government Regulation on Business." Study prepared for the Subcommittee on Economic Growth and Stabilization of the Joint Economic Committee, Congress, April 10, 1975. Washington: U.S. Government Printing Office, 1978.

Zander, Alvin. *Groups at Work*. San Francisco: Jossey-Bass, Inc., 1977.

CORPORATE POLITICAL STRATEGIES:

AN EMPIRICAL STUDY OF CHEMICAL FIRM RESPONSES TO SUPERFUND LEGISLATION

John F. Mahon

A great deal of recent research on the corporation-government-society relationship has been built around models linking structure-conduct-performance dimensions (Post, 1978a; Preston 1977; Thorelli). This research has explored the links between environment, industry structure and an organization's strategy and structure (Bain, Chandler, Porter) and between a firm's behavior (or conduct) and organizational performance (Post, 1976, 1978b; Sethi). This paper examines the relationship between corporate conduct and performance in the political arena.

Research in Corporate Social Performance and Policy, volume 5, pages 143-182
Copyright © 1983 by JAI Press Inc.
All rights of reproduction in any form reserved.
ISBN: 0-89232-412-0

INTRODUCTION

The organizational responsibility within the enterprise to deal with political issues and problems is increasingly being recognized through the growing development of public affairs departments (Baysinger and Woodman; Hegarty, Aplin and Cosier; Keim and Baysinger; Post, Murray, Dickie and Mahon, 1981, 1982; and Post and Mahon). The links between structure and conduct with regards to public affairs have been investigated through large questionnaire research (Murray) and statistical analysis (Mahon, 1982a, 1982b). This analysis has demonstrated that industry position and firm structure affect the existence and establishment of public affairs units, and that for each of three different public affairs structures identified there is a corresponding departmental conduct. They key remaining question, however, concerns the extent to which the structure and activities of a public affairs department affect the political strategies that a firm pursues in specific public issue conflicts.

Fox, Hanson, Sonnenfeld, Tiffany and others have argued that firms do pursue coherent political strategies, which are manifested in the action of an organization on specific political issues.

To date, only Sonnenfeld and Mahon (1982a) have examined the question of whether the existence of a public affairs unit affects the nature of corporate political strategies. The analyses of political strategies are especially susceptible to longitudinal case analysis. These political strategies are coherent patterns of action, intended and designed to yield predicted results in the context of given (or foreseeable) environmental conditions (Post, 1978b).

Since there seem to be numerous strategies, only analysis which sweeps in all available facts allows the researcher to know whether the types of strategies set forth are applicable.

In this study, the polticial strategies of six major chemical firms and their trade association, the Chemical Manufacturers Association, were analyzed for the purpose of determining whether the existence of a public affairs unit affected the behavior and performance of these organizations on the Superfund legislative debate. This analysis was intended to test theory and is, in Post and Andrews' terms, an explanatory and predictive case analysis.

Political Strategies

MacMillan interprets these political approaches as a function of organizational action.

> The objective of political action is to structure or restructure the situation with the view of furthering one's own goals. A political analysis aims at identifying what the political capabilities (power and influence) of the various critical elements in the situation are (p. 107).

Another approach to dealing with social and political strategies is offered by Page (Mahon, 1982c). Page notes that firms resist change because of the increase in the uncertainty level they face. In his investigation of automobile safety and drug promotion, he articulates a set of specific strategies and tactics that the firm can use to deal with unwanted social and political change.

The social issues literature provides an analysis of several strategic options available to the firm in dealing with social and political issues. Thomas for example, deals with individual responses to social pressures, particularly, social conflict. Post (1978b) and Gladwin and Walter have adapted Thomas's scheme to an analysis of political strategies that firms may follow in dealing with social and political pressures in both the national and international arena (See figure 1). The concern for management in these situations is twofold. The organization must be concerned with its continuing relationships with the opposition while achieving an outcome that is satisfactory to the firm (Gladwin and Walter). Figure 1 displays five styles of conflict management available to an organization based on its stake in an issue and the degree to which the firm has ''mostly conflicting'' or ''mostly common'' interests with industry critics. These strategies are objectively observable. In addition, the placing of organization or other social factors in this framework allows us to perform comparative analysis, assessing organizations' strategies. We should note that the placing of organizations in Figure 1 is representative of a particular point in time; that is, it is a snapshot of the strategies that these firms have exhibited as of a certain date.

Organizations can compete vigorously in an attempt to overwhelm the other side (resistance) and maintain the status quo. Management may likewise opt to avoid the problem by ignoring or withdrawing from the situation (avoid/neglect) or accommodating the opposition. The firm may also actively work toward mutually satisfactory solutions (collaborative), or the enterprise may seek out compromise, which represents an intermediate position on the chart and often arises out of a weaker positon in terms of outcomes or relationships. In the compromise strategy, the firm may have only a moderate stake in the outcome of the issue, or its power relative to others in the situation may be less. Additionally, we can look at firms' political actions in terms of response patterns.

Longitudinal Patterns of Response

It is clear from the literature that organizations alter political strategies over the course of a public issue. This suggests that some combination of internal and external factors are at work. The patterns of firm response can be characterized relative to the evolution of a public issue.

The failure of corporate performance to meet public expectations can give rise to a social issue and its ensuing ''life cycle.'' Throughout the political process and subsequent legislation leading to regulation, firms and industries can find themselves penalized and constrained. This has the effect of transferring some

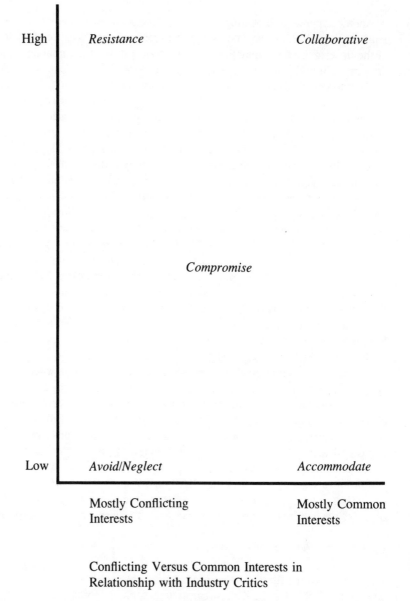

Figure 1. Political Strategies

146

of society's costs back to the firms themselves, with the result that the "externalities" of yesterday become internal costs of today—often through penalties and regulation of one form or another (The Reserve Mining Company's history provided an excellent illustration, See Schaumburg, 1976.)

Post (1979) agrees that the most fundamental concept is understanding the management of corporate responsiveness is the public issue life cycle.

> The concept, in brief, is that as a gap develops between public expectations of a corporation's performance in some area (e.g., product quality, emissions) and that of the firm's actual performance, pressure builds around the issue. If the gap is not closed, the issue begins a process of politicization that involves a phase in which political actors take an interest in the matter, a period of legislative and/or regulatory development, a litigation phase during which time the regulation or legislation is tested, and finally, a period of acceptance and internalization. The critical point in managerial terms is that corporate management has increasingly less discretion in resolving the issues—i.e., narrowing the gap between expectations and performance—as it proceeds through the life cycle. It is easier to resolve the complaint of a dissatisfied customer before a Ralph Nader or a Consumer Product Safety Commmission takes an interest in the matter, than after they have become involved. They too then become "actors" whose expectation must be satisfied before the issue can be resolved. The prescriptive lesson is clear: a management must learn to anticipate issues before they become fully politicized. If a manager waits until the issue is fully defined by a legislative or regulatory proposal, he or she has probably waited too long to respond (p. 12).

We can apply Post's (1976) concept of reactive, proactive, and interactive patterns of response to the life cycle concept of issues to offer another view of corporate behavior in response to social and political issues. We should, however, distinguish these response patterns from the political strategies noted earlier. The response patterns enable us to understand a particular firm's response over the entire life cycle of an issue. The political strategies allow us to position several organizations at a single point in the life of an issue. The underlying factor in both approaches (response patterns and political strategies) is that they are objectively observable from a firm's behavior over time.

How then, do these strategies become realized in the corporate-government-society relationship? Let us turn to an analysis of the situation facing the chemical industry as it began to engage in political strategy making and action over Superfund legislation.

SUPERFUND—PREHISTORY

The development of public awareness to the danger of toxic chemicals in our environment can be traced to the publication of Rachel Carson's *The Silent Spring* in 1962. This book, later critically examined on nationwide television, alerted society to the dangers of unregulated chemicals in our environment. Contamination incidents that have occurred since then seem to bear out her early warnings.

John E. Blodgett, in a report prepared for the Committee on Public Works and Transportation, U.S. House of Representatives, addressed the problem of hazardous wastes and toxic substances.

> In recent years, several episodes of environmental contamination by toxic substances have occurred in which health is threatened, products condemned, and resources destroyed or declared off-limits. The most notorious of these episodes include mercury in Lake St. Clair, PCB's in the Hudson River, PBB's in Michigan, kepone in the James River, carbon tetrachloride in the Ohio River, and HEXA-OCTA in the Louisville, Kentucky, sewers and in the Ohio River. These episodes have been nationally newsworthy, and stories of ill workers (kepone), condemned fish (mercury, kepone), destroyed cattle and possible health hazards (PBB's), sewage treatment plant breakdowns (kepone, HEXA-OCTA), and drinking water warnings (carbontet, HEXTA-OCTA), are generally well known. To these episodes must be added uncounted local ones of varying seriousness; these sometimes contaminate fish or shellfish, pollute streams, cause wells to be condemned, etc. (p. 25).

One should not get the impression that these incidents are confined to lakes, rivers, and streams. In August 1978 the national news media began reporting the leakage of hazardous chemicals from disposal sites in the abandoned Love Canal site in Niagara Falls, New York. At least 82 different chemical compounds were identified, 11 of them actual or suspected carcinogens. This was to lead eventually to one of the largest relocations of families from contaminated areas in our history, at immense cost to state and federal governments and in terms of human misery. This was, moreover, to be the first of many such sites uncovered. Other sites thus far identified are, for example:

- Elizabeth, New Jersey—Fire broke out in April 1980 at a dump that had been used by the former Chemical Control Corporation for highly explosive wastes. Catastrophe was averted when winds blew toxic clouds away from populated areas. Cost of clean-up estimated at $10-$15 million.
- West Point, Kentucky—Abandoned site known as "Valley of the Drums" contains 17,000 drums of unknown contents. Chemical leakage has been detected in streams feeding the Ohio River.

These incidents have had a noticeable impact on perceptions of the chemical industry. Earl Harbison, Jr., in remarks made at the Chemical Industry Strategic Planning Converence on May 23, 1979, pointed out that:

> Opinion research undertaken for Monsanto showed that the public continued to identify the chemical industry as *the prime* contributor to air and water pollution problems. For example, 71 percent said that waste from chemical plants is the greatest pollution hazard; it is ahead of all other industries.

Business Week also noticed the problems with the chemical industry's public image:

The chemical industry now ranks lowest in image of 13 industries surveyed by New York Pollster Yankelovich, Skelly & White, Inc. The "gap between the chemical industry and the one ranking second-last is quite large," says Laurence D. Wiseman, a Yankelovich vice-president (October 8, 1979, p. 73).

If the past does serve as a predictor of the future, the chemical industry had grave reasons for concern. During the period 1970-1980, there was a tremendous increase in the regulation of the industry. Some of this increased regulation, while attributable to strong public interest lobbies, is also a clear reflection of the industry's loss of public confidence and the perceived need for increased protection of the environment. Let us review, briefly, the legislation of this period.

In 1969 the National Environmental Policy Act was passed; its stated purposes were to declare a national policy which would encourage productive and enjoyable harmony between man and his environment, to promote efforts which would prevent or eliminate damage to the environment and biosphere, and to establish a Council on Environmental Quality. The practical impact was that if a company wanted to build or substantially alter an old site, it would have to prepare an "environmental impact statement" explaining how the proposed change would affect the environment.

The Clean Air Act of 1970 (with key amendments in 1977) also had a major impact. This act established an intricate system of federal-state regulation and enforcement designed to enhance the nation's air resources. Under the act, the Environment Protection Agency (EPA) sets national ambient air quality standards for pollutants like sulfur dioxide, lead, and carbon monoxide. The EPA could also set national emission limits for hazardous pollutants like asbestos, benzene, and vinyl chloride.

President Nixon in 1970 established the EPA to protect the nation's environment from pollution. The creation of this agency brought 15 different federal offices dealing with pollution under single management. The EPA establishes and enforces environmental protection policies and recommends them to the President.

In 1972 several pieces of legislation were passed that had an impact on the chemical industry. They were The Federal Environmental Pesticide Control Act; the Federal Insecticide, Fungicide, and Rodenticide Act; the Federal Water Pollution Control Act; and the Marine Protection, Research, and Sanctuaries Act.

The Clean Water Act of 1977 amended the Federal Water Pollution Control Act of 1972, established national goals, and authorized the EPA to adopt effluent standards and a national permit system. The national goals included prohibition of toxic pollutant discharges, elimination of discharges by 1985, and the development of "fishable" and "swimmable" water by July 1, 1983.

In 1976 Congress enacted the Toxic Substance Control Act over the bitter opposition of the chemical industry. It amended the act of 1971 and was the most complex and far-reaching of the environmental laws. It was meant to give the federal government control over chemicals not already regulated under other laws. It also gave the EPA a first-strike authority with respect to clearing an agent *before* it entered the market, as well as power to control existing chemicals if they were shown to be unreasonably hazardous. Additionally, 1976 saw the passage of the Resource Conservation and Recovery Act (RCRA) which created a federal hazardous materials disposal program for land disposal of discarded materials. It was a multifaceted approach toward solving the problems associated with the three to four billion tons of discarded materials generated each year and the problems resulting from the anticipated eight percent annual increase in the volume of such wastes.

It was against this backdrop of two decades of challenge and change that the industry began to prepare for a significant new environmental initiative—the regulation and clean-up of hazardous waste sites—or, as it came to be called, Superfund.

The Early Maneuvering

The beginnings of Superfund can be traced back to a variety of governmental and industry actions. Starting in 1973 the petroleum industry approached Congress seeking federal legislation in the area of oil spills. This regulation was actively pursued by the industry in order to achieve a dollar limit on liability and to obtain release from the numerous state regulations in effect. This interest by industry on oil spill regulations was the impetus to congressional action and thought on the entire problem of hazardous wastes and spills.

Superfund can also trace its legislative roots back to the Resource Conservation and Recovery Act (RCRA) of 1976. The General Accounting Office released a report on December 19, 1978, on the administration of RCRA

> . . . that shocked industry and made public debate and controversy over the recently proposed hazardous waste rules even more heated.
>
> The report said money should be available to pay claims resulting form disposal operations, to clean up resulting damages, and to prevent further contamination.
>
> The fund would be supported by fees assessed on disposal of hazardous wastes, but in developing the fee schedule, "an effort should be made to reflect the degree and duration of risk posed by specific wastes," the GAO report noted.
>
> Inadequate disposal practices in the past have caused harm to humans and the environment many years after sites have closed, the report said. In many cases, site ownership was transferred or relinquished, making legal liability and responsibility difficult to establish and causing clean-up costs and remedial costs to be passed on to taxpayers. A federal fund is needed to address the liability problem, the report stressed (*Chemical Regulation Reporter*, August 22, 1980, p. 708).

Starting in late 1978, according to Philip Cummings (Democrat) and Curtis Moore (Republican), counsels for the Committee on Environment and Public Works in the Senate, meetings were held between Congress, the EPA, and the

Chemical Manufacturers Association (CMA) to discuss a possible bill for hazardous wastes. Mank (of the EPA) recalled that Stauffer, Dow, Monsanto, Olin, Union Carbide, and Allied Chemical Corporations were also represented at these meetings, where the EPA laid out the government's position and asked the industry for their inputs on the issue. At that time, according to Cummings, Moore, and Mank, the CMA's first position was that the government should foot the bill. This was later modified to suggest a one-third split among the industry, the federal government, and state and local government. Finally, the industry said they thought they could contribute 40 percent of the total cost. Edmund Frost, general counsel and vice-president of the CMA, reportedly stated that "we are all but at agreement on this." Then, according to personnel both in Congress and in the EPA, the industry disappeared. They no longer would participate. It is not clear why the industry withdrew at this time, but this might be reflective of the changing attitude and strategy within the industry's trade association.

PUBLIC AFFAIRS IN THE CHEMICAL INDUSTRY

The chemical industry's long involvement with legislation, regulation, and community concerns has led many of the largest firms to establish formal public affairs units. Their philosophy and approach to public issues are an important determinant of the political strategies of the organization, and thus require brief summary.

At *Union Carbide* the public affairs department consists of approximately 90 staff members and, in addition to a headquarters unit, includes a Washington office and several regional offices for public affairs. A key aspect of their activities has been their focus on selected key issues, each monitored and managed by an "issue manager." In addition, Union Carbide has two very strong departments—Energy, Transportation, and Policy; and Health, Safety, and Environmental Affairs—to deal with energy and health issues. The guiding philosophy of this activity at Union Carbide has been ". . . come and let us reason together" (Menzies, p. 87).

DuPont's public affairs office spends time on traditional public relations activities (e.g., media relations, corporate communications, etc.), but has increasingly devoted time and manpower to environmental analysis and forecasting. DuPont does, however, differ from other firms' public affairs:

DuPont's public affairs department is unique relative to its competitors and other industrial firms' staffs. This is particularly true in the governmental affairs area, where the department is notable not for what it has, but for what is missing: a political action committee and the responsibility for legislative lobbying. The prominence of its crusading CEO has also posed a number of challenging questions, both for the DuPont department and public relations generally. In the context of a public chief executive, does the public affairs organization have any kind of leadership role? (Woelfel).

Dupont has subgroups to deal with environmental, health and safety, and energy concerns. The public affairs department has responsiblity for community relations, corporate contributions, media relations, stockholder relations, advertising (issue-related) and investor relations. DuPont has tried to make public affairs a strong point within the firm. The philosophy of their department makes clear why this is so.

> Corporate reputation is not, in our judgement, nebulous goodwill. Rather, it is based on clear perceptions by influential groups of basic corporate characteristics. First is the practical utility and value of a company's products. Second is a company's contributions to the national quality of life—social worth and benefit of business. Third is the fairmindedness and ethical behavior of company mangement (DuPont).

Monsanto, a large chemical firm, is organized along the lines of Union Carbide. Monsanto has a corporate office and a Washington, D.C., office for national and federal activities. In addition, the firm has offices at corporate headquarters and at the regional level for state and local relations. Monsanto, unlike DuPont, has a political action committee (PAC), and government relations is under the scope of the public affairs department. Monsanto, more than any other firm, has tried hard to persuade the public that chemicals are not all bad. It has been conducting an extensive public relations program entitled, "Chemical Facts of Life" for several years. A familiar refrain in their advertising was "Without chemicals, life itself would be impossible" (*Chemical Business*, November 12, 1979, p. 7). Monsanto is also recognized within the industry as very sophisticated in grassroots program operations (McGrath; *Chemical Business*, November 12, 1979; and Ember, 1980). So much involved is Monsanto in grassroots organizations and PAC's that they were the subject of a series of articles in the *St. Louis Post-Dispatch* several years ago. Several Monsanto executives were quoted as saying they were pressured to join the firm's PAC. One executive noted that the contribution was to be considered a "cost of employment" (Sansweet). It is also interesting to note that Louis Fernandez, Monsanto's vice-chairman, served as chairman of the CMA's Superfund Committee during this period.

Rohm and Haas, another large chemical firm, is organized for public affairs in much the same fashion as Union Carbide. Rohm and Haas has often taken moderate stances on legislation affecting the chemical industry, which is reflective of both the public affairs department and of the chairman of the board's, Vincent L. Gregory, Jr.'s views on the firm in a larger society.

The final two firms important to the Superfund deate are *Dow* and *Allied Chemical*. These two firms have the most unique reputations within the industry, Congress, and the EPA. *Chemical and Engineering News* (January 5, 1981) referred to these companies as "hardliners." Staff members of Congressional Committees and the EPA noted that during the battle of Superfund, these two firms were "the stormtroopers of the industry." These general impressions were also supported by some members within the CMA itself. Both of these firms have corporate levels and federal offices for public affairs, but no offices for state and local relations. They also have political action committees, Dow being the clear leader in chemical PAC spending during the period 1977-1978. Dow's president, Paul F. Oreffice, was also a member of the CMA's executive board during the Superfund legislative passage. Additionally, Dow's environmental relations director, Charles Sercu, was chairman of the Environmental Management Committee of the CMA.

We should also note that Allied chemical was going through tremendous internal reorganization under its new chief executive officer, Edward L. Hennessy, Jr. Under his leadership since May 1, 1979, Allied has divested huge chunks of the firm, settled litigation related to kepone, brought the firm into the electronics business and laid off 700 employees (Jasen). Hennessy appeared at this time to be devoting his efforts to strengthening Allied in the marketplace and internally improving managerial control.

In addition to these individual firms, it is important to understand the changes that were taking place in the industry's trade association. In June 1979 the Manufacturing Chemists Association changed its name to the *Chemical Manufacturers Association*. But this change involved a great deal more than just a name. The Manufacturing Chemists Association was formed in 1872 when a small band of oil or vitriol (sulfuric acid) producers banded together. In the past, the MCA's unofficial motto was "quiet excellence" and the group's lobbyists worked inconspicuously behind the scenes. According to William Stover, vice-president of CMA, "the industry was getting beaten up, and the MCA was not a forceful voice in Washington."

The industry brought in a new president, Robert A. Roland, who had twenty years experience with the National Paint & Coatings Association fighting similar battles in Washington. Roland shook up the organization, increasing dues revenue from about $4 million to $7.5 million, increasing staff from 65 to 130, and developing an entirely new committee and staff organization. The changes were rapid.

The change in faces at CMA over the last year or so has been dizzying, several insiders there say. Among the fifty-four professionals in the office, only six have been there for ten years or more.

"We're an association, not a chemical company," one executive explains. Some second career people who worked well in the corporate world did not do so well in that of the trade group, he says (Feare, p. 11).

The growth in staff was found in the technical department and the office of general counsel, areas that reflected the association's new aggressive stance. Edmund B. Frost, vice-president and general counsel who came to CMA in 1978 observes:

CMA will bring no frivolous cases and it will not move out of spite. It will not fight for the sake of a fight, but neither will it hesitate to sue when it thinks the general interests of the chemical industry are damaged and there is a chance of winning in court (Feare, p. 12).

THE LEGISLATIVE BATTLE

Congressional hearings began in March of 1979 before the House (Commerce) Subcommittee on Oversight and Investigation chaired by Bob Eckhardt (D., TX) and before the Senate Subcommittees on Environmental Pollution and Resource Protection, chaired respectively by Edmund S. Muskie (D., ME) and John C. Culver (D., IA).

Given the media exposure to Love Canal, it made sense that Congressional hearings on hazardous waste disposal would begin by looking at that particular situation. Eckhardt's committee met on several occasions to examine the Love Canal problem and the broader issue of hazardous wastes. The hearings produced several revelations that were quite damaging to the credibility of Hooker Chemical, the company directly involved, and that of the chemical industry as a whole. Internal Hooker documents dated December 4, 1972, noted that:

> The physical characteristics of the fill which was placed here through the years is not the type which would be desirable for a recreational area. Hooker is still being plagued with problems associated with the fill at the Love Canal area in spite of their best efforts to shed themselves of any responsiblity (U.S. Congress, House, April 10, 1979).

The press was not silent on this issue. In an editorial entitled "Who Pays for Poison?" in the *Washington Post*, the editors, commenting on some of Hooker's testimony noted above, observed:

> The question left by this sad experience is how companies can be moved to take a larger view of their responsibilities and clean up their old toxic dumps before people are actually hurt. New laws, public pressure and the example of Love Canal have already raised the potential costs of doing nothing and changed corporate perspectives somewhat. Even so, it is still likely that many clean-up efforts will bog down in arguments over how the blame and the costs—which will be large— should be apportioned among the companies and the governments involved.
>
> By now, companies such as Hooker ought to realize that times have changed. Instead of waiting to be pushed, they should voluntarily disclose all they know about their past and present dumps, and shoulder responsiblity for cleaning up the problems—residues that they know or had reason to know about. That would put them in the stronger moral position from which to ask for public help if the problems exceed their resources: It wouldn't be bad public relations either (April 12, 1979, p. 16).

This editorial brought swift response from the chemical industry. Robert Roland, President of the CMA, responded in an editorial reply on April 21, 1979:

One of the things that we must all realize in discussing the solid-waste disposal problem, including toxic or hazardous wastes, is that it is not just the problem of the chemical industry. It is a result of society's advanced technology and pursuit of an increasingly complex lifestyle. The *Post's* editorial implies that a more positive public posture by manufacturing companies would engender a more positive public response if the solution to the problems exceeded resources. I think it is manifestly clear from testimony given recently that such will clearly be the case, with estimates of a Superfund to stabilize and secure existing hazardous dumps running to the tune of almost $50 billion (Roland, p. 15).

At the end of May or the early part of June, an important meeting was held at the White House. According to EPA staffers Marc Tipermas, Director of the Office of Program Analysis, and Andy Mank, Special Assistant to the Administration for Water and Waste management, the issue was "Superfund" and who was going to pay for it. It was, in light of what was to follow, a very significant confrontation. Representatives of the Department of Commerce, the Council of Economic Advisors, the Council on Wage and Price Stability, and the Office of Mangement and Budget argued for a fund totally generated from general governmental revenues. On the other side were representatives of the EPA; the Department of Health, Education and Welfare; the Occupational Safety and Health Administration; and the Council on Environmental Quality arguing for a shared funding approach between industry and the government. According to sources in attendance, President Carter himself decided on an 80 percent/20 percent industry/government split. Both the EPA and the CMA were surprised. This decision was to lead to a shift in tactics by the CMA once legislation was introduced.

In a May 18, 1979, Senate subcommittee meeting, Bruce D. Davis, President of Hooker's Industrial Chemicals Group, testified that these "ultrafund" (as CMA called Superfund) proposals needed to come to grips with four major issues:

1. The exact use of the ultrafund.
2. Should the ultrafund be comprehensive in its coverage?
3. Which sites should be covered by legislation?
4. The fund size and method of funding.

In regard to the fourth point, Davis pointed out what was to become a cornerstone of the industry's argument against Superfund:

Because the problem is a truly national one, we feel that a fund should be comprised of public as well as industry funding. In fact, in view of the national scope of the problem, substantial Federal funding appears to be appropriate (U.S. Congress, Senate, May 18, 1979).

In June bills to deal with hazardous wastes started surfacing all over Congress. The administration bills (S 1241 and HR 4566) were introduced on June 14 and 21 respectively and would create a $1.6 billion fund. Representatives Staffers and Florio introduced their bill (HR 4571) on June 21, 1979, which was essentially the same as the administration's bills. Representative La Falce and Senator Moynihan introduced their bill (HR 5290) somewhat later (September 14, 1979), and it had two significant differences from the previous proposals. First, it specified a smaller fund ($500 million), but did not require any industry contribution. Second, it provided for the payments of damages to individuals.

In the Senate, Senators Culver and Muskie introduced S 1480 on July 11, 1979. Their bill at this point provided for a fund of $500 million, collected exclusively from industry fees for damages to individuals. It did not include oil spills.

The CMA's response to this flurry of activity was immediate and predictable. Robert A. Roland wrote:

> The administration's bill unfairly singles out the chemical and related industries to bear a disproportionate burden of clean-up costs. In doing so, it fails to adequately reflect the society's responsibility for resolving a problem which everyone has helped create and for whose solution everyone should help pay (*Chemical and Engineering News*, June 25, 1979, p. 27).

The industry's strategy in dealing with the legislation, according to John Doyle, minority counsel, Subcommittee on Water Resources in the House, was to "try and get legislation to as many committees and subcommittees as possible, complicating the legislation, increasing the number of hurdles necessary for passage, and hopefully killing the legislation." The industry's task was simplified by the complexity of the legislation which would overlap the jurisdiction of six House committees and three Senate committees. The industry, Congress, the EPA, and the public were at the end of 1979 entering what *Chemical Week* (October 3, 1979, p. 44) termed ". . . the eye of the 'Superfund' storm."

Given this situation, the chemical industry could view 1979 as a successful year. The proposed legislation, because of its complexity, was subject to several jurisdictional disputes in Congress. Rival bills in opposition to the Administration's proposals were introduced, and the industry was on record for proposing clean up of orphan or abandoned sites. The outlook for 1980 also appeared bright. It was to be a congressional and presidential election year, and Congress was traditionally reluctant to deal with controversial legislation during those times.

The CMA was, according to inside observers, being pushed to take a hard-line stand against any legislation in this area. Dow and Allied chemical, supported by Union Carbide and DuPont, were making effective and influential arguments for a strong position against the bill. Moderates like Olin, Rohm and Haas, and Monsanto were unable to make their views prevail within the CMA. A clear decision was made within the trade association to fight legislation, and the CMA would take the lead. The positions of various actors in the Superfund issues at this point in time are shown in Figure 2.

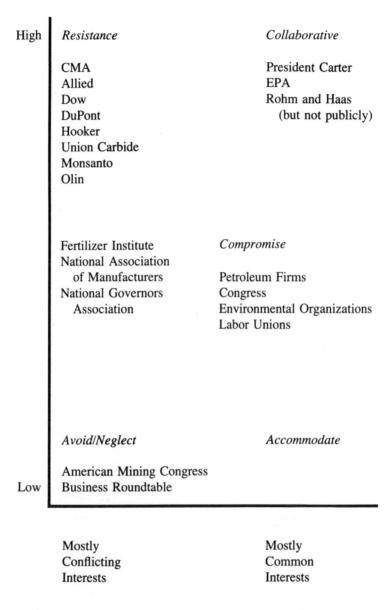

High | *Resistance* | *Collaborative*

CMA
Allied
Dow
DuPont
Hooker
Union Carbide
Monsanto
Olin

President Carter
EPA
Rohm and Haas
    (but not publicly)

Fertilizer Institute
National Association
    of Manufacturers
National Governors
    Association

Compromise

Petroleum Firms
Congress
Environmental Organizations
Labor Unions

Avoid/Neglect

Accommodate

American Mining Congress
Low | Business Roundtable

Stake of the Organization in the Issue

Mostly
Conflicting
Interests

Mostly
Common
Interests

Figure 2. Political Positions of Key Actors in the Superfund Debate,
January 1980

1980: Year of Decision

The opening of the CMA's campaign against Superfund began in earnest on March 7, 1980, with the release of a summary of a study on hazardous waste sites around the country. CMA president Roland noted that the study

> . . . confirms our belief that the size of the Superfund problem is not as great as the Environmental Protection Agency has estimated and that state agencies are acting in this area in a responsible manner to handle their own problems.
>
> The hazardous waste disposal problem is manageable at the state level, and this precludes the need for massive new federal intervention.
>
> The Association opposes Superfund legislation because it would create an unnecessary new level of federal bureaucracy and squander the nation's resources at a time when sound fiscal management is imperative (CMA News Release, March 7, 1980).

The summary released by the CMA was responded to in depth by the EPA in late March 1980. The EPA's response was unusually harsh and detailed. The EPA accused the CMA of releasing a report that

> . . . is both inaccurate and misleading and has been circulated by CMA in a self-serving attempt to scuttle proposed Superfund legislation.

The EPA response went on to address and refute every major point in the CMA document. More importantly, the EPA circulated its response to all committees involved in Superfund legislation in both the House and Senate.

The EPA and members of Congress asked for a copy of the full survey (not just the summary supplied on March 7, 1980). In all instances, the CMA refused to provide the material.

On April 2, 1980, Congressman Florio introduced HR 7020, the Hazardous Waste Containment Act of 1980. Florio's bill provided for a $600 million fund, co-financed equally by the industry and the federal government. The bill also set strict standards of liability (joint, several, and strict). The bill was referred to Florio's own subcommittee for review. Florio was, however, facing a deadline. He had to move the bill to the House Commerce Committee before May 15, 1980. That was the deadline for committees to approve bills involving federal appropriations (*Environmental Reporter*, May 2, 1980, pp. 4-6).

Once again, a media event would serve as a focal point of attention to Superfund for all interested parties. On April 23 a fire broke out at a dump that had been used by the former Chemical Control Corporation in Elizabeth, New Jersey. The wastes were highly explosive and did in fact explode as the fire raged. A major catastrophe was averted when winds blew the deadly toxic clouds away from heavily populated areas. The cost of cleanup for this incident was estimated at $10 to $15 million (Parisi).

On April 30, one week after the Elizabeth, New Jersey, fire, Florio obtained approval for HR 7020 from his subcommittee by a 5 to 3 vote. The bill then went to the full committee (Interstate and Foreign Commerce) for consideration.

The united front by CMA against Superfund began to erode at this point. According to a CMA participant, a difference of opinion occured at this time (Florio's subcommittee) over strategy. Florio's bill was essentially stopped in subcommittee, but Union Carbide, DuPont, Rohm and Haas, Monsanto, and Olin wanted to compromise on funding and receive other concessions. When the bill went to the full committee, a compromise occured. According to *Chemical Week*:

> The first crack in the chemical industry's opposition to a Superfund began at about 4 p.m. on May 13, when Vincent L. Gregory, Jr., chairman of Rohm and Haas, and Kenneth Davis, the company's Washington representative, visited Representative James J. Florio (D., NJ), chairman of the House Subcommittee on Transportation and Commerce. Gregory and Davis expected to continue an argument with Florio over the form of HR 7020.
>
> . . . Florio told Gregory and Davis that he understood industry's position and that he was willing to support amendments on funding and liability, which were major points of concern. By midnight, the revised bill was ready and on May 13, the Commerce Committee moved swiftly to adopt the measure, easily overcoming attempts to toughen it (June 18, 1980, p. 63).

These "cracks" in the industry's position were not public knowledge in May. The compromise involved the use of funds for remedying failing (or orphan) sites, and for the removal of third-party liability. Additionally, this bill would not change liability laws to make it easier to recover damages for injuries and, where several companies were found responsible for damages, courts could apportion the costs among them rather than hold one firm liable for all damages. This compromise did not meet with unanimous approval with CMA.

> But such support for HR 7020 appears to have caused serious dissension within the chemical industry. One company official says there has been "blood in the streets" (*Chemical Week*, June 18, 1980, p. 63).

Those favoring the compromise argued that the industry's position—that they were not responsible for the dumping—

> . . . appeared to antagonize many congressmen, who were being pressured as a result of media coverage of hazardous-waste-site issues. In addition, Union Carbide's Washington representative, Jeremiah Kenney, points to EPA's "skillful, two-pronged campaign" in the media and in direct lobbying to push for the Superfund. And, congressional sources say the chemical industry "stonewalled" on the Superfund, making it difficult even for sympathetic congressmen to work out an acceptable compromise (*Chemical Week*, June 18, 1980, p. 63).

The compromise HR 7020 passed the full committee by a 21-3 vote and was placed on the Union Calendar.

In the Senate, concerns was raised about the future of the Superfund legislation when Senator Edmund S. Muskie left the Senate to accept an appointment as secretary of state for the Carter Administration. Muskie was considered by many as the leading figure on environmental issues. Also, for the first time the industry picked up support from several senators. As a congressional aide noted, "You do not negotiate with outside interests, but with other congressmen." Senator Domenici's own experience as an attorney and his philosophical position caused him to express concern over Superfund. In addition, he had several firms within his state (New Mexico) that would be affected. Senator Simpson personally and politically backed the industry position. Senator Bentson wanted a bill, but as a prior insurance man, he was concerned with the impact of this legislation on small businessmen. Senators Domenici, Simpson and Bentsen articulated a position that had merits, and they were bi-partisian Senate members. This became an important and troublesome coalition to deal with. On the other side, Senators Muskie, Bradley, Culver, Moynihan, and Chafee were strong advocates for passage of the legislation. But as one staffer clearly noted, "Muskie's loss (to secretary of state) changed for all time the deliberative aspects of this and all future bills."

The strains within the CMA were beginning to show publicly. Mosher points out

> The Chemical Manufacturers Association, which has fought every proposal, undoubtedly has contributed to the slow pace of legislation. And it has also contributed to some ill will in Congress, even among opponents of Superfund legislation.
>
> "Those who have stonewalled the legislative process have also made it very difficult for those of us who wanted a reasonable bill," Representative Edward R. Madigan (R., IL) said during the debate on the Florio bill (p. 855).

The first public break within the CMA position was voiced at this time as well.

> A considerable segment of the chemical industry is coming to believe that if Congress doesn't act this year, it will soon. Officials of many chemical companies are putting pressure on the Chemical Manufacturers Association to abandon its hard-line position against any legislation. If regulation is inevitable, they want to have a voice in shaping it. "I think society will demand some level of federal effort to clean up waste sites like Love Canal," predicted Jerry Kenney, Union Carbide Corporation's Washington representative. "Politically, the chemical industry is not going to escape without paying a fee" (Mosher, p. 857).

The Final Committee Hearings

The chemical industry brought considerable pressure to bear on the House in order to have Florio's bill (HR 7020) referred to the Ways and Means Committee. This was yet another shift in tactics. In the 95th Congress, bills dealing with an oil fund were not sent to the Ways and Means Committee. The industry forced the bill to Ways and Means because of its revenue aspects, since they thought that they could get a better deal. John Doyle (Monority Counsel, Water Resources Subcommittee) noted that "Ways and Means was especially sensitive and knowledgeable of industry needs." Stover, vice-president of CMA, was pleased at the time.

> We were delighted to see it go the Ways and Means. We thought we would get a more balanced view there that would limit the bill to "orphan sites" and hang the wrongdoer. If you can't find the wrongdoer, then use federal money.

As a consequence of this lobbying effort, the bill was referred to the House Ways and Means Committee, but sequentially. This sequential referral was important to the bill's sponsors. It meant that Ways and Means had only 30 days to take action on the bill, otherwise it would return to the House floor for consideration. Hearings were held on HR 7020 and HR 85 on June 2, 1980. Very early in the hearings, Representative Downey (D., NY) announced his intention to increase the fund size to $1.2 billion and to increase the industry's contribution to 75 percent.

On June 17, the House Ways and Means Committee formally voted (20-15) on HR 7020 and increased the size of the fund to $1.2 billion, and by a 21-14 vote increased the industry's contributions to 75 percent of the total.

According to several observers, the CMA had bi-partisan support within the Ways and Means Committee for a $900 million Superfund. CMA, however, decided it could win this one. Unfortunately, according to congressional sources, "a key congressman took a walk" and Representative Downey's amendment to increase the fund to $1.2 billion and require 75 percent industry contributions were passed in less than four minutes.

Chemical Week noted that the Superfund compromise won, but still voiced optimism.

> Chances of final, compromise legislation reaching President Carter's desk before Congress adjourns in October are slim. But the chemical industry's opposition to a Superfund is crumbling.
> The Chemical Manufacturer's Association is granting what is called "grudging approval" to HR 7020 and is seeking a similar measure from the Senate (June 18, 1980, p. 63).

Other comments from industry members demonstrate the growing thrust for compromise on this issue.

> Rohm and Haas's Davis says his company unequivocally supports HR 7020. "It would have saved lots of agrravation if we had gotten the measure months ago," he says. And DuPont's Washington representative, John Klocko, says the Commmerce Committee's markup of Florio's bill was the turning point for Superfund, because the industry decided it could get improved legislation it could live with.
> Companies that were pushing for a compromise—particularly Rohm and Haas, Olin, and Monsanto—appear to have won their point (*Chemical Week*, June 18, 1980, p. 63).

This support for compromise caused serious dissension within CMA. Allied, Dow, and DuPont, within the councils of CMA, were still urging the membership to help kill any Superfund legislation. Figure 3 documents the position of key actors in the Superfund process as of June 18, 1980.

At the same time, the Superfund bill was moving through the Senate. The Senate Environment and Public Works Committee agreed on how Superfund would be financed and who would operate and maintain these sites after remedial action was taken. President Carter also entered this battle and sent a letter to Senator Randolph, chairman of the Senate Environment and Public Works, urging him to do everything in his power to report S 1480 by the July 4 recess.

On June 27th, the Senate Environment and Public Works Committee approved a $4.1 billion fund to finance the clean-up of toxic waste dumps and to compensate their victims. The committee vote was 10 to 1 with Senator Simpson (R., WY) the lone objector. This bill brought sharp reaction from CMA.

> "We haven't stopped a godddamn thing in that committee," said CMA President Robert Roland before the bill passed, "but we have indications that a lot of people will support us on the floor." The current House version is "a more reasoned approach," Roland added, calling the Senate committee product yesterday "impractical, unnecessarily broad and punitive." Any fund financed by the industry is "still repugnant," he said (Omang, June 28, 1980).

In order to make sense of the various bills now proposed in Congress, a comparison of them is shown in Table 1. The election year pressures were adding new factors to be considered at the point in time, and the delays and obstructions by CMA hurt.

> Lobbyists for the Chemical Manufacturers Association have already stumbled badly over the Superfund. For months after the Administration first proposed it more than a year ago, the industry refused to consider and compromise (*Business Week*, July 14, 1980, p. 42).

The industry now realized that not only would it have to pay something, but also that it may have lost the opportunity to determine how much.

> The industry already has suffered for its miscues. For example, chemical lobbyists urged sending the Commerce Committee bill to Ways and Means. Some claim that this was a tactic to delay the bill, but CMA's Roland says that the industry wanted the fee scrutinized as a tax. In any case, the strategy backfired. Ways and Means, under pressure to come up with $1.2 billion in revenue to conform with the fiscal 1981 budget resolution, voted to triple the fee.
>
> Industry's best chance for derailing the Superfund now is delay (*Business Week*, July 14, 1980, p. 42).

Irving S. Shapiro, chairman of DuPont, addressed the National Conference of Lieutenant Governors on August 17, 1980. His speech was entitled "We Can Manage Hazardous Wastes" and strongly supported a Superfund Bill. The speech

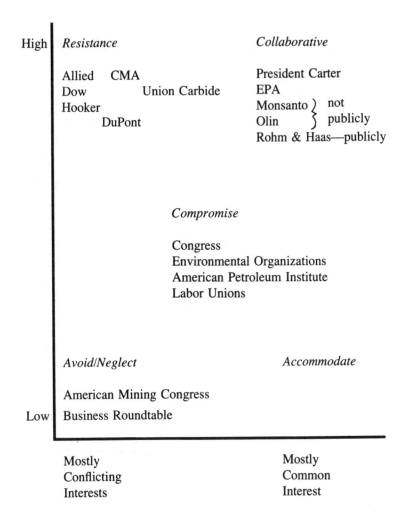

Figure 3. Political Positions of Key Actors in the Superfund Debate (HR 7020), June 18, 1980

Table 1. Proposed Superfund Legislation as of July 1, 1980

	Administration Bills S 1341 (Introduced June 14, 1979) HR 4566 (Introduced June 21, 1979)	HR 7020 As Passed By Interstate and Foreign Commerce Committee, May 16, 1980	HR 7020 As Passed By House Ways and Means Committee June 20, 1980	S 1480 As Passed By Senate Environment and Public WorksCommittee, June 27, 1980
Fund Size:	$1.625 billion over four years	$600 million over four years	$1.2 billion over five years	$4.085 billion over six years
Fund Source:	80% from industry fees on crude oil, petrochemical feedstock, inorganic chemicals, heavy metals	50% from industry excise taxes on specified substances	75% from industry excise taxes on specified substances	87.5% from industry excise tax on oil and specified chemicals
Coverage:	Oil and hazardous substance spills, containment and emergency response for inactive and abandoned disposal sites	Release (or threat) from inactive hazardous waste sites	Release (or threat) from inactive hazardous waste sites	Any hazardous substance (broadly defined) and any pollutant which may present imminent and substantial danger: generally does not apply to oil pollution
Liability:	Joint, several and strict for owners, operators and lessees	No third party liability, provides for liability defenses while maintaining strict, joint and several liability	No third party liability, provides for liability defenses while maintaining strict, joint and several liability	Joint, several, and strict (except where person can apportion and show his contribution—then limited to that position): federal cause of action

Preemption of State Funds:	Yes	No	No	No
Damages and Claims:	Spills: removal and restoration costs, third party damages, no personal injury damages. Sites: emergency assistance, containment, no third party damages	Funds limited to remedying problems to failing sites	Funds limited to remedying problems to failing sites	Removal, containment and emergency response; all damages for personal injury or loss of natural resources, out of pocket medical expenses, loss of income

165

was not widely publicized, but it did serve as a signal of Shapiro's position and as an indicator of where DuPont was going to go next on Superfund.

> Nonetheless, the chemical industry is willing to pay its fair share to make the environment safe from these orphan dumps. To that end, we support a Federal "Superfund" to help the states clean up abandoned disposal sites. Presently, there are three such bills in Congress and DuPont believes the best of these to be the bill sponsored by Congressman Florio of New Jersey—HR 7020. The Florio bill addressed the primary problem of providing funds today to clean up inactive sites (Shapiro, August 19, 1980, p. 8).

The pace of legislation began to slow in the Senate. The Senate Finance Committee and Commerce Committee scheduled hearings on S 1480 in September on the bill for which they were seeking jurisdiction. The jurisdiction of the Commerce Committee was to be denied, but the Finance Committee's request was upheld. Additionally, the House Rules Committee cleared both HR 85 and HR 7020 for floor action by the House of Representatives (*Environment Reporter*, September 5, 1980, p. 666).

The industry continued to set up its pressure campaign; the *St. Louis Post Dispatch* reported that

> The chemical and oil industries have begun a well-organized and well-targeted campaign to dramatically change a Senate bill. . .
>
> The chemical company campaigns include what *Congressional Quarterly*, in a report published this past week, termed a "highly sophisticated computerized mailing" by St. Louis based Monsanto Company to its 40,000 shareholders.
>
> "There's been no groundswell of public support to offset the massive campaign being waged by the chemical industry," said a staffer for the Senate Environment Committee. "Unless people are sitting near a chemical dump, they won't write. As a result, the lobbying is very lopsided right now."
>
> "This campaign is much more sophisticated, much more effective than a postcard campaign," said Curtis Moore, minority counsel for the Senate Environmental Committee. "It speaks of a high degree of knowlege of how the Senate operates. It shows an awareness that a single contact from a personal friend, or a single letter from the right kind of organization may be worth more than a hundred postcards."
>
> The campaign is effective because instead of flooding Capitol Hill with letters from housewives, the letters are from engineers, lawyers and architects—"the people who influence policy," Moore said (September 14, 1980, pp. 1-7k).

Pressure continued to mount for action on Superfund by industry, the public, and the media. The Finance Commititee, which finally got jurisdiction over the bill (S 1480), did not want to bring it to a vote or allow it to go to the Senate floor for action. There were several reasons for this reluctance. Some senators were opposed on ideological grounds, while others were concerned with the legal precedent that would be set and with the impact on small firms. The CMA was very concerned that the committee would act, as the bill was seen as ". . . a son of Muskie strong arm move." That is, the industry was fearful that the Committee would act out of respect for Muskie and favorably pass the bill to the Senate floor. The CMA and member firms, as already noted, mounted an intense lobbying campaign to delay the bill. This was not lost in the media.

> Time is running out on one of the more important pieces of legislation before Congress this year. The legislation would create a fund—nicknamed Superfund—for dealing with emergencies caused by spills and leaks for oil and hazardous chemicals. Though no one publicly disputes the need for such a fund, it is being delayed to death by a massive lobbying campaign waged by the oil and chemicals industries. (*Washington Post*, September 15, 1980, p. 42).

The media was also quick to assess the situation and assign blame if the law did not pass.

> Enactment has been frustrated by splintered congressional jurisdiction—three or more different committees on each side of the Capitol—and by a determined lobbying campaign against any but the weakest versions of the bill. With so many different committees in the act, there are almost endless opportunities to kill the legislation through inaction without anyone's saying to come out and vote against it, and this is precisely the chemical and oil lobbyists' strategy.
>
> The present arena is the Senate Finance Committee, which finally held hearings last week after two months of delay. Senators outdid each other in extolling the importance of the bill but then solemnly noted the complexity and momentousness of its precise administrative details and funding mechanisms. These matters can be worked out on the floor and in House-Senate conference, however; the committee's job is to take prompt enough action so that final passage is possible in the remaining few days of the session. If this committee and other key members of the leadership continue to vacillate, no amount of rhetoric will hide the fact that the Senate let the chemical industry pressure it into running out the clock on a bill that would serve everyone's best interest (*Washington Post*, September 15, 1980, p. 28).

The CMA then made a critical "credibility" blunder. Roland, appearing on ABC's September 11 "Nightline" stated that

> . . . in testimony before the Senate Finance Committee on S 1480, we indicated once more that we support 7020—HR 7020—The Florio bill on the House side. . . .The breakdown would be 75 percent industry and 25 percent government. It would be $1.2 billion (*Chemical and Engineering News*, January 5, 1981, p. 17).

The association was sending out mixed signals that hurt their supporters, damaged the CMA's credibility, and provided more ammunition for their detractors. The day after his television interview, Roland sent out a letter stating that his remarks had been misinterpreted and that the CMA still supported only the $600 million measure.

On September 19, the House of Representatives overwhelmingly adopted HR 85, the oil pollution spill fund, by a vote of 288 to 11. On September 23, the House considered HR 7020 as reported by Ways and Means (the $1.2 billion 75/25 split contribution bill). During the House's consideration of the bill, Representative Stockman consistently referred to the bill's creation of the EPA as a "czar" in the hazardous waste area. He offered two amendments to the bill, the first of which would have gutted the bill and removed all industry contribution. This amendment was rejected. Stockman's second amendment requiring the EPA administrator to define "hazardous waste site" within 120 days of enactment of the bill and subjecting that definition to congressional review and one House veto, was also rejected. The bill did pass by a large majority (351-23) and it was sent to the Senate for their consideration.

Robert Roland, after passage of the bill in the House observed that ". . . the bill, although not perfect, represents a conscientious bi-partisan effort to address the problem realistically and to establish adequate protection for the public and environment" (*Environmental Reporter*, September 26, 1980, p. 729). Figure 4 portrays the firm's positions as of September 1980 concerning HR 7020.

As Congress adjourned for its election recess, the media kept the Superfund issue alive. The *Washington Post* in an editorial entitled "Last Days for Super-fund" continued to apply pressure on the Finance Committee.

> However, the measure is now stalled in the Senate, in the Finance Committee to be precise. So far, Finance Chairman Russell Long and his committee have refused to indicate what changes they would like to see in the existing Senate bill, or even to agree to act in time to allow final action on the bill during the post-election lame-duck session. Senator Dole and others have further hurt the bill's chances by threatening to use Superfund as the vehicle for the controversial tax cut should it be taken up on the Senate floor. These senators and others regularly proclaim their support for some kind of Superfund. But after months of delay, their actions—or failure to act—tell the real story.
>
> The Finance Committee owes it to the rest of Congress—and to the public—to let Superfund be voted by the full Senate before the end of this year (September 24, 1980, p. 26).

The *New York Times* also applied pressure in their editorial "While Poison's Fester. . ."

> Finally, the House has approved "Superfund" legislation to clean up abandoned hazardous waste sites for oil and chemical spills. The only barrier now is the Senate, where, alas, there is no sign that Russell Long is prepared to allow the "Superfund" bill to reach the floor for a vote. If his Finance committee fails to act, the nation will lose a precious opportunity to defend against toxic hazards that are becoming increasingly common.
>
> Diehard proponents of one bill or another threaten to block final action unless their versions prevail. That would be the worst outcome of all. Either legislative approach would be far better than no bill at all (HR 7020 or S 1480). Congress has stalled enough. Poisons are festering. So is injustice. The nation is waiting (September 26, 1980, p. A34).

In spite of this strong rhetoric and the fact that the Superfund legislation had become ". . . one of the best spectator sports now being played on Capitol Hill" (Ember, September 29, 1980, p. 2), the chance for passage was seen as only 50-50. This slowing of momentum was not lost in the White House. The President contacted legislators and asked if his administration could work directly for a compromise. This work, at the suggestion of several Senators, took the form of meetings among the key actors. These meetings were very helpful in moving

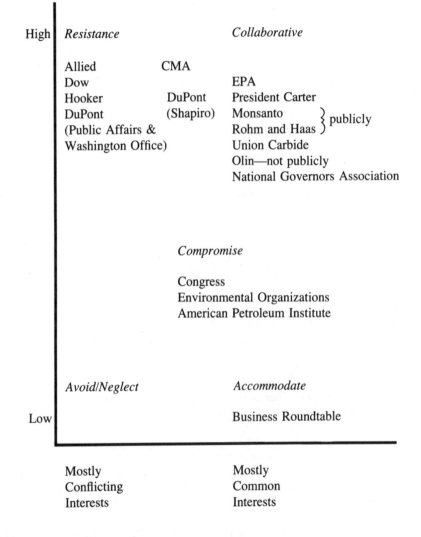

Figure 4. Political Positions of Key Actors in the Superfund Debate
          (HR 7020), September 1980

the industry to accept a compromise. But in early October, the industry apparently decided that Reagan would win and that they would not have to make any more concessions or perhaps not have to deal with any legislation at all.

Shabecoff noted the prevailing mood concerning Superfund.

"Superfund is dead for now, but we think we can get a compromise bill when Congress comes back," said Robert Maher, a White House aide (October 1, 1980, p. A28).

Finally, on October 1, the Senate Finance Committee was given formal approval by the Senate to consider S 1480. The Senate agreed unamimously to give the Finance Committee a November deadline to consider the bill (*Environmental Reporter*, October 10, 1980, p. 668).

The Final Push

The presidential and congressional elections on November 4, 1980, dramatically altered the power structure of Superfund politics. The Republican party achieved a landslide victory in the presidental election and achieved substantial gains in the House. More importantly, the Republicans achieved control of the Senate where the Superfund legislation was being delayed. The election of Ronald Reagan, with his avowed philosophy of reducing governmental intervention in business afairs, must have been a bright spot for the CMA and member firms. Further good news came when Senators Byrd and Baker (outgoing and incoming majority leaders) announced that the Senate would not consider controversial legislation in the lame duck session beginning November 12, 1980. The forecasts for Superfund were poor.

However, another Carter environmental goal, the so-called "Superfund" to finance cleanup of toxic waste dumps apparently is dead. Both situations are products of the new Republican strength in the Senate (Omang, November 8, 1980, p. 21).

At this point the CMA was positive that Superfund would be stopped.

"The question is whether the Senate wants to take up something as time consuming and controversial as this is going to be," he [Roland] said. "I would say that they have other more important budget matters to take care of (Omang, November 8, 1980, p. 21).

Once again, the CMA's over-confidence would lead them to make critical errors. On November 14, 1980, a critical meetings took place between Roland and Congressman Florio, the sponsor of HR 7020. Aides from both sides agreed on the following facts: (1) Florio wanted the CMA to issue a statement clearly presenting its support of HR 7020; and, if CMA would do this, (2) Florio could guarantee the delivery of the Senate on HR 7020. In response to this, all sides agreed that Roland stated he could not issue a statement for the CMA but would need to get approval from the executive committee of the Board of Directors of CMA. Roland also stated that the CMA could not provide a statement of support because it was opposed to HR 7020, and he doubted that Florio could "deliver" the Senate when he could not control his own subcommittee. What was disputed by the CMA were comments attributed to their organization by Florio to the effect that the industry felt it could get a better deal from the incoming Republican administration. According to Ember

> Florio left the meeting enraged and held a press conference to announce that Roland had reneged on his deal to support his $1.2 billion bill. Florio tells *C&EN* that Roland did make the statement about industry's getting a better deal next year. Roland, through CMA spokesman Jeff Van, insists he never made that comment (1981, p. 18).

Whether or not Roland made these statements about the incoming administration to Florio is unimportant. Two points stand out. First, the CMA did, given previous comments to the press and others, appear to reverse its position. Second, influential congressmen such as Senators Baker, Dole, Domenici, and Moynihan believed that the CMA did make the statement about the incoming administration. This statement put the Republicans in an untenable public position. To fail to act now would make it seem that they were in the industry's hip pocket. Additionally, when asked about this statement, Roland acknowledged that the political climate next year would be more favorable to business and that the CMA opposed the bill passed by the House. He insisted that the CMA hasn't "reneged on a thing" because it always opposed the House bill as too "radical" (*New York Times*, November 15, 1980, p. 26).

This hard-line approach to compromise caused great tension within the CMA membership that was soon to surface publicly.

> But representative James J. Florio (D., NJ) apparently sensed that the Chemical Manufacturers Association would not support his bill (HR 7020) and would try instead to put the bill over into the next Congress, hoping for a better deal. So Florio created sufficient publicity over the issue to tip the balance in favor of passage of a Superfund bill. "If you're going to cut a person off at the knee," says one industry source, dismayed at CMA's handling of Florio, "at least you shouldn't do it publicly" (*Chemical Week*, December 3, 1980, p. 16).

All this publicity and controversy over Superfund caused the incoming administration to request a position paper from the EPA addressing two questions: (1) Why does the bill have to pass now?, and (2) How would the Reagan Administration pass it? The EPA response highlighted four major points.

- The passage of the bill next year would require a great deal of re-battling over the same issues and prevent the development and progress of the Reagan legislative program.
- Any Superfund bill would affect industry-government relationships. Passing Superfund now would make it a Carter vice a Reagan bill.

- If passage is delayed until next year, Reagan would have to use "chips" to get congressional support. ("Chips" are promises of support for individual congressmen's legislation or appointments or other political favors.)
- The current Superfund can be made acceptable to a broad spectrum of industry.

Senior Republican congressional members bought the position laid out in the EPA position paper, but expressed reservations about getting industry support. Without this support, Republicans were reluctant to push for passage.

More public pressure was brought to bear on the Finance Committee to release S 1480 in mid-November. The *New York Times*, the *Washington Post* (November 17, 1980, p. A5), the *Boston Globe* (November 17, 1980, p. 20), and other major papers all released articles dealing with chemical industry political action committee contributions in the 1980 elections to 18 Finance Committee members. No impropriety was suggested, but the circumstances at this time did not portray these members in a favorable light. The total contribution to the Committee was $300,000, the maximum of which, $73,950, was given to incoming Senator Charles Grassly (R., IA) who defeated an outspoken sponsor and supporter of Superfund, Senator Culver.

In spite of these revelations CMA attempted to remain aloof and somewhat neutral. William Stover, vice president of CMA said,

> I feel sure that the new power figures in Washington are not going to permit the Congress to move ahead with major precedent-setting legislation. . . . Our support or lack of support at this time is really beside the point, (*Boston Globe*, November 17, 1980, p. 20).

The reaction by the Finance Committee was immediate. The next day in an unusual move:

> The Senate Finance Committee washed its hands of the controversy over a "Superfund" to clean up chemical dumps yesterday, reporting out without comment a $4.2 billion bill that is certain to be either killed or significantly amended on the Senate floor.
>
> Finance Committee Chairman Russell Long (D., LA) brought the issue to a vote after only two hours of a scheduled three-day markup in order, he said, to get action on the controversial subject before Congress adjourns. "This legislation should be decided by this Congress and this Senate, and we hope the Senate can act on it in these remaining days," he said (Omang, November 18, 1980, p. 24).

Senators Randolph and Stafford, the outgoing and incoming chairmen of the Senate Environment and Public Works Committee, introduced a compromise bill on November 17, 1980. This compromise removed many of the objections that the industry had to S 1480, slashed the size of the fund, removed all victim compensation provisions except out-of-pocket medical expenses, and strictly limited the liability provisions. The two Senators also threatened to "introduce a more stringent 'Superfund' bill next year if the chemical industry blocked the compromise" (*New York Times*, November 18, 1980, p. 18).

The public stand against any Superfund legislation began to crack on November 19, 1980. Irving Shapiro, chairman of DuPont, in an interview with New York Times reporter Philip Shabecoff, stated that a fund for cleaning up toxic waste sites should be enacted in the current congressional session.

> "I want legislation in this session, rational legislation dictated by the facts," Mr. Shapiro said.
>
> He said that a compromise proposal for a $2.7 billion fund offered by Senator Robert T. Stafford and Senator Jennings Randolph was unacceptable, but added that if the chief executives of the chemical companies get together with White House and Congressional representatives "we could have a sensible bill in two hours" (Shabecoff, November 20, 1980, p. A30).

The industry continued to suffer public embarrassment from its shift in position on Superfund.

> Senator Moynihan said: "I have to say that I can't imagine a greater disservice that the business community can do to President Reagan than to signal its expectation of what his Administration will be like by withdrawing support for this legislation.
>
> Senator Moynihan added, "In the annals of corporate cynicism, I have not encountered anything as brazen (Shabecoff, November 19, 1980, p. A30).

The industry association was surprised and its credibility damaged by Shapiro's break. It was surprised because DuPont, within CMA's executive board, had been supportive of a hard-line approach. The prestige and influence of both DuPont and Mr. Shapiro opened the door for further fragmentation of the CMA position. On November 20, Vincent L. Gregory, Jr., chairman of Rohm and Haas Company, announced in a company news release that "We support prompt passage of legislation creating a fund to clean up hazardous waste sites." Rohm and Haas had long been a supporter of a more evenly balanced approach with CMA and of some sort of Superfund. William S. Sneath, chairman of Union Carbide Corporation also announced his support of Superfund legislation in the current Congress on November 20 as well. The industry support for compromise legislation that the EPA addressed in its position paper for the Reagan administration was clearly demonstrated. This fragmentation, according to a CMA member, was one of extreme sensitivity, with firms angry at the developments. Now, Congress would count on the largest (DuPont) and third largest (Carbide) chemical firms' support of Superfund. The positions of the firms are shown in Figure 5 as of November 22, 1980. CMA president Roland gamely kept up the "industry position."

> We are concerned that the Senate has decided to debate Superfund legislation at this time. We believe. . . that the haste and hidden political agendas of a lame duck session mitigate against thoughtful. . . consideration" (*Morning News*, November 20, 1980).

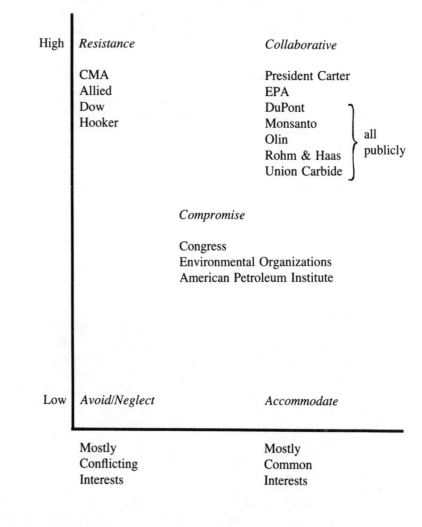

Figure 5. Political Positions of Key Actors in the Superfund Debate, November 1980

On November 21 Stafford and Randolph, sensing victory on compromise legislation, further modified their substitute bill reducing the fund to $1.6 billion, eliminated compensation for individuals, eliminated joint and several liability, and limited the scope of liability. This compromise, which involved 18 senators, was reached after eight and one-half hours of negotiations. A key stumbling block was Senator Jesse Helms, who argued long and forcefully against the bill. Only after his demands were met was consensus achieved. On November 24 the Senate considered Superfund legislation. The Senate passed the compromise bill by a vote of 78-9.

The Senate bill was brought to the House floor for consideration on December 3, 1980. The night before, President Carter, apparently concerned about its prospects, phoned 65 representatives in 90 minutes attempting to gain their support. The impact of an outgoing president is difficult to measure, but the House, after considerable debate, passed the Superfund bill by a vote of 274-94.

The Chemical Marketing Reporter offered its reasons for the successful passage of Superfund:

> Industry sources, meanwhile, pointed to the key role played by Senator Howard Baker of Tennessee, the next majority leader on the legislation. As one put it, "This should be called the Howard Baker Bill."
>
> Among the latest theories suggested by industry men for Senator Baker's reversal to push for a "Superfund" bill this year is that he struck a political deal with those on the other side of the aisle. Also suggested is that those in the transition team for the Reagan Administration wanted the bill "left on President Carter's doorstep" as one executive put it (December 3, 1980, p. 12).

Chemical Week attempted to analyze the situation in an article entitled "Superfund Finale Wrenches CMA." In this article it was pointed out that CMA did not cover itself with glory during the debate over Superfund and may well have sown the seeds for future problems within its own membership and in its dealings with Congress:

> Caught unprepared by the wave of support for the compromise bill, CMA found itself alone in support of a $600 million Superfund bill approved months ago by the House Commerce Committee. "From my standpoint, CMA did not negotiate with us in any real sense," says an aide to Senator Stafford. The aide maintains that, as debate progressed, the Chemical Specialities Manufacturers Association is reported to have moved away from CMA's position. In short, he says, "CMA did not serve itself well."
>
> Nevertheless, CMA has antagonized a number of congressmen by underestimating political realities and presenting no unified position on Superfund. An aide to a Republican congressman, sympathetic to industry, says that the industry was "disorganized" when the House was considering Superfund. He recalls there were "too many people supposedly speaking for the industry, too many points of view, and too great a reluctance to make concessions." Another source says: "Had (CMA) been more constructive, this wouldn't have been so bitter at the end" (December 3, 1980, p. 16).

BEHAVIOR AND PERFORMANCE
IN A POLITICAL SETTING

The response capability and range of options available to the organization when dealing with political issues are at least in part, driven by the structure and conduct of public affairs. This research, then, would seem to question Thompson's earlier observation that ". . . organizations with similar technological and environmental problems should exhibit similar behavior: patterns should appear" (p. 2). This view would have to be modified to note that similar mechanisms for interpreting the environment would have to be in place, and that the structuring of the organization's institutional subsystem could lead to different patterns of response given similar technology and environment issues.

The case study presented herein demonstrates two major points. First, various patterns of corporate behavior reflect the *different* political strategies pursued by the individual organizations. Second, these patterns also reflect the *evolution* of political strategies over the life cycle of an issue. The actions of the six chemical firms serves to highlight these observations.

Allied Chemical's strategy throughout the Superfund debate was one of resistance. The explanation for this resistance comes from two major observations. First, Allied's new chief executive officer had just taken over as Superfund was beginning, and his concerns were primarily focused on restoring Allied's competitive health. As such, he concentrated on divestiture of failing business segments and tightening of internal managerial control. Second, both Allied and Dow Chemical have reputations as industry hardliners with respect to governmental regulations and intervention. Therefore, it made sense that Allied would support the CMA position and pursue a strategy of resistance based on reaction to occurring events, and that their public affairs were not influential in altering this policy.

Dow Chemical also pursued a strategy of resistance to Superfund and reaction to events as they occured. Dow reasoned that it was not contributing to the problem that Superfund was meant to address. Dow incinerated most of its wastes, and what it did not burn, it maintained on Dow-owned and Dow-controlled property. As such, Dow's chief executive officer and the public affairs department attempted to present this information to interested parties and argued that no new law was necessary. Public affairs here was used as a tool of company policy.

Dow and Allied were both organized for public affairs in the same nationally focused manner. One difference, as noted earlier, was that Dow had an extensive political action committee network for the solicitation and distribution of funds to political candidates. Its position on Superfund, then, was a reflection of context (Dow—handles its own wastes; Allied—concerned with competitive problems), public affairs department structure and activities (or conduct), and motivational factors (their histories and the goals of their chief executive officers). It is curious that both firms organized with a national public affairs focus selected a political strategy of resistance.

Dupont was an interesting case. Although its structure of public affairs includes national, federal, and state and local elements, a vital link was missing. DuPont's public affairs department, unlike those of the other chemical firms, did not have responsibility for government relations and legislative lobbying, nor did it have a political action committee. The responsibility for government relations and legislative lobbying lay in the legal department. During the Superfund debate, both the public affairs and legal departments supported the strategy of resistance as espoused by the CMA. However, no other chemical firm had to deal with the likes of Irving Shapiro. In the final weeks surrounding Superfund, his public support for such legislation proved crucial. Why did he do it? There are several possible answers to this, but two stand out. First, Shapiro has long and often spoken of chief executives as having a public responsibility to speak out and act on critical issues. Second, Shapiro and Carter genuinely liked and respected one another, and this was Shapiro's opportunity to help out an old friend. DuPont's action then can be seen as primarily influenced by motivational factors (Shapiro wanted to do it) in the end, but during most of the debate the legal department, aided by public affairs, gave support within CMA for a resistance strategy.

Monsanto's position on Superfund was principally a reflection of the activities and influence of its public affairs department. Monsanto, for some time prior to Superfund, had been attempting to clean up the chemical industry image through creative advertising. As such, Superfund was a massive attack on the industry's image. Monsanto supported the CMA publicly almost to the end, but privately was arguing for moderation and reasonable legislation within the CMA and in Congress. But when the industry was faced with a critical choice, Monsanto reacted: Either support HR 7020 and defeat the much stronger Senate bill S 1480, or continue to oppose all legislation and run the risk of seeing S 1480 passed into law. Monsanto chose to support HR 7020 publicly, but it brought its public affairs expertise to bear on S 1480. Recall that Monsanto's strengths lay in political action committees and grassroots campaigns. Monsanto mounted a very effective grassroots campaign against S 1480, which contributed to the delay in its consideration by the Senate and gave all participants more time to deal with the issue. Therefore, Monsanto's actions were a direct reflection of situational factors, in particular the strengths of its public affairs organization.

Rohm and Haas assumed a strategy of collaboration from the outset and attempted to interact with interested parties to achieve a reasonable and workable solution. This was Chief Executive Officer Gregory's personal philosophy and his actions were supported by the public affairs department.

Union Carbide was a distinctively different story. Union Carbide started out using a resistance strategy based on support for the CMA position. As time passed, the public affairs department became increasingly sensitized to the fact that the industry could not win on Superfund. Kenney, their Washington lobbyist,

Table 2. Political Strategies of Six Major Chemical Firms During
Superfund Legislation

Firm	Public Affairs Structure	Dominant Political Strategy	Observed Conduct	Key Influence
Allied Chemical	National	Resistance	Reactive	CEO
Dow Chemical	National	Resistance	Reactive	CEO, Public Affairs
DuPont*	All**	Resistance/ Collaboration	Reactive/Proactive	CEO, Public Affairs Legal Affairs
Monsanto	All	Collaboration/ Resistance***	Interactive/Reactive	Public Affairs
Rohm and Haas	All	Collaboration	Interactive	CEO, Public Affairs
Union Carbide	All	Resistance/ Collaboration	Interactive	Public Affairs

Notes:

* It must be noted that DuPont's actions prior to Shapiro interview were entirely supportive of CMA stand. Shapiro caught his own organization by surprise by his announcement of support for "Superfund."

** DuPont's Public Affairs Department does not have responsibility for federal government relations and legislative lobbying. Those activities are in the legal department. In addition, DuPont does not have a Political Action Committee.

*** Monsanto's resistance strategy was aimed at preventing S 1480 from being passed into law. This bill was opposed by all firms within the industry. Monsanto, like Rohm and Haas, was a strong supporter of achieving a workable piece of legislation from the start of the debate.

noted early on that the industry would have to pay something for Superfund. Union Carbide did not have a "public" executive like Shapiro, nor did it have a history of resistance like Dow and Allied. Carbide's strengths in public affairs lay in its attempts to involve operating managers in public affairs activities. This institutionalization of public affairs contributed to Carbide's shift on the Superfund issues over time. The public affairs department was able to make its voice heard and acted on.

Table 2 summarizes the political strategies of the six chemicals firms. In Dow and Allied Chemical, public affairs department had little influence because of stronger influences from other factors. This lack of influence may also be a reflection of the public affairs department organization. In Monsanto, DuPont, Rohm and Haas, and Union Carbide, public affairs did have an impact on both the strategy and patterns of response exhibited by the firm. We should note that all of these firms (with the exception of DuPont) are organized in public affairs with a "do it all" focus. In Monsanto's case, public affairs expertise shaped its proactive behavior through the use of grassroots programs. In DuPont's cases, public affairs and the legal department carried what they thought was the firm's position until Shapiro's public announcement. Rohm and Haas's department supported Gregory's position, while Union Carbide's public affairs had a direct impact on management strategy and response over time.

It should be clear, as the DuPont experience during "Superfund" demonstrates, that a public affairs department cannot slow down or stop a chief executive officer who decides to take a "public activist" role. Conversely, as Union Carbide's experiences seems to demonstrate, a public affairs department can help a less "activist" chief executive to move the corporation in a specified direction.

Finally, stonewalling, or outright resistance to legislation, does not seem to be a successful strategy in terms of the firm's "political" image. Allied and Dow Chemical had objectively reasonable bases for being opposed to hazardous waste legislation. Their past actions on previous bills in Congress had earned them a reputation as hardliners within both Congress and Environmental Protection Agency. Their actions on Superfund, though reasonable given their situation, contributed further to their political image as unreasonable and stubborn. Although we cannot place a cost on "political" image, it does appear that Allied and Dow have developed their reputations so that, even if they do offer constructive and forward-thinking proposals, congressmen, staff personnel, and EPA personnel will tend to discredit their efforts. That is, in dealings with the government, these firms operate at a disadvantage. Contrast this with the views of DuPont, Union Carbide, and Rohm and Haas, who are seen as innovative, flexible organizations that can compromise on tough public policy issues. They will continue to have a sympathetic audience when they approach Congress or the EPA.

NOTE

This paper is based on the author's doctoral dissertation which received the annual prize awarded by the Social Issues Division and the A.T. Kearney Award from the Business Policy and Planning Division, both of the Academy of Management, for 1982.

REFERENCES

Ackerman, R. W. *The Social Challenge to Business*. Cambridge, MA: Harvard University Press, 1975.

Bain, Joe S.. *Industrial Organization*, revised edition. New York: John Wiley and Sons, 1968.

Baysinger, B. D., and R. W. Woodman. "Dimensions of the Public Affairs/Government Relations Function in Major American Corporations." *Strategic Management Journal* 3 (1982): 27-42.

Blodgett, J. E. (ed.) *Compensation for Victims of Water Pollution*. Report prepared for the Committee of Public Works and Transportation, U.S. House of Representatives, Washington, D.C.: U.S. Government Printing Office, May 1979.

Carson, R.. *Silent Spring*. Boston: Houghton Mifflin, 1962.

180 JOHN F. MAHON

Chandler, A.. *Strategy and Structure*. Cambridge, MA: MIT Press, 1962.

Cummings, Philip, Democratic Counsel for the Senate Committee on Environment and Public Works. Interview, January 8, 1981, Washington, D.C.

Doyle, John, Republican Counsel for the House Subcommittee on Water Resources. Interview, January 6, 1981, Washington, D.C.

DuPont. "Public Affairs Department Manual." May, 1975.

Ember, L.. "Chances Only 50-50 for 'Superfund' Legislation." *Chemical and Engineering News* (September 29, 1980): 29.

———. "Industry's Superfund Lobbying Goes Awry." *Chemical and Engineering News* (January 5, 1981): 17-19.

Feare, T., "Can CMA Remove the Tarnish." *Chemical Marketing Reporter* (July 28, 1980): 8-14.

Fox, J.R., *Managing Business-Government Relations: Cases and Notes on Business-Government Problems*. Homewood, IL: Irwin, 1982.

Gladwin, T., and I. Walter. "How Multinationals Can Manage Social and Political Forces." *Journal of Business Strategy* 1, No. 1 (1980): 54-68.

Hanson, Kirk. "Corporate Strategy and Public Policy." Paper presented at the Academy of Management Meetings, Atlanta, GA, August 1979.

Harbison, E.. "Image is a Problem, But There is Still Time to Act." Remarks made at the Chemical Industry Strategic Planning Conference, May 23, 1979.

Hegarty, W. H., J.C. Aplin, and R. H. Cosier. "Achieving Corporate Success in External Affairs." *Business Horizons* 21 (October, 1978): 65-74.

Hofer, Charles W., Edwin A. Murray Jr., Ram Charan, and Robert A. Pitts. *Strategic Management: A Casebook in Business Policy and Planning*. St. Paul,: West Publishing Company, 1980.

Jasen, G. "Allied Chemical Has Rapid-Fire Reactions Under Chief Hennessy." *Wall Street Journal* (April 23, 1980): 1, 33.

Keim, G. D., and B. D. Baysinger. "Corporate Political Strategies Examined: Constistuency-Building May be Best of All." *Public Affairs Review* 3 (1982): 77-87.

MacMillan, I.. *Strategy Formulation: Political Concepts*. St Paul: West Publishing Company, 1978.

Mahon, J. F.. "The Corporate Public Affairs Office: Structure, Behavior, and Impact." Unpublished Doctoral Dissertation, Boston University, 1982a.

———. "Public Affairs Structures and Activities in Large American Corporations" in Kae Chung (ed.), *Academy of Management Proceedings*. New York: Academy of Management, 1982b.

———. "Social Issues Research: The Thompson-Page Contribution," in Lee E. Preston (ed.), *Research in Corporate Social Performance and Policy*. Greenwich, CT: JAI Press, 1982.

Mank, Andy, Special Assistant to the Administrator for Water and Waste Management, Environmental Protection Agency. Interview, January 8, 1981, Washington, D.C.

McGrath, Phyllis. *Redefining Corporate-Federal Relations*. New York: The Conference Board, 1977.

Menzies, H.. "Union Carbide Raises Its Voice." *Fortune* (September 25, 1978): 86-88.

Moore, Curtis, Republican Council for the Senate Committee on Environment and Public Works. Interview, January 8, 1981, Washington, D.C.

Mosher, L. "Love Canals by the Thousands--Who Should Pay the Costly Bill?" *National Journal* (May 24, 1980): 855-857.

Murray, E. A., Jr.. "The Public Affairs Function: Report on a Large Scale Research Project," in Lee E. Preston (ed.), *Research in Corporate Social Performance and Policy*. Greenwich, CT: JAI Press, 1982.

Omang, J.. "Senate Unit Wants Industry to Pay for Chemical Damages." *Washington Post* (June 28, 1980): A5.

———. "Shifts on Hill May Help Alaska Lands Bill, Doom Toxic Superfund." *Washington Post* (November 8, 1980): Al.

———. "Senate Committee Sends 'Superfund' Bill to Floor." *Washington Post* (November 18, 1980): 24.

Parisi, A.. "Who Pays? Cleaning Up the Love Canals." *New York Times*, Section 3 (June 8, 1980): 1.

Porter, M.. "The Contributions of Industrial Organization to Strategy Formulation: A Promise Beginning to be Realized." Paper presented at the Academy of Management Meeting, Atlanta, GA, August, 1979.

Post, J. E.. *Risk and Response: Management and Social Change in the American Insurance Industry.* Lexington, MA: D.C. Health, 1976.

———. "Research on Patterns of Corporate Response to Social Change," in Lee E. Preston (ed.), *Research in Corporate Social Performance and Policy* 1. Greenwich, CT: JAI Press, Inc., 1978a.

———. *Corporate Behavior and Social Change.* Reston, VA: Reston, 1978b.

———. "The Internal Management of Social Responsiveness: The Role of the Public Affairs Department." Paper presented at a seminar on The Corporation in Society. Planning and Management of Corporate Responsibility at the University of Santa Clara, October 31 to November 2, 1979.

——— and P. N. Andrews. "Case Research In Corporation and Society Studies," in Lee E. Preston (ed.), *Research in Corporate Social Performance and Policy* 4. Greenwich, CT: JAI Press, 1982.

——— and J. F. Mahon. "Strategic Management of External Relations: How Companies Manage Public Affairs." Paper presented at the International conference on Global Strategic Management in the 1980's, London, England, October 1-2, 1981.

———, E. Murray, R. Dickie, and J. Mahon. "Public Affairs Offices and Their Functions: Highlights of a National Survey." *Public Affairs Review* (1981):88-99.

———. "The Public Affairs Function in American Corporations: Development and Relations with Corporate Planning." *Journal of Long Range Planning* 15, No. 2 (April, 1982): 12-21.

Preston, L. E.. "Strategy-Structure-Performance: A Framework for Organization/Environment Analysis," in Hans B. Thorelli (ed.), *Strategy + Structure = Performance.* Bloomington, IN: Indiana University Press, 1977.

Roland, R.. "Toxic Scapegoats." *Washington Post* (April 21, 1979): 15.

Sansweet, S.. "Political-Action Units at Firms are Assailed by Some Over Tactics." *Wall Street Journal* (June 24, 1980): 1, 12.

Schaumberg, Frank. *Judgement Reserved.* Reston, VA: Reston, 1976.

Sethi, S. P.. "Dimensions of Corporate Social Performance: An Analytical Framework for Measurement and Evolution." *California Management Review* 19, 3 (1975): 52-62.

Shabecoff, P.. "Bill for Hazardous Waste Cleanup Stuck in Senate with Recess Near." *New York Times* (October 1, 1980): 20.

———. "DuPont Chairman Backs Cleanup Fund." *New York Times* (November 20, 1980): A30.

Shapiro, I.. "We Can Manage Hazardous Wastes." Speech presented before the National Conference of Lieutenant Governors, Atlantic City, New Jersey, August 19, 1980.

Sonnenfeld, J.. *Corporate Views of the Public Interest: Perceptions of the Forest Products Industry.* Boston: Auburn House, 1981.

Stover, William, Vice President, Chemical Manufacturers Association. Interview, January 7, 1981, Washington, D.C.

Tiffany, P.. "History and Strategy: Recent Business-Government Relations in the American Steel Industry." Paper presented at the Academy of Management Meetings, New York, New York, 1982.

Thomas, Kenneth. "Conflict and Conflict Management," in Marvin Dunnette (ed.), *Handbook of Industrial and Organization Psychology.* Chicago, IL: Rand-McNally, 1976.

Thompson, James D. *Organizations in Action.* New York: McGraw-Hill, 1967.

Thorelli, H. (ed.). *Strategy + Structure = Performance.* Bloomington, IN: Indiana University Press, 1977.

Tipermas, Marc, Director, Office of Analysis Program Development, Environmental Protection
    Agency. Interview, January 6, 1981, Washington, D.C.
U.S. Congress, House, Committee on Interstate and Foreign Commerce. *Hazardous Waste Disposal,
    Part 1, Hearings Before a Subcommittee of the House Committee on Interstate and Foreign
    Commerce*, 96th Congress, first session, March 21, 22; April 5, 10; May 16, 23, 30; June 1,
    4, 5, 15, 18, 19, 1979.
————. *Hazardous Waste Disposal Report*, 96th Congress, first session, September, 1979.
U.S. Congress, Senate, Committee on Environment and Public Works. *Hazardous and Toxic Waste
    Disposal Field Hearing, Hearings Before Subcommittees of the Senate Committee on Environ-
    ment and Public Works*, 96th Congress, first session, May 18; June 29, 1979.
————. *Hazardous and Toxic Waste Disposal Field Hearing, Hearing Before Subcommittee of the
    Senate Committee on Environment and Public Works*, 96th Congress, first session, June 22,
    1979.
Woelfel, R.. "DuPont and Its Publics: A Lot of Good Chemistry Between Them?" M.S. Thesis,
    Massachusetts Institute of Technology, 1981.

EVOLUTION AND ROLE OF THE CORPORATE ENVIRONMENTAL AFFAIRS FUNCTION

Raj Chaganti and Arvind Phatak

The quality of the environment has been a public issue confronting American business for over two decades. With the passage of laws dealing with air and water pollution, interest in the issue peaked in the 1970s and has leveled off since then. With the passage of time, uncertainties concerning legislative compliance, rules of enforcement, and aceptable standards of corporate performance have steadily diminished. Availability of appropriate technology to control emissions and other environment-related problems and plentiful supply of specially trained manpower have facilitated the implementation of corporate environmental policies. The top executive of environmental affairs at Scott had this to say about future trends in this area: ''I do not think that there is much more evolution coming.... There is always going to be some fine tuning, and somebody will find some exotic chemicals for us to worry about. Solid waste is really becoming more and more of a problem. . ..but I do not view that as requiring any major

Research in Corporate Social Performance and Policy, volume 5, pages 183-203
Copyright © 1983 by JAI Press Inc.
All rights of reproduction in any form reserved.
ISBN: 0-89232-412-0

change." Although one company's view may not represent the entire situation, most indicators suggest that the environmental issue has reached a "maturity stage." Some have even gone further and argued in favor of easing environmental pressures in light of growing concern for productivity, mounting costs of regulatory compliance, and changing public expectations (Weidenbaum). Thus the issue has gone through the typical issue life cycle stages: changing public expectations, political controversy, development of legislation, and governmental action and litigation (Post, p. 26).

During these years, corporations, particularly those such as chemical manufacturers which were prone to environmental pressures, have experienced two related but distinct kinds of changes: (1) decision procedures concerning certain core activities—e.g., manufacturing plant, investments, product design—have significantly changed to bring them in line with the environmental regulations; and (2) a function called "environmental affairs," concerned with the management of the physical environment—air, water, noise, radiation, thermal pollution, solid waste disposal, restoration of land, scenic beauty, and land-use planning—has been gaining in importance and recognition in top management decisions. A Conference Board survey published in 1974 (Lund) confirms this trend: In more than 50 percent of the companies surveyed, the president or chairman of the board was making the major environment-related decisions, and in 96 percent of the companies, environmental policy decisions were being made at the corporate headquarters. However, fewer than 40 percent of the companies reported having written environmental policy statements. In spite of this absence of general evidence, in our judgement there has been a trend toward institutionalization of the environmental affairs function in a number of companies.

Such cross-sectional studies are fruitful in identifying the types of organizational structures that are in vogue to manage environmental concerns. However, any causal inferences drawn from such studies would be problematic due to the time lags and leads that are inherent in the process of organizational adaptation to the external changes (Miller and Friesen) and because different organizations may be at different life cycle stages (Kimberly and Miles). Organizations are not static. They grow, develop, and change. Organizational structures evolve over time, and the evolutionary process is as significant as the structure that results from it. In short, cross-sectional studies do not tell us where the structure came from and where it is heading.

Keeping the limitations of the cross-sectional studies in view, this paper tracks the course of evolution of the corporation environmental affairs function in four companies—Campbell Soup, FMC, Scott, and SmithKline-Beckman—and describes the roles currently played by the departments. In-depth interviews with the top environmental executives revealed that the corporate environmental affairs function typically evolves in five distinct and identifiable stages: birth of the function, establishment of the department, growth, maturity, and consolidation. While the actual and potential environmental pressures seem to have led to the birth of the function, business strategy plays a major role in shaping the pattern of its evolution. Ten different roles played by the environmental affairs department were identified. We have grouped them into three broad categories: technical, administrative and institutional. In all four corporations the departments were responsible for "enforcing" the corporate environmental policies; the other dominant roles played by the personnel were unique in each company suggesting that the departmental charter in each case was dictated by the internal context of the corporation.

A REVIEW OF THE RELEVANT LITERATURE

Chandler, in his much-cited research work on strategy and structure based on historical examination of 70 large corporations, has identified the process by which American enterprises grow and develop. His principal findings were that organizational structure follows strategy of the firm; corporate strategies and structures develop in stages; and organizations tend to move from one stage to the next in response to pressures such as higher costs and inefficiencies. Subsequent studies in Chandler's tradition by Scott, Salter, and Berg have refined and elaborated on the idea of "stages of development" which has now become entrenched in business policy literature and practice. The idea of the "stages" offers a framework for arraying the corporations along a continuum and predicting the characteristics of a corporation at each stage and the expected pattern of evolution.

In many organizations the evolution is smooth. Other organizations go through development steps rather abruptly and with considerable strain (Filley and Adage). Some theorists have argued that organizations develop through a series of evolutionary and crisis stages (Greiner). The smoothness with which the development occurs depends on the specific strategy followed and how well it is implemented in an organization. In a comprehensive review of literature on the development of organizations over time, Child and Keiser identified four broad strategies, referred to as developmental strategies, that lead to structural shifts in organizations. These strategies are adopted by the top executives to safeguard or enhance the position of the organization in its environment. They include strategies to reap benefits that come from growth, to enhance competitive power and public approval, to identify and occupy niches that are safe and appropriate for the firms, and to institutionalize certain management approaches to respond flexibly to external changes (Child and Keiser). Each of these developmental strategies calls for a different type of an organizational structure. For example, an organization which has grown through acquisitions may divisionalize its major operation units, institute a centralized planning group, and give considerable autonomy to its divisional heads. As the organization moves from one developmental stage to another, concomitant changes occur in its structure. The apparent relationship between the "stages of development" and "organizational structure" makes it imperative that we compare the structure of organizations that are at similar stages.

Evidence has been documented by McNulty and Franko to suggest that structure tends to lag strategy. In the context of the institutionalization of corporate responsiveness, Ackerman and Bauer observed that ". . .large corporations. . .unless provoked to do otherwise. . .approach today's problems with yesterday's solutions even though the context in which the new problems arise may be different" (p. 125). Allison's study of the Cuban missile crisis also lends support to the conclusion that some parts of large organizations lag or lead others during the evolution. Indeed, the corporate strategy and the associated structure may act as barriers to implementing corporate responsiveness (Ackerman, Ackerman and Bauer). In the same vein, some strategies and structures may facilitate the implementation by speeding up the responsiveness.

Major economic and social changes, such as those witnessed in the environmental area during the 1960s and 1970s provide another context for understanding the evolution of the "environmental affairs" function. Dierkes and Preston have made a distinction between "environmental" and "nonenvironmental" firms. In the former, physical environmental impacts are central, pervasive, and dominant features of the organizations and their economic activities. In the latter, such impacts are relatively insignificant. Accordingly the development and role of the environmental affairs function would be different in these two types of firms.

Moreover some economic and social changes may have a greater impact on some parts of the organization than others. For example, environmental pressures during the 1960s and 1970s have had the most impact on the technical systems of corporations as compliance with the newly imposed air pollution standards called for new equipment and new manufacturing procedures. A wide array of social changes and corporate responses have been described by Post. His studies suggest that institutional, administrative, and technical subsystems must learn to manage the changes, regardless of the subsystem most impacted by the changes. From the perspective of the management of change in organizations Tichy echoes a similar theme. He argues that three interrelated cycles—technical, political, and ideological—are in effect in all organizations at all times. The problems associated with the three cycles are *technical*, which pertain to the production of outputs; *political*, which are concerned with the specific uses that the organization is put to and who shall benefit from its outputs; and *ideological*, which deal with the task of building consensus on the characteristic values held by the various members of the organization. Changes—both external and internal—tend to accentuate the problems in one or more of these areas, setting off a problem-solving cycle. Organizations tend to spend varying amounts of their energies at different times in efforts to resolve the problems. Tichy, however, does not specify the steps involved in the problem-solving process nor does he present the concomitant structural changes in organizations.

Ackerman and Bauer, Ackerman, and Murray (1974), whose works focused on implementation of corporate social responsiveness, identified three distinct phases in resolving the managerial dilemmas posed by social issues. The three phases as they apply to the environmental affairs function are.

1. *The commitment to respond.* This is indicated by the interests and involvement of the chief executive officer (CEO) of the company in environmental affairs. His interests and involvement may be marked by several indicators such as the position he takes on the matter in public and in front of the stockholders, and the resources he makes available for the purpose. The CEO's role in that sense may set the scene for a formal policy on the matter and give it a direction. More recent writings that appeared in the corporation and society literature (e.g., Merenda, Taylor) confirm the significance of the conclusion.

2. *The acquisition of specialized skills and knowledge.* Going beyond the policy statements, corporations need the "know-how" and personnel that make things happen. Corporations need the "specialists" to deal with issues within the organization. In this phase, the organizations go through a technical learning process and the "environmental affairs" group emerges.

3. *The institutionalization of purpose.* In this phase, the basic purpose of the "environmental affairs" function is made an integral part of the corporation's objective set. The "standard operating procedures" are revised appropriately to make the purpose an integral part of jobs at all levels in the corporation. Reward systems are suitably changed so that the managers are motivated to achieve environmental and other business objectives.

The three phases together characterize the pattern of organizational response to the issues at hand. Following the lead provided by their work we will study the evolution of the corporate environmental affairs function.

Specifically, we will examine two aspects of the evolution.

- *Evolution of the function.* We will identify the distinct stages in which the function evolves. The stages enable us to array various corporations along a continuum and predict where the function might be heading next.
- *Types of roles the department plays.* A number of managerial roles have been identified in the literature (Mintzberg, Parsons). Murray (1982) identified a number of roles played by the corporate public affairs departments. Following Parson's framework, the roles may be categorized as technical,

administrative, or institutional. The set of roles played by the environmental affairs departments describes its task in the company.

DATA AND METHOD

Top environmental executives in four corporations—Campbell Soup, FMC, Scott, and SmithKline-Beckman—were interviewed in-depth. The discussions were taped and transcribed in their entirety. The interviews focused primarily on the way the organizational structure of the department had evolved within the last 20 years, the role played by the group in the organization, and other related issues.

In each case, the top environmental executives had been with the company since the inception of the function in the organization. This made the task of tracking the evolution of the function very easy. Also, published corporate records and reports were used to describe the pattern of development of the corporation. Based on this data, we profile the pattern of development of each company and its environmental affairs function.

PROFILES OF THE FOUR COMPANIES

Campbell Soup Company

Campbell Soup Company began in 1853 as a partnership. The company's history indicates that it has been able to grow in a mature industry (where "new product ideas are hard to come by") primarily by expanding its product line and through acquisitions of companies with established markets. In 1981 the company had 33 subsidiaries, compared to a mere 11 in 1975, and a total of 70 plants at different sites. The company responded to changing life styles of society by capitalizing on easily prepared foods and entering into the restaurant business.

As of March 1981, Campbell's global operations are divisionalized into two groups: foreign and domestic. The International Campbell Division is segmented geographically. The Campbell-U.S. Division is broken down into eight business units (soups, beverages, pet foods, frozen foods, fresh produce, main meals, groceries, and food service) as well as retaining Vlasic Food, Pepperidge Farm Inc., and restaurants as separate business entities.

The company is not only concerned with pollution as an environmental problem, but considers efficient discharge to be a particularly important function to be monitored along with other aspects of corporate citizenship, such as charitable donations, youth employment, and urban affairs projects. The stress on "efficient discharge" arises because the company is a heavy user of water, and about 35 percent of its plants are in small towns and rural areas where public water treatment facilities often are not equipped to handle large volumes of discharge.

Environmental Affairs Function. In Campbell the environmental affairs function started in the 1950s with the appointment of a sanitary engineer in the engineering department. His job centered around water pollution control. He was reporting to the Manager of Engineering who in turn was reporting to the Director of Engineering. Since its inception, the one-person environmental affairs unit evolved into a five-person team which is now part of a 200-person engineering department. The top environmental executive is the Director of Environmental Affairs who reports to the Vice-President of Capital Improvements who, in turn, reports to the president of the company.

The scope of the Environmental Affairs Department covers a broad spectrum of problems which include water pollution control, negotiating sewage rates with the municipalities, conducting feasibility and engineering studies to improve the existing effluent systems, ensuring compliance with governmental regulations, surveying the potential plant acquisitions to determine the costs involved in upgrading them to Campbell's standards. and training the plant personnel on environmental regulations.

The changes that have occurred over the years in the structure and scope of the department have been attributed to the growth in the size of the company and the increase in its diversity and complexity which necessiated direct evaluation of environmental affairs by the top management.

The creation of the environmental affairs function at Campbell predates the general rise in the regulatory pressures. The technical task of managing the large volumes of effluent was the major impetus for creating the Environmental Affairs Department in the company. The evolution of the department over time has been influenced largely by the organizational context, viz., size, diversity, complexity, and growth of the company through acquisitions, rather than by the regulatory pressures. The location of the department in the Capital Improvements Department indicates that its predominant role is designing technical systems.

FMC Corporation

FMC Corporation was formed in 1928 when a leading manufacturer of agricultural sprayers and a leading manufacturer of canning and dried fruit processing equipment merged to form a diversified company whose main line of business was manufacturing equipment for the food industry. Rapid acquisitions in the 1930s and 1940s steadily diversified the company's product-lines into agricultural and industrial chemicals. Growth and diversification through acquisitions continued in the 1960s when FMC acquired American Viscose in 1963 and the Link-Belt Company in 1967. The acquisitions significantly altered the company's mix of businesses. They increased the company's involvement in commodity-like products in which success was dependent on the company's ability to sell in large volumes and at very low prices. In the early 1970s, FMC went through an extensive restructuring of its operations, all aimed at improving profitability. Fourteen plants were built, 22 inefficient ones were closed, and more than 20 businesses and major product lines were sold or discontinued. The company was reorganized into nine operating groups and each group manager was given responsibility for planning and running his business. As of 1981, the company is involved in five major lines of businesses: specialized machinery, industrial chemicals, defense equipment and services, performance chemicals, and petroleum equipment and services.

Environmental Affairs Function. Until about 1970, each division in the company was managing its own environmental problems. In the beginning, the environmental pressures were mostly centered in the Chemicals Division. Though the fiber and film lines had also experienced environmental pressures, they were managing them on their own. This was also true with the Machinery Division.

With the company's reorganization in 1970, the environmental affairs function was centralized and placed in the Corporate Administrative Group based in Philadelphia. This is one of the nine divisions in the company. The top environmental executive is called the Director of Environmental Planning. He came from a line position in the Chemicals Division. Presently the department has 14 individuals and each one is responsible for 18-20 locations. Major specializations such as regulatory affairs, air pollution, operations, and toxic substance control, are the responsibility of the department.

The department views the line departments as its "customers." According to the top executive of the department, ". . .we serve the line department's needs. . . .They are to be kept satisfied. At the same time we are to keep them out of jail. They don't like trouble, fines, consent orders, and trouble with the regulations." The Environmental Planning Department establishes environmental standards for the company as a whole. According to the executive, it is "one of the few staff departments (in the company) that has a major role and we decide what is going to be the standard (on environmental matters)." In 1981 the department formalized its charter as part of the company-wide strategic planning process. The director periodically appears before the board's Public Affairs Committee to discuss his department's activities. In addition, the "user" departments rate the Environmental Planning Deparmtent's performance from time to time.

In sum, till 1970, the environmental affairs function was carried out in each division separately in a highly decentralized fashion. With the reorganization of the company in 1970, the Environmental Planning Department was created at the corporate level to serve all business divisions in the company. It now plays a major role in the corporate strategic planning process and sets environmental performance standards for the company as a whole and its various divisions.

Scott

Scott Paper was formed in 1879 in Philadelphia by two brothers. The company grew very rapidly during the forties and fifties by acquiring mills throughout the country. In 1965 Scott acquired the Plastic Coating Corporation, the Technifax Corporation, and related companies engaged in a wide range of products for the collection, storage, reproduction and dissemination of information. This acquisition gave Scott entry into the vast market created by the "knowledge explosion" that occurs every 15 to 20 years. In 1967, Scott merged with S. D. Warren, a company in the printing, publishing, and converting paper business. This merger alone added nearly 20 percent to Scott's volume. In 1969, through a new subsidiary, the Brown Jordan Company, Scott moved into the leisure furniture business. At the same time a Land Utilization Division was created to profitably utilize and develop the company's three million-plus acres of timberland for recreational purposes. This marked the diversification into yet another line of business, viz., leisure. Between the years 1972 and 1976 the company committed large amount of capital to upgrade its old plants and to build new ones. These capital expenditures became necessary partly due to the pressures from the Environmental Protection Agency. 1976 was the peak year for capital expenditures in the company.

As of 1981, Scott is organized along divisional lines, the principal divisions being packaged products; printing, publishing, and converting paper; international operations; leisure furniture; and foam products. The packaged products division is the largest of all the divisions.

Environmental Affairs Function. The first formal identification of a corporate environmental affairs function goes back to 1963, when one person was appointed to do the job. He was assigned to the satff of the Vice-President of Operations. That was when Scott was essentially a one-division company. The individual had experience with a paper industry research association and with a waste treatment equipment manufacturer.

The position of the environmental specialist has evolved from that of a staff group in the manufacturing division to that of a department reporting to a corporate vice-president whose job includes environmental resources, among his other responsibilities. In 1977, a position called the Staff Vice-President for Environmental Resources was created. He was reporting to the Senior Corporate Vice-President for Finance whose work also involved planning. In the latter part of 1982, the Environmental Affairs Department was taken out of the Planning and Finance Group. Now, it is back where it started. The Staff Vice-President of Environmental Affairs now reports to the Vice-President of Operations in the Packaged Products Division which is the largest operating division.

The Environmental Affairs Department has the responsibility for assisting and guiding the plants to achieve and maintain an environmental plan. It means working with the plants to secure required permits, working with the plants and the engineering group to design and select appropriate technology, and working with the plants and the Operating Division to ensure that the company is in compliance with the law. Auxiliary functions performed by the department include working with the corporate public affairs department in lobbying, with corporate staff attorneys in litigating environmental charges, and with research and development in designing appropriate technical systems.

A variety of reasons have been offered by the executives for the way the function has evolved in the company. The creation of the department was thought of as a means of achieving uniformity in the management of environmental affairs throughout the company. The objective was to bring a higher level of technical competence in this area into the corporation and ensure that the company did not get any surprises.

During the years when the company was incurring huge capital expenditures on new plant construction, the Environmental Affairs Department was reporting to the Vice-President of Finance and Planning in recognition of the importance of the department in selecting new plant sites and assessing related environmental impacts. More recently, in response to a general need to reduce corporate overheads and because of the learning that has already occurred in the company on the environmental matters, the department has been transferred back to the largest operating division, from which it currently services the whole company.

Recognizing the ''overlap'' between environmental affairs and the Occupational Health and Safety Department, the company is considering the possibilities for clustering them under one umbrella. That may very well occur in the next phase of the evolution.

In sum, the corporate identification of the Environmental Affairs Department in the 1960s responded to anticipated environmental regulations. The later development of the department, however, was shaped by the business strategy and the organizational context of the company.

SmithKline-Beckman

During 1980 SmithKline-Beckman celebrated its 150th anniversary. From a small apothecary shop in Philadelphia, it has grown into a very large health care company. Till 1960 the company had grown primarily through new product research and development.

The year 1960 marks the beginning of SmithKline-Beckman's diversification into different product lines and geographical areas. In the mid 1960s the company aggressively committed its resources to nonpharmaceutical business. The trend has continued into the 1970s with the acquisition of companies in consumer products such as cosmetics, medical diagnostic products and services, and ultrasonic products and services. The company name changed in 1973 from SmithKline-French to SmithKline, and in 1982 to SmithKline-Beckman to reflect the strategic changes that have been occurring in the company during the period. To maximize the growth and profitability of the diversified company, the corporate organizational structure was realigned toward a worldwide product-line organization. Responsibility for human pharmaceutical research was centralized, and corporate business development activities were broadened. In the last few years the company has sold some of its cosmetic product lines in an effort to rationalize its consumer products division.

Environmental Affairs Function. The environmental affairs function started in the 1970s as a one-man department with the appointment of an engineer as the Manager of Corporate Environmental Services. He was reporting to the Director of Corporate Engineering, who in turn reported to the Vice-President, Corporate Technical Services. This was in response to the considerable uncertainties created by the environmental movement of the 1970s. As time progressed, the company recognized the wide-ranging impacts of the environmental regulations and expanded the size of the department to three persons. In 1978 the position of the Director of Corporate Engineering Services was created. He now reports to the Vice-President of Corporate Technical Services. At the same time, the size and competence of environmental personnel at each plant were strengthened to make the plants more responsible for environmental matters.

In the early stages of the evolution of the function, environmental affairs was viewed predominantly as an engineering function because, according to the top environmental executive, "it was seen as having to bring ourselves up to speed as far as our systems were concerned." Later, management recognized that it was a function that was more important from the standpoint of regulatory "interface" rather than the mechanics of meeting regulatory specifications. Says the executive, "... while I was in the Engineering Department they would present me the environmental problem and I would solve it. But as we saw this necessity for getting involved at the actual regulation level, by interfacing with the various governmental agencies, we felt it necessary to expand the department." Consistent with this characterization of the department's role, public affairs and environmental affairs collaborate frequently on environment-related matters that potentially impact the company. The department plays a major role in "shaping" new legislation and not merely in "responding" to existing regulations.

The company has facilities in more than 40 states, and the diversity that exists in the state and local environmental regulations enhanced the need for giving greater autonomy and responsibility to each plant in managing its own environmental problems.

Looking at the next stage in this evolution the executive commented, "Certainly there is an overlap between environmental affairs and public affairs. There should be some interface there. Certainly the overlap between my function and the occupational health and safety function and likewise between my function and what R and D is doing in developing new systems and procedures. What I would like to see is the bringing together of these various functions, possibly under one head.''

In sum, the environmental affairs function came into being in response to the environmental regulations of the 1970s. During the early 1970s, when the company was "running" to catch-up with the laws and designing the systems to bring itself in line with the regulations, the role of the department was largely a technical one. In the later years, the task of the department was redefined to give it a prominent role in "defining the problem" and proactively shaping the regulations. Plant level personnel were trained to take on greater responsibilities in managing environmental affairs at the plant level.

Table 1 summarizes the profiles of the four companies.

STAGES IN THE EVOLUTION

Based upon the four case histories presented above and discussions with executives in the companies, we have identified the following five typical stages to describe the evolution of the environmental affairs function. The stages are sequential in nature; however, in our judgement not all companies may pass through all the stages. In fact, depending upon the context in which the corporations choose to institute the function, they may skip one or more of the stages. The movement of the environmental affairs function (EAF) from one evolutionary stage to the next is affected by changes occuring in the stages of the issue cycle and the stages of corporate development. Keeping these influences in view, we shall now describe the five evolutionary stages.

Stage I: Birth of the Function

The evolutionary development of the EAF begins when company management sees the need to respond affirmatively to the perceived on-coming pressures in the environmental area (air, water, noise, pollution) from interested pressure groups such as the Audobon Society, the Sierra Club, the Friends of the Earth Society, and local communities. The motivation is for the company to keep these groups at bay and do what must be done by the company, in terms of systems improvements, to keep the company in harmony with the pressure groups. Company management acts by appointing one person at the operating or corporate level to manage the EAF within the company. Thus the EAF as a separate function, distinct from all other functions, is created by a top management policy decision to adapt to a new set of factors in its external environment.

The person in charge of the EAF generally reports to the head of the largest operating unit or a corporate staff group depending upon the types of problems that he is expected to resolve and the prevailing organizational structure. He is

Table 1. The Profiles of the Four Companies

	Campbell	FMC	Scott	SmithKline-Beckman
Business strategy	Related-business	Unrelated-business	Dominant-business	Dominant-business
Relative impact of environmental affairs on company	Low	High	Medium	Medium
Division in which environmental affairs is located	Capital Improvements	Administration	Largest Operating Division	Corporate Technical Services
Background of chief environmental affairs executive	Specialist in an environment-related field	Executive with a long line experience in the company	Specialist in an environment-related field	Specialist in an environment-related field
Size of department (number of persons)	5	14	4	3

technically trained to initiate, develop, implement, and control improvements in plant operations to manage potential environmental problems. Thus his role is primarily to keep the firm's operations ''clean'' with respect to the external physical environment. The person in charge of this function is given a title commensurate with his duties, e.g. environmental engineer, environmental service officer.

Stage II: Establishment of the Department

As the environmental pressures mount or as the environmental legislation goes into effect, the one-man EAF expands and becomes a full-fledged environmental affairs department (EAD) as more people are added to handle the increased workload. The head of the EAD is given a new title such as director or staff vice-president. The principal responsibility of the EAD at this stage is to influence the pending environmental legislation and eventually to ensure that the operating divisions are in compliance with legislation. To that end, once the legislation is on the books, the EAD moves to develop and disseminate policies and procedures that must be followed through the company.

Stage III: Growth

Growth of the company and a simultaneous increase in the diversification of its business portfolio places new demands upon the services provided by the EAD. Top management expects the department to bring any newly acquired businesses up to the ''environmental'' standards of the company. The expertise of the department is also used to conduct environmental surveys of potential acquisitions which are then reviewed by top management as one of the critical inputs in deciding whether the company should enter a particular business. The department may be given the authority to review and to sign off capital expenditure projects to assure that adequate resources are made available for environmental legislative compliance. During the period that the company is in an expansionary mode and allocating large amounts of resources for new acquisitions or diversifications, the EAD may be transferred to the corporate level (if it is not already there) so that it may serve the corporation as a whole.

With many business divisions under the corporate umbrella, the EAD develops corporate environmental policies and procedures for the divisions to follow. The EAD coordinates and controls divisional environmental programs and ensures that the divisions are in compliance with existing environmental legislation. Some large multi-plant divisions may have their own environmental coordinators in which case the corporate EAD works in conjunction with the coordinators in training the plant environmental personnel on maintaining and operating the environmental systems at the plant level.

Companies that do not experience the problems associated with growth in size or business diversity may skip this stage and evolve directly from Stage II to Stage IV.

Stage IV: Maturity

Now the legislative actions and changes in the environmental arena have been all but completed and there is a fair amount of certainty and stability in this domain of the company's total environment. Also, internally, the company has matured both at the plant and corporate levels withh respect to learning how to adapt effectively to the legislative and pressure group demands and has already translated the learning into effective action programs, procedures, and systems. The company may have reached internal stability as management has turned its attention away from new business development or acquisition.

When the above conditions arise in a company, the EAD may lose some of its significance as a corporate function. Internal contingencies and context may dominate the top management's thinking. In order to reduce corporate overheads or for reasons of "administrative convenience," the EAD may once again be moved back to an operating division. In spite of its new status in the organization, EAD continues to play a key role in the company's environmental affairs.

Stage V: Consolidation

The next stage in the evolution of the EAF may be the consolidation of several staff groups into one department by the formation of an "umbrella group" comprising functions such as environmental affairs, occupational health and safety, and public affairs. A reason for bringing these functions together is the synergy that may accrue from the fact that the three departments are heavily involved with legislative compliance and have skills for lobbying and interacting with public agencies. Administrative costs and duplication of effort might be eliminated through each consolidation. Size of the company may determine the real benefits that will accrue from such reorganization.

Table 2 summarizes the evolutionary paths followed by the four companies in our study.

TYPES OF ROLES PLAYED
BY THE ENVIRONMENTAL AFFAIRS GROUP

The personnel in the EAF play a variety of roles. The specific set of roles played by EAF personnel at a certain time are largely determined by the way the function is organized in the company and by the nature of the services demanded of the department. Following Parson's framework we have classified the roles into three categories: (1) Technical, (2) Administrative, and (3) Institutional.

Table 2. Evolutionary Paths of the Environmental Affairs Function in the
Four Companies

Evolutionary Stage:	Time Frame 1950s	1960s	1970s	Early 1980s	Late 1980s
Ia Birth of the function at an operating level		FMC Scott			
Ib Birth of the function at a corporate level	Campbell		SmithKline-Beckman		
IIa Establishment of the department at the operating level		FMC	Scott		
IIb Establishment of the department at the corporate level		Campbell		SmithKline-Beckman	
III Growth			FMC Scott		
IV Maturity		Campbell	FMC	SmithKline-Beckman Scott	
V Consolidation					Scott SmithKline-Beckman

Technical

A technical subsystem is "...the core of what the entity does and which ususally accounts for its distinctive character" (Post, p. 8). For example, the core activity of a paper manufacturer is the capacity to convert wood pulp into paper.

The EAD helps the plants in selecting and designing systems and technology in conjunction with appropriate line and staff groups in the company, such as managers, engineers, and technical personnel at operating and plant levels, and with corporate technical and engineering groups. The purpose of this activity is to offer *consulting* services in designing systems that meet legislative requirements.

Administrative

"An administrative subsystem coordinates the technical activities, and provides support services to the technical subsystems of an organization" (Post, p. 8). The roles played by the subsystem include:

Enforcing. It is the responsibility of the EAD to assure that the company is always in compliance with local, state, and federal legislative and regulatory requirements. To fulfill this major responsibility, the EAD establishes corporate environmental standards for the various operating units in the company. When new acquisitions are made by the company, the EAD helps the newly purchased business units to come up to the company's environmental standards. The EAD develops and puts in place administrative procedures that serve as guides for operating units and which helps to minimize the chances of violations of the law.

Auditing. Closely related to the above is the auditing role of the department. The EAD monitors whether the operating units are meeting and following the company's environmental standards, policies and procedures, and takes the necessary corrective actions. The EAD also makes certain that company units actually spend monies that are budgeted for setting up environmental systems that meet the company's environmental standards.

Interpreting. Among the duties of the department is the task of helping the operating units to define the environmental problem that would be presented by legislative and regulatory requirements that have been either newly enacted or modified. This process involves interpreting new legal requirements and developments and assisting operating units in forecasting and assessing the impact of the regulatory changes on their respective operations.

Coordinating. The EAD coordinates activities at the plant level that are related or stem from the need to keep plants in compliance with legal environmental requirements. This involves promoting the expertise and services of the department to induce the plant level managers to come to the department for assistance in this area. Also included is the task of interacting and sharing relevant information with other staff units in the organization whose functions are interdependent and/or overlapping with those of the EAD, such as occupational health and safety, public affairs, industrial relations, and research and development.

Disseminating.   The EAD distributes information throughout the company of new developments in the environmental area, and of the corporate response, if any, to such developments.

Training.   This role involves developing and implementing programs designed to improve the knowledge and skills of operating personnel in maintaining and operating environmental systems within each plant.

Institutional

An institutional subsystem ". . .is concerned with maintaining legitimacy and managing the organizations relations with the environment" (Post, p. 8). Roles played by institutional systems have strategic impacts on the total organization. Information generated by the EAD in playing institutional roles can result in significant changes in these external environmental trends, events, and forces which, if left unchallenged, could have long-range consequences for the firm as a whole. The following institutional roles may also influence the fundamental direction that the company follows in the future.

Scanning.   The scanning role involves the monitoring of the external environment for the purpose of detecting and interpreting trends and events that may have strategic positive or negative impacts on the company's operations. In playing this role, the EAD stays on top of social and economic trends that may influence future environmental legislation, forecasts future legislative trends, and monitors the public, legislative, and regulatory environmental priorities and proposals. The department analyzes the proposed legislation and regulations and provides management with data which can be used to develop alternative response strategies.

Allocating.   In this role the EAD is in a position to influence how and where the organization's resources are allocated. The department has an impact in decisions concerning plant expansion and location, capital improvement projects, and site selection. It analyzes the actual and potential environmental costs and liabilities of business expansions and divestitures; conducts environmental surveys of potential acquistions as an input to a corporate acquisition decision; and reviews, approves, and signs off proposed capital expenditure projects, when there is an environmental impact, to assure that adequate funds are made available for compliance with environmental standards and adequacy of engineering solutions.

Representing.   The EAD serves as the company's representative in city and regional environmental councils and industry associations. It keeps in close

Table 3. Dominant Roles Played by The
Environmental Affairs Function in the Four Companies

	Role		
	Technical	Administrative	Institutional
Company			
Campbell	Consulting	Enforcing	Allocating
FMC		Enforcing	Scanning Allocating
Scott	Consulting	Enforcing	Allocating
SmithKline-Beckman	Consulting	Auditing	Scanning Representing

contact with various relevant governmental agencies. An important activity of the EAD is influencing the content of the proposed environmental legislation and regulations by the U.S. Congress. To this end it works with corporate groups, e.g. public affairs, and with industry associations. The department provides these groups with assistance in the development and support of programs to modify proposed environmental legislation. They may also do some public relations work on behalf of the company by publicizing the company's environmental management programs before appropriate constituencies.

Dominant roles played by the EAF in the four companys studied are shown in Table 3.

CONCLUDING REMARKS

In this paper we tracked the course of the evolution of the environmental affairs function in four companies—Campbell, FMC, Scott, and SmithKline-Beckman—and identified the roles played by the departments. In-depth interviews with the top environmental executives revealed that the corporate affairs function evolved in five distinct and identifiable stages: birth of the function, establishment of the department, growth, maturity, and consolidation. While the nature of the environmental pressures brought upon the organization by forces outside it led to the creation of the function, the strategy and structure of the corporation shaped the subsequent evolutionary course of the function. In all four corporations, the departments were responsible for "enforcing" the environmental policy. The other dominant roles played by the departments in each company were unique, suggesting that the departmental charter of each firm was dictated by its internal context.

We also sensed a trend toward combining the occupational health and safety function which deals with the "micro" environmental concerns, the environmental affairs function which deal with the "macro" physical environmental issues, and possibly the public affairs function which deals with the institutional aspects of the broad external environment. The degree of overlap among the functions in terms of their public policy orientation and the need to reduce the corporate overheads may be moving some companies in the direction of consolidating these activities.

Finally, in none of the companies was the environmental affairs function an integral part of the corporate planning department. The only notable exception was Scott, in which the environmental affairs department was a part of the corporate finance and planning group during the period when the company was committing large capital expenditures.

ACKNOWLEDGMENTS

The authors wish to thank Mr. Lou Gilde, Campbell Soup; Mr. Neil Elphick, FMC Corporation; Dr. Nicholas Lardieri, Scott; and Mr. Peter Quinn and Mr. John Watson, SmithKline-Beckman. This study was made possible by a research grant from Temple University to Dr. Phatak.

REFERENCES

Ackerman, Robert W., *The Social Challenge to Business*. Cambridge, MA: Harvard University Press, 1975.

Ackerman, Robert W., and Raymond Bauer. *Corporate Social Responsiveness: The Modern Dilemma*. Reston, VA: Reston Publicshing Company, Inc., 1976.

Allison, Graham. *The Essence of Decision: Explaining the Cuban Missile Crisis*. Boston: Little Brown and Company, 1971.

Berg, Norman. "Strategic Planning in Conglomerate Companies." *Harvard Business Review* 43 (1965):79-92.

Chandler, Alfred D. *Strategy and Structure*. Cambridge, MA: M.I.T. Press, 1962.

Child, John, and Alfred Keiser. "The Development of Organizations Over Time," in P. Nystrom and W. Starbuck, *The Handbook of Organization Design*, Volume I. New York: Oxford University Press, 1981.

Dierkes, Meinoff, and Lee E. Preston. *Accounting, Organizations and Society* 2, No. 1 (1977) 3-22.

Franko, Lawrence G. "The Move Toward Multidivisional Structure in European Organizations." *Administrative Science Quarterly* 19 (1974): 493-506.

Filley, A. C., and R. J. Adage. "Organizational Growth and Types: Lessons from Small Institutions," in L. L. Cummings (ed.), *Research in Organizational Behavior*, Volume 2. Greenwich, CT: Jai Press, 1980.

Greiner, Larry. "Patterns of Organizational Change." *Harvard Business Review* (May-June 1967):121-138.

Kimberly, John R., and Robert H. Miles (eds.). *The Organizational Life Cycle: Issues in the Creation, Transformation, and Decline of Organizations*. San Francisco: Jossey-Bass Publishers, 1980.

Lund, Leonard. *Corporate Organization for Environmental Policy Making*. New York: Conference Board, Inc., 1974.

McNulty, James E. "Organizational Change in Growing Enterprises." *Administrative Science Quarterly* 7 (1962):1-21.

Merenda, Michael J. "The Process of Corporate Social Involvement: Five Case Studies," in Lee Preston (ed.), *Research in Corporate Social Performance and Policy*, Volume 3. Greenwich, CT: Jai Press, Inc., 1981.

Miller, Danny, and Peter H. Friesen. "The Longitudinal Analysis of Organizations." *Management Science* 28 (September 1982):1013-1034.

Mintzberg, Henry. *The Nature of Managerial Work*. Englewood-Cliffs: Prentice-Hall, 1973.

Murray, Edwin. "The Public Affairs Function: Report on a Large Scale Research Project," in Lee Preston (ed.), *Research in Corporate Social Performance and Policy*, Volume 4. Greenwich, CT: Jai Press, Inc., 1982.

———."Implementation of Social Policies in Commercial Banks." Dissertation, Harvard Business School, Boston, 1974.

Parsons, Talcott. *Structure and Process in Modern Societies*. New York: Free Press, 1960.

Post, James E. *Corporate Behavior and Social Change*. Reston, VA: Reston Publishing Company, 1978.

Salter, Malcolm. "Stages of Corporate Development." *Journal of Business Policy* 1 (1970):40-57.

Scott, Bruce R. "Stages of Corporate Development," 9-371-294, BP 998. Intercollegiate Clearing House, Harvard Business School, Boston, 1971.

Taylor, Marilyn L. "Implementing Affirmative Action: Impetus and Enabling Factors in Five Organizations," in Lee Preston (ed.), *Research in Corporate Social Performance and Policy*, Volume 3. Greenwich, CT: Jai Press, Inc., 1981.

Tichy, Noel M. "Problem Cycles in Organizations and the Management of Change," in John R. Kimberly and Robert H. Miles (eds.), *The Organizational Life Cycle: Issues in the Creation, Transformation and Decline of Organizations*. San Francisco: Jossey-Bass Publishers, 1980.

Weidenbaum, Murray L. *The Future of Business Regulation: Private Action and Public Demand*. New York: AMACOM, 1979.

OWNERSHIP, CONTROL, AND SOCIAL POLICY

Neil Mitchell

The question this paper addresses is whether the theory of "managerialism" offers an explanation of corporate social policy. The theory of managerialism refers to the observation that ownership has become separated from control in the business corporation and the behavioral implications derived from this institutional change. With managers rather than owners in control, it is theorized that profit now competes with other motives, one of which may be social responsibility. The growth of corporate social policy may thus be a result of the rise of the modern corporation under managerial control.

The strategy pursued in addressing this question falls into three parts. The first part examines the factual basis for accepting the separation of ownership from control; that is, the foundation of managerialist theory. This paper shows, through a survey of empirical studies of the issue, that the fact of this institutional change is not established but controversial. Moreover, even if the separation of ownership and control is accepted, the evidence that control type has the behavioral implications attributed to it is at least ambiguous. The second part

Research in Corporate Social Performance and Policy, volume 5, pages 205-230
Copyright © 1983 by JAI Press Inc.
All rights of reproduction in any form reserved.
ISBN: 0-89232-412-0

discusses the theoretical and factual basis of these implications. The last part, using data from the 1920s, tests the hypothesis of a relationship between control type and the existence of corporate social policy. As far as the author is aware, 1920s data has not been used before to test managerialist expectations, and the extent of corporate social policy at this time may be quite a surprise in itself.

THE SEPARATION OF
OWNERSHIP FROM CONTROL

In Volume 3 of *Capital* Marx briefly discusses the separation of ownership from control. Some (Dahrendorf) claim this discussion as support for the doctrine of managerialism. Others (Zeitlin) maintain that Marx's point is to note an institutional change that is a development, not a transformation, of capitalist economic and social relations. Veblen recognized a division of interest between the owners of business enterprises and the industrial experts who ran them. But absentee owners "continue to control the industrial experts and limit their discretion, arbitrarily for their own commercial gain regardless of the needs of the community," according to Veblen (p. 100). Some eminent contemporaries of Veblen had remarked on the separation of ownership and control. While Keynes was noting "the tendency of big enterprise to socialize itself," Walter Rathenau observed,

> The de-individualization of ownership simultaneously implies the objectification of the thing owned. The claims to ownership are subdivided in such a fashion, and are so mobile, that the enterprise assumes an independent life, as if it belonged to no one. . .The executive instruments of the new hierarchy become the new center (p. 121)

Anticipating Adolf Berle and Gardiner Means, he argued that among "the chiefs of the great corporate undertakings. . .we already encounter an official idealism identical with that which prevails in the state service. . . .Covetousness as the motive force, has been completely superseded by the sense of responsibility" (pp. 122-23). But *The Modern Corporation and Private Property* was the first full-length attempt to study the issue systematically. This work is of particular interest, for it was done within the corporate context of the 1920s and the methods, findings, and hypotheses remain influential.

Berle and Means observed that the ability to exploit the capital resources of the public through selling shares in a public market distributes a single corporation's shares among large numbers of investors. In aggregating their wealth with numerous others, shareholders lose their power to control the use of their wealth within the firm, that is, control over the firm's physical assets and become to that extent "merely recipients of the wages of capital." With this development the old concept of property in which the proceeds of wealth and control over its use were combined is broken into its parts. "There has resulted the dissolution of the old atom of ownership into its component parts, control and beneficial ownership'' (p. 8). On the expansion and dispersal of stock ownership—the number of stockholders doubled between 1918 and 1925—the notion of the separation of ownership and control rests, and the edifice of managerialism is constructed.

The locus of control within a corporation for Berle and Means lies, in most cases, with those who have the power to select the board of directors. Formally this power is exercised by stockholders who elect the directors annually. But with an increasing number of stockholders and a diminishing size of individual holdings, stockholders become progressively weaker. As Berle described it in *Economic Power and the Free Society,*

> We go through the ancient forms and it is good that we do so but everyone knows that a stockholder's meeting is a kind of ancient, meaningless ritual like some of the ceremonies that go on with the mace in the House of Lords (1957, p.8).

At the annual meeting the stockholder can attend and vote, not attend and not vote, or vote by proxy. Unless the stockholder owns a lot of stock, his or her vote will not mean much, which leaves the options of not voting or surrendering his or her vote to the proxy committee selected by the existing management. Where stock is widely dispersed, ownership of a small percentage (nowadays put as low as 5 percent or 10 percent though Berle and Means had it at 20 percent) can provide working control of a corporation. In this case the majority of stockholders have been separated from control over the corporation. The process of separation is complete when even such minority holdings disappear and management, through its power over the proxy machinery, becomes a "self-perpetuating body" (Berle and Means, p. 87).

Berle and Means were convinced that this institutional change was of great significance. Institutions, changing themselves, have changed capitalism. "The dissolution of the atom of property destroys the very foundations on which the economic order of the past three centuries have rested" (p. 8). And this cooperative atom is splitting itself.

There are some difficulties with Berle and Means' argument. Empirically it is based on an analysis of the largest (according to assets) 200 American non-financial corporations. They categorized 44 percent of these corporations as under management control at the beginning of 1930. But as critics have pointed out, the study was carried out at a time when sources of information were more limited (Chevalier). Berle and Means claim "reasonably definite and reliable information" on about two thirds of the companies; for the rest they relied on newspaper reports or "street knowledge" (pp. 91-93). Maurice Zeitlin says that they "had information which permitted them to classify as definitely under management control only 22 percent of the 200 largest corporations. . ."(p. 1081-82). A conservative estimate of the percentage of stock ownership necessary for minority control, 20 percent, and unreliable information may have resulted in an overestimation of the extent of management control.

In the 1960s Robert Larner attempted to repeat Berle and Means' study. His definition of control, the power to select the board of directors, was the same as theirs, and he generally adopted their procedures and classifications. The Berle and Means study set minority control between 20 and 50 percent of stock ownership, but because of the increase in size of corporations and the wider dispersion of stock, Larner reduced the lower limit to 10 percent (p. 11). According to Larner, 84 percent of the 200 largest nonfinancial corporations were management-controlled by 1963. In summary, says Larner, "it would appear that Berle and Means in 1929 were observing the so-called "managerial revolution" in process. Thirty-four years later that revolution seems close to complete. . ." (p. 22).

Coexistent with work like Larner's, there has also been research that has questioned the extent of the separation of ownership and control. A Securities and Exchange Commission study, done for the Temporary National Economic Committee (TNEC) in the late 1930s, concluded that "ownership of voting stock remains the basic, the stablest, and the most secure vehicle of control" (p. 7). Defining control as "the power of determining the broad policies guiding a corporation," the study classified the 200 largest corporations according to control type existing in the period 1937-1939. About 60 corporations were found to be without a "visible center of ownership control," and thus were presumed to be management controlled.

> In about 140 of the 200 corporations the blocks in the hands of one interest group were large enough to justify, together with other indications such as representation in the management, the classification of these companies as more or less definitely under ownership control (p. 104).

According to the TNEC study, there were three kinds of ownership. About 40 companies were controlled by single families. Three single families, the du Ponts, the Mellons, and the Rockefellers, controlled over 15 of the largest 200 corporations. Some 35 corporations were identified as controlled by an interest group which consisted of several families, though critics have claimed that the TNEC study did not demonstrate the cohesion of this sort of interest group (Gordon, p. 43). Finally 60 firms were controlled by other corporations holding their stock. Larner, following Berle and Means, suggests that if the controlling corporation were management-controlled, then the corporation in which they held a large share of stock should also be classified as management-controlled (p. 6). However, ownership in this case still is the basis of control, and there is no good reason to suppose that managers as owners would act differently than individuals or families as owners. It is conceivable that these managers may act within the corporations they manage in the manner predicted by managerialist theory, whereas with regard to the firms in which their corporations own stock, they may well act as it is assumed other owners act.

Another significant finding of the TNEC study was that officers and directors held 6 percent of the common stock and about 2 percent of the preferred stock of the 200 corporations. While relatively small, the size in absolute terms of this stockholding may be sufficient to tie managerial interest to ownership interests, depending on what stock ownership represents in relation to other forms of managerial compensation.

In the early 1960s Don Villarejo looked at the 250 largest industrial corporations and concluded that from 54 percent to 61 percent were owner-controlled. Larner questioned these findings on the grounds that Villarejo "aggregated the stockholdings of directors, investment companies and insurance companies in each corporation without providing specific evidence, such as family or business relationships, to suggest a community of interests or to indicate the likelihood of either intragroup or intergroup cooperation" (p. 22). Maurice Zeitlin finds this criticism remarkable, suggesting that it is a criticism also applicable to Larner's own work. "Larner certainly does not present systematic evidence of the kind he requires of Villarejo. . ." (p. 1084).

In *Fortune* Robert Sheehan, using what he described as a conservative definition of control (putting the lower limit of minority ownership at 10 percent), wrote that in approximately 150 companies of the "Fortune 500" controlling ownership is in the hands of an individual or of a single family. It should be mentioned that Sheehan did not "include in the group any of the various coalitions that may indeed assure working control for small groups of associates in many companies; nor does the figure include some businessmen known to wield great influence with holdings of less than 10 percent" (p. 180).

Jean-Marie Chevalier in his study of control type in the 200 largest nonfinancial corporations for 1965-66 found only 80 to be management-controlled (p. 186). His definition of minority ownership was "liberal" in that he fixed the lower limit at 5 percent. The Patman Committee on Banking and Currency of the House of Representatives also used a 5 percent definition of minority control in its 1968 investigation of financial power in the American economy. Interestingly this report found that "the major banking institutions of this country are emerging as the single most important force in the economy" (p. 5). This finding contradicts Galbraith and others who have claimed fading financial power. Usually the attachment of a low percentage to minority control is justified by the example of the Watson family at IBM, who own approximately 3 percent of the stock but have a controlling position. Others suggest that the Watson family's control of IBM depends on their "strategic position," not their stock ownership. As John M. Blair says "Whether under today's conditions the proper control threshold is 10 percent, 5 percent, or any other figure will remain a matter of dispute" (p. 80).

Critical of studies like Larner's that rely heavily on corporate reports to the

Securities and Exchange Commission, which for a variety of reasons understate the concentration of stock ownership, Philip Burch searched the business press (*Fortune, Business Week, Forbes, The New York Times, Time*), Standard and Poor's *Corporation Records*, Moody's manuals, as well as SEC reports, over the period 1950-1971 in his study of the separation of ownership and control. He classified corporations on *Fortune's* 1965 list as either management-controlled or family-controlled. His criteria for family control were that 4 percent to 5 percent or more of the stock was held by a family, group of families, or affluent individuals, and that there was inside or outside representation for the stock-holding group on the board of directors usually over an extended period of time (p. 30). Burch found 58 percent of the 50 biggest industrial concerns to be management-controlled, while only 43 percent of the top 200 and 41 percent of the top 300 industrial concerns were in this category (p. 68). Aware of the disparities between his study and the projections of Berle and Means and the findings of Larner, Burch devoted his appendices to a reassessment of these studies and a critical discussion of their methods.

In 1974 Maurice Zeitlin made a strong case against acceptance of the separation of ownership and control as characteristic of corporations. Managerialists, according to Zeitlin, have underestimated the continuing importance of ownership in relation to control of the large corporation as a result of deficiencies in method and in data collection. He suggested a case-by-case analysis sensitive to the interrelatedness of corporations and focusing on kinship patterns between top officers, directors, and the principal shareholders (p. 1099). He noted the understandable secrecy of large share-owners and their use of voting trusts, foundations, and holding companies as devices for holding stock. Through these and other devices the "presence of principal proprietary families may be hidden or rendered scarcely noticeable among the reports of stock ownership filed with the Securities and Exchange Commission. . ." (p. 1086). He also pointed out that the customary use of the *Fortune* list in order to find the largest corporations, there being no official list, means that privately owned companies that do not publish certified financial statements are left out. There were approximately 17 of these that could have made the *Fortune* list in 1965, and therefore should have appeared in Larner's study, for example, but did not (p. 1085).

By the late 1970s the Patman Committee findings had rekindled interest in financial control in the economy. David Kotz claimed that about 35 percent of the 200 largest nonfinancial corporations were under financial control (p. 411). According to Kotz, what bank spokespersons say about their lack of influence over corporations whose stock they hold in trust, merely selling it if they disapprove of management, is widely accepted, but there are reasons for doubting it. If a bank holds 5 percent or more of a corporation's stock, selling rapidly could depress the stock price, causing a capital loss for the trust accout. Kotz argued that exerting influence over management may be more efficient. Few small groups, Kotz maintained, "possessing a great and growing power whose exercise could bring substantial gain to the possessor, allow that power to remain unexercised for long'' (pp. 412-413).

Corroboration for the view that the degree of separation of ownership and control has been overstated has come from a recent British industry "which shows that the extent of managerial control is more limited than has been thought and may not have an inexorable tendency to increase" (Nyman and Silberston, p. 74). Using a minority control threshold of 5 percent, Nyman and Silbertson calculated that 56.25 percent of the top 250 British firms can be classified as owner-controlled (p. 74).

Most recently the issue has been raised in Edward S. Herman's book *Corporate Control, Corporate Power*, perhaps the single best treatment of the subject since Berle and Means' analysis. Examining control type in the 200 largest nonfinancial corporations in 1975, he classified 82.5 percent as management-controlled. There are a number of reasons for the discrepency between his figures and those of others. He argues that Burch's criteria of 4 percent to 5 percent plus inside or outside representation is too liberal. Herman's category of minority control "includes cases where the ownership is large enough to establish a presumption of control (10 percent or more), or where a group demonstrably in control (usually the active managers) own 5 percent or more of the voting stock" (p. 304).

Where a large block of stock is held by an individual or family who are not active in the management of the corporation, even though they may have some board representation, Herman regards this as a case of latent, as opposed to active, power; such cases are classified as a type of management control. For example, Allied Chemical is classified under management control although the Solvay group had stock worth 9.7 percent and in 1967 appeared to engineer a change in management of Allied Chemical. Herman claims that this "management displacement occurred at a time of serious company malaise" and that Solvay needed the help of other family interests (p. 21). Allied Chemical is classified by Burch, on the other hand, as family-controlled. In cases where the holding is over 10 percent, coupled with board representation, Herman has "tended to posit control" (p. 304). He uses a "conservative" definition of minority control and this, in part, accounts for the discrepancy.

In his study Herman distinguishes between the mechanism and the location of control, the "how" and the "who" of control.

> Ownership is often both a mechanism of control and the locus of control; but in the numerous and important cases where minority concentrations run from 1 to 15 percent, the overlapping of how and who becomes less assured. . . . Somebody may own 6 percent of a company's voting shares and have no power whatsoever in its affairs. . . .The failure to separate how control is maintained and who controls has probably led to an overrating of ownership as a mechanism of control. . .(p. 24).

Particularly with relatively small stockholdings, 1 percent to 5 percent, Herman maintains that it is not the stock that is important in terms of control, but strategic position (role and status in an organization). According to Herman those in control through strategic position may well have sizeable stockholdings in absolute terms which make up much of an individual's wealth. The 4.2 percent of R. J. Reynold's Industries' stock held by its officers and directors was worth $180 million in 1975 (p. 63). Controllers, then, may have ownership interests; ownership in this sense is not separated from control, although it is not through that ownership that control is exercised. Ownership, for Herman, in this case constrains but does not control corporate policy. It is possible to calculate, using Herman's subcategories under management control, the extent of "substantial ownership interests" on the part of managers and directors in the 200 largest nonfinancial corporations. Approximately 37 percent are in this category—where ownership is not separated from control even though it may not be the stockholding that provides the mechanism of control.

Herman argues, contrary to Kotz, that the investments of commercial banks and others, while large, are characterized by "passivity in voting behavior" and have not led to cases of financial dominance over non-financial corporations. Consequently these large blocks of stock do not show up in his classification scheme of power in corporations. But through other means (bankers on corporate boards, lending powers), Herman says, "significant influence by financial institutions was present in a substantial minority of large companies," usually operating as "a constraining and negative power short of ultimate authority" (p. 159).

Clearly Herman's distinction between constraint and control is very important for his argument.

> Literal control as used here means the power to make the key decisions of a company, which include choices of products, major markets, volume and direction of investment, larger commercial and political strategies and selection of top personnel. The power to constrain is used to mean the power to limit certain decisions' choices, as in a ceiling on dollars that may be spent on new facilities or paid out in dividends, or a power of veto over personnel choices. The two terms are not mutually exclusive as defined here. A constraint is a form of control even if only negative in exercise.... A constraint also merges into control when it extends to the power to displace the active management (p. 19).

So Herman's distinction, in some cases, does not distinguish, though his classification scheme identifies cases of financial constraint and places them in a subcategory of management control. Some 19 percent of the 200 corporations are classified as subject to financial constraint. Herman develops a theory of "constrained managerial control of the large corporation" and his system of classification is derived from this theory. Under this theory "ownership persists as a powerful influence and constraint on managerial ends and behavior" (p. 15). What Herman calls constraint, others call control, and the discrepancies in results are a partial reflection of these conceptual differences. His work is a major contribution to, but not a settlement of, a controversy.

Table 1.   Summary of Management Control in Empirical Studies of
Control Type in the Largest U.S. Non-financial Corporations.

	Percent of Management Controlled Corporations		
Studies	Top 200	Top 250	Top 500
Berle and Means (1932)	44%		
TNEC (1940)	30%		
Villarejo (1960)		46%	
Sheehan (1967)			70%
Chevalier (1969)	40%		
Larner (1970)	84%		
Burch (1972)	43%		
Herman (1981)	83%		

As Table 1 shows, variety is the spice of empirical work on this issue. And it will remain so, as long as there is disagreement over definitions and procedures. Until generally acceptable criteria for control and generally acceptable approaches to the study of the separation of ownership from control are found, variation will continue to characterize results. As the issue of the separation of ownership from control is irretrievably political, to hope for Rhadamanthine standards of classification is unrealistic and even compromise is unlikely. It is a political as well as an economic issue, because announcing that institutions are changing by themselves, and that as a result managers may no longer be singularly wedded to the profit motive, serves to undermine traditional opposition to capitalism. To draw the contrast starkly, managerialism at its most enthusiastic swaps the self-interested robber-baron image of the businessman for the public-interested industrial-statesman image. If managerialist theories are correct, then, not only is capitalism a thing of the past, but so is its antithesis, socialism. Consequently "management control" is perhaps one of those "essentially contested concepts" and if not a "pseudo" fact, as Zeitlin suggests, the separation of ownership and control is certainly an elusive one.

BEHAVIORAL IMPLICATIONS

The central behavioral proposition of managerialists is that managers' selfish interests, in management-controlled firms, are different from owners' selfish interests and will lead managers to pursue goals other than profit maximization. This part of the paper examines the theoretical and empirical aspects of this proposition.

Keynes anticipated much of the later discussion in his essay "The End of Laissez-Faire."

A point arrives in the growth of a big institution. . .at which the owners of the capital, i.e. the shareholders, are almost entirely dissociated from the management, with the result that the direct personal interest of the latter in the making of great profit becomes quite secondary. When this stage is reached, the general stability and reputation of the institution are more considered by the management than the maximum of profit for the shareholders. The shareholders must be satisfied by conventionally adequate dividends; but once this is secured, the direct interest of the management often consists in avoiding criticism from the public and from the customers of the concern (p. 314).

During the 1920s American social scientists began to posit a relationship between corporate social responsibility and the separation of ownership from control. In 1925 Robert Brookings claimed that the separation of ownership from control in the United States "is bringing about a change in the ideas of managers about their own responsibility" (p. 13). Managers were beginning to feel a responsibility to labor and the public as well as to stockholders, according to Brookings. In a similar vein Berle and Means maintained that,

The separation of ownership from control produces a condition where the interests of owner and of ultimate manager may, and often do, diverge, and where many of the checks which formerly operated to limit the use of power disappear. . .New responsibilities towards the owners, the workers, the consumers, and the State thus rest upon the shoulders of those in control. In creating these new relationships, the quasi-public corporation may fairly be said to work a revolution (p. 6).

Claiming that managers' stock ownership is negligible, Berle and Means suggested that the way is clear for the assertion of community interests. Community interests are defined in terms of "fair wages, security to employees, reasonable service to their public, and stabilization of business." If the corporate system is to survive, then management must develop into a "purely neutral technocracy," according to Berle and Means, "balancing a variety of claims by various groups in the community and assigning to each a portion of the income stream on the basis of public policy rather than private cupidity" (p. 356). The threats to corporate survival were not clearly specified in *The Modern Corporation and Private Property*, but a continuing theme in Berle's later works has been the importance of what he calls the "public consensus." It is this public consensus, or "public opinion" as it is called in *The Twentieth Century Capitalist Revolution*, that channels managerial discretion in socially useful directions, preventing the corporation from becoming a "tyrannous institution" (1954, p. 54). To sum up, the separation of ownership and control permits management motives other than profit. It is probable that these motives will include community well-being, particularly as they are policed by public opinion backed up by the potential of political intervention.

Berle's development of the notion of public consensus is uncritical. His insight was to see that the corporation is a political institution, in need of legitimacy and sensitive to public opinion. However, this insight leads not to a critical detachment in analyzing corporate actions, but to a rationalization of contemporary corporate power structures. Berle's own work satisfies the corporate need he describes. Berle sees the public consensus as an actual working democratic device which ensures corporate actions do not drift from considerations of community interests (1959, p. 153). The public consensus is conceived as an independent, external, measure of corporate actions. The possibility of corporate actions themselves framing the public consensus is not considered. When Peter Bachrach says that "A.A. Berle has developed a theory of public consensus in an effort to legitimize the growing concentration of corporate power," he may be right or wrong about the intent, but he is correct about the effect (p. 59).

Since Berle and Means' work others have put forward the case for expecting divergent patterns of behavior in owner-controlled and management-controlled firms. Ralf Dahrendorf says that the effect of the separation of ownership and control is

> . . .that it produces two sets of roles the incumbents of which increasingly move apart in their outlook on and attitudes toward society in general and toward the enterprise in particular. . . Never has the imputation of a profit motive been further from the real motives of men than it is for modern bureaucratic managers (p. 46).

Galbraith, like William Baumol, sees corporate growth, measured in sales, as the primary goal of the modern managerial corporation.

> . . .the paradox of modern economic motivation is that profit maximization as a goal requires that the individual member of the technostructure subordinate his personal pecuniary interest to that of the remote and unknown stockholder. By contrast, growth, as a goal, is wholly consistent with the personal and pecuniary interest of those who paricipate in decisions and direct the enterprise (p. 174).

R. Joseph Monsen and Anthony Downs construct, in a more formal manner, a theory of managerial firms. "Our theory," they say, "is really nothing more than the application of the self-interest axiom in traditional theory to a new type of firm: one in which ownership is separate from management. . .(p. 236). Managers attempt to maximize their own incomes instead of the firm's profits. According to Monsen and Downs, managerial firms are more cautious, have larger expense accounts, and are more conciliatory to their workforce and the public. We may have come some distance from Berle and Means' "purely neutral technocracy," and Monsen and Downs differ from Galbraith in terms of the growth motivation. But playing down profit and the notion that management control rather than owner control will be more socially responsible, or more conciliatory to employees and the community, remain common themes.

CRITIQUES

Critiques of these theories split along two levels of analysis. One level fastens on individual motivations; the other, at system level, on the imperatives of the market. While it is convenient for our analysis to group these arguments in this way, of course there are intersections between the two levels; the imperatives of the market system are transformed into individual motivations.

It is suggested that the managerialists have misapplied the self-interest axiom at the level of the individual. Managers whose authority may be bureaucratic, derived from their office or strategic position rather than property ownership, continue to own stock. Property-related interests constitute such an important part of their income that "managements' ownership and ownership-based income is absolutely so large as to gear manager and owner interests together" (Herman, p. 93). Herman estimates that company stock counts for about one half of a top executive's personal assets in the 100 largest industrials (p. 95). Larner, who examined the components of an executive's wealth and income, says the "results suggest that the corporation's dollar profit and rate of profit are the major variables explaining the level of executive remuneration and compensation" (p. 61). The claim by some managerialists that growth as opposed to profit has become the rational corporate executive's chief goal is further countered by the argument that growth can only be realized through profits. Thus managers' selfish interests are the same as those that owner-controllers are assumed to have.

At the level of the system there are constraints which, if not enforcing profit maximization, at the least ensure that corporate policy cannot deviate substantially from the pursuit of profit. Like the "vulgar owner-entrepreneur of the bad old days, the modern manager, however bright and shiny," says Ralph Miliband, "must also submit to the imperative demands of the system of which he is both master and servant. . ." (p. 34). The chief of these imperatives is profit. The twin threats of takeover and bankruptcy enforce corporate obedience to this imperative (Blackburn, p. 123). In short, there are both system-level constraints that restrict managerial discretion and a framework of personal incentives that direct managerial actions towards profit.

Fortunately the discussion need not halt at this somewhat abstract stage, for a number of studies have attempted to actually measure the profit performance of firms subject to the different control types. Of 12 such studies only 5 have found that there is a significant variation in profit performance between owner-controlled and management-controlled firms; that is only 5 support managerialist expectations (see Table 2).

Herman categorizes Larner's work as supporting managerialist expectations since he does find some evidence for profitability varying with control type, but Larner's own assessment of his findings is that "managment-controlled corporations seem to be just about as profit-oriented as are owner-controlled corporations" (p. 29). Although Radice finds a relationship between control type and

Table 2. Summary of the Findings of Empirical Work on the Affect of Control Type on Profit Performance

Study	Does Affect	Does Not Affect
Boudreaux (1973)	x	
Elliot (1972)		x
Herman (1981)		x
Holl (1975)		x
Kamerschen (1968)		x
Kania and Mckean (1976)		x
Larner (1970)		x
Monsen, Chiu, and Cooley (1968)	x	
Palmer (1973)	x	
Radice (1971)	x	
Sorensen (1974)		x
Stano (1976)	x	

profitability, and is categorized accordingly in Table 2, he makes the following qualification: "differences. . .do appear to exist between the two control types in profitability," but "our hypothesis. . .was not confirmed completely: we cannot conclude that owner-controlled firms show a greater tendency to maximize profits" (pp. 560-61). One other study, not included in Table 2, but relevant to the discussion, examined corporate ideology in relation to control type and found no relationship. Maynard Seider found that owner-controlled firms were as likely to express a social responsibility ethic as management-controlled firms (p. 123). The evidence, though mixed, favors the view that the separation of ownership from control has no significant effect on managerial motivations and practices.

CONTROL TYPE AND SOCIAL POLICY IN THE 1920s

The preceding discussion presented the hypothesis of a relationship between control type and the existence of corporate social policy, and also showed why there are some difficulties with it. This section attempts to test the hypothesis using data from the 1920s. The findings provide additional evidence that control type is not an important influence on behavior, which is defined not in usual terms of profitability and growth, but in terms of social policy. First, some discussion of the context and content of corporate social policy in this period is necessary.

In 1914 Ford reduced the working day to eight hours—three shifts instead of two—and introduced a five-dollar basic daily wage. Company policy stated that nobody seeking a job should be turned down because of his physical condition, unless he had a contagious disease, and that no one should be discharged for physical disability. Allan Nevins, saying that unions were not much of a force in Detroit at the time and denying that the primary motivation was to reduce labor turnover, attributes these policies to the humanity of the employer: ". . .not since New Lanark had a bolder effort been made to raise the standards of working-class life than that now instituted by the Ford Company" (p. 552). Robert Owen, the founder of New Lanark, was an odd man, and so no doubt was Henry Ford. But while New Lanark was an isolated but significant curiosity of early capitalism, Ford's Detroit car company was more or less in tune with its times. Ford's labor policies were not eccentric.

In 1922 Standard Oil of New Jersey established a welfare program "based on the fundamental proposition of a square deal for all concerned—the employees, the management, the stock-holders and the public" (Hicks, p. 55). This program included the eight-hour day, disability benefits for work-related accidents, sickness benefits, paid vacations, employee stock-ownership schemes, pensions, and a guarantee not to discriminate against union members. Clarence Hicks, a propagandist for corporate social policies, helped formulate the Standard Oil program, having previously assisted with the International Harvester scheme. According to Hicks, International Harvester "was the first great corporation in America to assume responsibility for industrial accidents, far in advance of any state or federal legislation on workmen's compensation" (p. 42). In his autobiography Hicks does admit to failing to persuade Tolstoy, whom he visited on a trip to Russia, of the worth of this approach to the problems of modern industrial society—Tolstoy advised a return to the farm. American businessmen, however, were more tractable than Russian novelists.

Corporate social policy had organizational as well as individual promoters. Formed in 1900, the National Civic Federation (NCF) recognized at the outset "the importance of developing welfare activity" (Green, p. 267). Among its members the NCF included Andrew Carnegie, George Perkins, Samuel Gompers, John Mitchell (president of the miner's union), and John R. Commons. The NCF had a welfare department, set up with the labor members' approval though the department itself consisted only of employer members. The purpose of the department was educational and promotional. The NCF considered it an obligation of employers to provide for the well-being of their employees. It held conferences of employers and distributed literature in an attempt to stimulate the interest of employers. By 1915 the organization claimed that it was entitled to much of the credit for changing "the thoughts and conduct of the great army of progressive employers who are today giving consideration to the conditions surrounding their employees in this country" (Green, pp. 267-69).

Corporate social policies, sometimes referred to as welfare work, included a large number of activities: maximum hours and minimum wage stipulations, gardens, profit sharing, stock ownership, insurance and disability schemes, unemployment funds, pensions, works' councils, housing, gymnasiums, schools, libraries, dental services, athletics, picnics, and gifts to charity, to name some. The U.S. Bureau of Labor Statistics provides a useful definition: "Anything for the comfort and improvement, intellectual and social, of the employees, over and above wages paid, which is not a necessity of the industry nor required by law'' (p. 8). This definition captures the essentially voluntary nature of corporate social policy in the sense of an absence of market or legal constraints. The definition is extended here to include the community as well as employees. In this analysis of the relationship of control type to social policy four separate types of social policy are identified: pension schemes, life insurance schemes, employee stock-ownership schemes, and contributions to charity.

There were very few industrial pension plans established before the turn of the century. But after 1900 there was a rapid increase in the popularity of pension schemes. By 1927 there were approximately 500 industrial pension plans in existence, covering approximately 4 million employees (Todd, p. 356). Common eligibility requirements for these pension schemes were age and length of service. International Harvester established a company scheme in 1908 under which all employees (except executives) of 70 years or over were entitled to pensions, provided they had 20 or more years of service (Ozanne, p. 83). As with many schemes the employer paid the full cost and according to Robert Ozanne the pension was financially quite generous (p. 84). In 1927 the average industrial pension benefit was $605. Public utility companies paid relatively higher pensions than manufacturing companies or railroads (Latimer, p. 222). Usually under noncontributory plans pension benefits were paid as they came due out of the firm's current operating expenses. Many industrial pension plans ran into financial trouble arising from an underestimation of the rapidity with which costs could grow. However, there was a tendency during the 1920s toward the requirement of contributions from employees. Between 1926 and 1930, 75 percent of the new pension plans introduced in this period required contributions from the employee (National Industrial Conference Board, 1931, p. 45). The *Monthly Labor Review* estimated that 90,000 old people were receiving benefits from industrial pension schemes in 1927 (p. 54).

Industrial life insurance schemes became widespread in the United States in the second and third decades of the twentieth century. Under these schemes life insurance was provided by an insurance company for a group of employees on behalf of their employer. The amount of insurance in force rose from $13 million in 1929 to about $7 billion in 1928 (National Industrial Conference Board, 1919, p. 3). At this time it was estimated that approximately 8 million employees were benefiting from this form of insurance with an average coverage of $1200 per person. The rate of growth of group life insurance was much greater than that of ordinary life insurance during this period (Rubinow). Industrial life insurance did not require individual medical examinations in order to ascertain eligibility. Instead the factory itself was often inspected. Particularly high-risk industries paid higher premiums. In the National Industrial Conference Board (NICB) study of 618 companies operating insurance schemes, 439 had eligibility requirements of a length of service varying from two weeks to five years, most requiring between three and six months. Of these companies 417 had schemes which covered their entire work force (1929, pp. 20-21). The premium, based on the average age of the participants, was paid either entirely by the employer or jointly by the employee and the employer under a contributory plan. As with pensions the tendency during the 1920s was to move from noncontributory to contributory plans. Industrial life insurance was gradually extended to include disability, providing the worker payment of his insurance if he was permanently disabled.

Approximately 1 million employees owned stock in 1927 (Foerster). The largest single gift of stock ever made to employees was by George Eastman who, in 1919, gave $1 million of his personal holdings in the Eastman Kodak Company to employees who had been with the company two or more years. When sold, the stock was often priced at less than market price, or if the market price was maintained, then special financial advantages were often granted the employee (NICB, 1928). "Selling securities to its employees nearly always involves some cost to the company" (p. 125). The reasons companies were willing to incur these costs, according to the NICB study, included favorable publicity, increased employee loyalty, and increased savings on the part of employees. However, in some cases, notably among public utilities, selling stock to employees was used as a way of obtaining capital (p. 157). These should not be considered instances of social policy. But of the 14 cases in this analysis of control type and social policy in which the presence of social policy is identified by employee stock ownership alone, none were public utilities.

In 1929 about 22 percent of the money raised by 129 community chests included in a study undertaken for the National Bureau of Economic Research was contributed by corporations. Corporate contributions to community chests increased from $2,535,819 to $12,954,769 between 1920 and 1929. This increase in corporate contributions accompanied the growth of the community chest movement (Williams and Croxton, p. 11). The depression in the early 1920s temporarily stalled corporate giving as it stalled other corporate social policies. Aside from community chests the YMCA was the chief beneficiary of corporate philanthropy. In 1917 over 100 YMCA's were supported jointly by employers and employees (Williams and Croxton, p. 52). There were 500 lump-sum gifts of $1 million or more to various charities in 1928, illustrating what Robert Bremner describes as the "charitable zeal of business leaders" (p. 154).

DATA FOR ANALYSIS

While this paper has pointed out the difficulties with the process of classifying corporations in terms of control type, Berle and Means' classification of the largest 200 nonfinancial corporations according to ultimate control was used. Three corporations were classified by Berle and Means as "special situations,"

Table 3.   Control Type and Social Policy in Top 200 U.S. Firms, 1929

	Management Control	Ownership Control
No Social Policy	38%	51%
Social Policy	62%	49%
	100%	100%
	(n = 112)	(n = 85)

Gamma = –0.24 $X^2_{,1df}$ = 2.4   not significant at the 0.05 level

and these were excluded from the sample. Some firms were classified by Berle and Means as controlled by "legal device," an intermediary category between minority ownership control and management control, though in one "there appeared to be a very considerable separation of ownership and control" (p. 108). Where this classification occurred, Philip Burch's evaluation of control type in his reassessment of Berle and Means' study was used (approximately one fifth of the cases).

Out of a total of 197 corporations, 111 are identified as having social policy. Of these, 77 had pension schemes, 11 had life insurance schemes, 69 had employee stock-ownership schemes, and 40 contributed to charity. The appendix provides a list of corporations included in the analysis and identifies the presence or absence of social policy. These types of social policy were selected primarily because information on them identifying individual firms was available. The data on pensions and employee stock ownership is the most complete, as it is based on comprehensive surveys of American industry at the time. For life insurance schemes only a selected list of firms, compiled by the NICB, was available. But this selection was not influenced by control type. Contributions to charity were identified from a list of contributors to a Red Cross war fund. It is possible that more of the corporations, both owner- and management-controlled, had social policy than is indicated here. Ford, for example, is not included in the ownership control with social policy category. But there is no reason to suppose that additional data on other types of social policy would vary with control type any more than the data do on the four types identified. Although the existence of any one of these types is sufficient for the corporation to be classified as having social policy, in over half the cases the corporation had more than one type. The fit between the date of information on control type (1929) and the dates of information on social policy is not exact. The drift is least with pensions (1929) and greatest with charity (1918).[2] Any distortion resulting from this drift should favor managerialist expectations if the managerialist claim of trend towards management control is correct.

Table 3 shows that more management-controlled firms have social policy than

Table 4.   Size, Control Type, and Social Policy in U.S. Firms, 1929

	Small		Medium		Large	
	M-C	O-C	M-C	O-C	M-C	O-C
No Social Policy	42%	60%	35%	46%	41%	30%
Social Policy	58%	41%	65%	55%	60%	70%
	100%	101%	100%	101%	101%	100%
	(n=24)	(n=42)	(n=51)	(n=33)	(n=37)	(n=10)

M-C = management-controlled
O-C = owner-controlled

owner-controlled firms. But the 13 percent difference provides poor support for managerialist theory. There is no significant relationship between type of control and the presence or absence of social policy. That is, the gamma (-0.24) suggest that there is only a weak relationship, and the low chi-square indicates that even that relationship is not statistically significant.

While this analysis is based on the largest 200 American corporations, size varies considerably within this group. In their study Berle and Means also provided information on the size of corporations. Size is interesting both because it is expected to influence control type—larger firms are more likely to have a wider distribution of stockholdings and are more likely to be management-controlled, and because it might also be taken as an indication of the capacity to produce social policy. Using Berle and Means' figures on size in terms of assets, these firms were placed in three categories; small (up to $160 million), medium (from $161 to $500 million), and large (over $500 million). Differences in size, even among the largest 200 firms, appear to influence both control type and the existence of social policy. Between the three size-categories, there is an increase both in the percentage of management-controlled firms and in the percentage of firms with social policy. The 36 percent of small firms that are management-controlled rises to 61 percent management-controlled in the medium category and 79 percent in the large category. The 47 percent of small firms with social policy rises to 61 percent for medium-size firms, and 62 percent for large firms.

Interestingly, as size increases any relationship between control type and social policy disappears (see Table 4). The data shows that among the largest firms, owner-controlled firms are actually slightly more likely (10 percent) to have social policy. Size may be important for social policy because it reflects both on the ability of firms to provide social policy and on the power of the firm and perceptions of its legitimacy—thus increasing the need for social policy.

CONCLUSION

This paper has examined the separation of ownership from control in the modern corporation and the behavioral implications of this institutional change. The question addressed is whether this change can account for corporate social policy, as various managerial theories might lead us to expect. A review of research on the extent of the separation of ownership from control revealed considerable variation in findings. The most recent study, Herman's *Corporate Power, Corporate Control*, finds that over 80 percent of the largest 200 American corporations are management-controlled, a finding that accords with Berle and Means' suggested trend in the direction of managerial control. But at the same time Herman's study robs the observation of the separation of ownership from control of much of its significance through the development of a theory of "constrained managerial control" under which ownership remains a powerful influence in managerial decision making.

This paper discusses the behavioral significance of control type in the context of the 1920s and in terms of corporate social policy. Although often considered a recent phenomenon, perhaps as an outgrowth of the post-1960s, post-Watergate wave of popular distrust of social, political, and economic institutions, corporate social policy and the social responsibility ethic have been a characteristic of corporations at least since the 1920s. Of course, the nature and content of corporate social policy have altered over time, in relation to the state's activity and in relation to changing cultural and political norms. The data from the 1920s does not indicate any strong association between the making of social policy and managerial control. Rather it reveals a tendency among large firms, irrespective of control type, to make social policy.

APPENDIX A
BERLE AND MEANS' 200 LARGEST CORPORATIONS AND SOCIAL POLICY

Size: Assets in millions of dollars

Indicators of Social Policy: P = Pensions, I = Life Insurance, E = Employee Stock Ownership, C = Charity.

Economic Sector: R = Railroad, U = Utility, N = Industrial

Where Berle and Means use the categories "legal device" or "pyramiding," Burch's evaluation was used. These are marked with an asterisk (*).

	Size	Social Policy	Sector
Management Control With Social Policy			
Illinois Central Rd. Co.	680.9	PE	R
Kansas City Southern Ry. Co.*	146.1	P	R
Norfolk & Western Ry. Co.	497.0	P	R
Western Maryland Ry. Co.	168.2	P	R
Pacific Gas & Electric Co.*	428.2	PEC	U
Goodyear Tire & Rubber Co.*	243.2	PIE	N
Boston & Maine Ry. Co.	256.4	PE	R
Lehigh Valley Ry. Co.	226.0	PE	R
Reading Co.	565.0	PE	R
Interboro' Rapid Transit Co.*	458.6	P	U
Phila. Rapid Transit Co.*	95.6	P	U
American Tobacco Co.	265.4	EC	N
Ligget & Myers Tobacco Co.*	150.3	C	N
Public Service Corp. of N.J.	634.6	PE	U
Radio Corp. of America	280.0	PE	N
Chi., Rock Isl. & Pac. Ry. Co.	477.4	PE	R
N.Y., N.H. & H. Ry. Co.	560.8	PE	R
Atchison,To.& Santa Fe Ry. Co.	1,135.4	PE	R
Baltimore & Ohio Ry. Co.	1,040.8	P	R
Chicago & N. Western Ry. Co.	641.0	P	R
Delaware & Hudson Co.	269.4	PEC	R
Great Northern Ry. Co.	812.4	P	R
Missouri-Kansas-Texas Ry. Co.	314.0	P	R
Newe York Central Ry. Co.	2,250.0	PE	R
Northern Pacific Ry. Co.	813.9	P	R
Pennsylvania Ry. Co.	2,600.0	PE	R
St. Louis-San Fran. Ry. Co.	439.9	P	R
Southern Pacific Co.	2,156.7	PEI	R
Union Pacific Ry. Co.	1,121.1	P	R
American Tel. & Tel. Co.	4,228.4	PEC	U
Boston Elevated Ry. Co.	109.7	P	U
Consolidated Gas Co. of N.Y.	1,171.5	PEC	U
Western Union Tel. Co.	332.2	PEC	U
General Electric Co.	515.7	PEIC	N
U.S. Steel Corp.	2,286.1	PEC	N
Chi.,Burl'ton & Quin. Ry. Co.	645.4	P	R
Spokane, P'land & Seattle Ry.	140.2	P	R
Bklyn. Man. Transit Co.	288.5	P	U
Consol. Gas, Elec. Lt., & Pr.	135.9	PE	U
Edison Elec. Ill. of Boston	156.3	P	U
Inter. Tel. & Tel. Corp.	521.2	PE	U
So. Calif. Edison Co., Ltd.	340.6	PE	U
American Can Co.	191.3	P	N
American Car & Foundry Co.	119.5	C	N
American Locomotive Co.	106.2	C	N
American Sugar Refining Co.	157.1	PEC	N
Anaconda Copper Mining Co.	680.6	C	N
Armour & Co. (Ill)	452.3	PEI	N
Bethlehem Steel Corp.	801.6	PEC	N
Eastman Kodak Co.	163.4	P	N

	Size	Social Policy	Sector
Firestone Tire & Rubber Co.	161.6	E	N
B.F. Goodrich Co.	163.6	PIE	N
International Harvester Co.	384.0	PEC	N
International Paper & Pr. Co.	686.5	EC	N
Kennecott Copper Corp.	337.8	C	N
National Biscuit Co.	133.2	CIE	N
Pullman, Inc.	315.5	PE	N
Pure Oil Co.	215.4	E	N
Sears, Roebuck & Co.	251.8	EC	N
Studebaker Corp.	134.2	PIE	N
Swift & Co.	351.2	PEC	N
Union Carbide & Carbon Corp.	306.6	C	N
United Fruit Co.	226.0	E	N
Westinghouse Elec. & Manu. Co.	253.9	PE	N
F.W. Woolworth Co.	165.4	C	N
Youngstown Sheet & Tube Co.	235.7	E	N
American Woolen Co.	113.9	E	N
American Rad. & St. San. Corp.	199.4	C	N
United Shoe Machinery Corp.	94.1	E	N

Management Control Without Social Policy

	Size	Social Policy	Sector
Amer. Commonwealths P'r Corp.*	184.4		U
American Water Wks. & Elec. Co.*	378.5		U
Assoc. Gas & Elec. Co.*	900.4		U
Cities Service co.*	989.6		U
Tri-Utilities Corp.*	346.0		U
U.S. Elec. Power Corp.*	1,125.8		U
Utilities Power & Lt. Corp.*	373.1		U
Gen'l Theatre Equipment, Inc.*	360.0		N
Int'l Match Corp.*	217.6		N
Shell Union Oil Corp.*	486.4		N
Erie Railroad Co.*	560.9		R
St. Louis Southwestern Ry. Co.*	139.4		R
Wabash Ry. Co.	334.6		R
American Gas & Electric Co.	431.0		U
American Power & Light Co.	754.1		U
Columbia Gas & Elec. Corp.	529.2		U
Commonwealth & Southern Corp.	1,133.7		U
Detroit Edison Co.*	296.1		U
Elec. Power & Light Corp.	560.0		U
Nat'l Power & Light Co.	500.0		U
Niagara Hudson Power Corp.	756.9		U
North American Co.*	810.3		U
United Gas Improvement Co.	802.0		U
Prairie Oil & Gas Co.*	209.8		N
N. American Light & Power Co.*	308.4		U
Prairie Pipe Line Co.	140.5		N
Chi., Mil'kee, St. Pl. & Pac. Rd. Co.	776.1		R
Southern Ry. Co.	655.5		R

	Size	Social Policy	Sector
Electric Bond & Share Co.	756.0		U
Chicago Union Station Co.	96.8		R
Sinclair Crude Oil Purchasing	111.9		N

Management Control Without Social Policy

	Size		Sector
Baldwin Locomotive Works	98.8		N
Borden Co.	174.0		N
Chrysler Corp.	209.7		N
Drug, Inc.	158.0		N
P. Lorillard Co.	110.0		N
Montgomery Ward & Co.	187.5		N
National Dairy Products Corp.	224.5		N
Phila. & Reading Coal & Iron Co.	129.0		N
Richfield Oil Co. of Calif.	131.9		N
Sinclair Consolidated Oil Corp.	400.6		N
Texas Corp.	609.8		N
Wilson & Co.	98.0		N

Ownership Control With Social Policy

	Size	Social Policy	Sector
Florida East Coast Ry. Co.	123.6	P	R
Gulf Oil Corp. of Pa.	430.9	P	N
Jones & Laughlin Steel Corp.	222.0	PE	N
R.H Macy & Co.	97.0	C	N
Marshall Field & Co.	137.2	C	N
Phelps Dodge Corp.	124.7	PC	N
Crane Co.	115.9	PEC	N
Deere & Co.	94.6	PIE	N
Del., Lackawanna & W. Rd. Co.	189.3	PI	R
N.Y., Chi. & St. Louis Rd. Co.*	350.0	P	R
Commonwealth Edison Co.*	440.0	PEC	U
Middle West Utilities Co.*	1,120.0	PE	U
Pacific Lighting Corp.	203.4	C	U
Peoples Gas Light & Coke Co.*	192.1	PE	U
Public Service Co. of N. Ill.*	190.0	PE	U
Atlantic Refining Co.	167.2	P	N
E.I. du Pont de Nemours & Co.	497.3	PEI	N
General Motors Corp.*	1,400.0	E	N
Inland Steel Co.	103.2	C	N
Standard Oil of Indiana	850.0	PE	N
Standard Oil of N.J.	1,767.3	PEC	N
Standard Oil of N.Y.	708.4	PEC	N
Tide Water Associated Oil Co.	251.4	PEC	N
U.S. Rubber Co.	307.8	PEC	N
Vacuum Oil Co.	205.7	PEC	N
Crown Zellerbach Corp.*	117.7	E	N
Denver & Rio Grande W. Rd. Co.*	223.4	P	R
Amer. Smelting & Refining Co.	241.0	PC	N
Continental Oil Co.	198.0	E	N
Corn Products Refining Co.	126.7	IEC	N

	Size	Social Policy	Sector
Int. Mercantile Marine Co.	100.0	C	N
International Shoe Co.	111.3	E	N
Long-Bell Lumber Corp.	116.1	E	N
National Lead Co.	108.4	PE	N
Pittsburg Coal Co.	171.5	PE	N
Proctor & Gamble Co.	109.4	PEC	N
Ownership Control With Social Policy			
Republic Iron & Steel Corp.	331.7	E	N
Standard Oil Co. of Calif.	604.7	PE	N
Wheeling Steel Corp.	128.3	E	N
American Rolling Mill Co.	104.3	E	N
Atlantic Coast Line Rd. Co.*	840.0	P	R
Crucible Steel Corp	124.3	C	N

Ownership Control Without Social Policy

	Size	Sector
Virginian Ry. Co.	152.7	R
New Eng. Gas & Elec. Assoc.	108.7	U
Railway & Bus Association	112.2	U
Aluminum Co. of America	300.0	N
Ford Motor Co.	761.0	N
Gt. Atlantic & Pac. Tea of Amer.	147.3	N
Koppers Co. of Del.	250.0	N
Minnesota & Ontario Paper Co.	90.3	N
Nat'l Steel Corp.	120.8	N
Seaboard Airline Ry. Co.	283.1	R
Duke Power Co.	212.1	U
Eastern Gas & Fuel Associates	158.7	U
Lone Star Gas Corp.	109.0	U
Singer Mfg. Co.	210.0	N
Alleghany Corp.*	1,600.0	R
United Light & Power Co.*	520.1	U
Cliffs Corp.*	98.0	N
R.J. Reynolds Tobacco Co.*	163.1	N
Union Oil Associates	240.0	N
United Stores Corp.*	161.5	N
Chicago & Eastern Ill. Ry. Co.	97.4	R
Chicago Great Western Rd. Co.	149.2	R
Western Pacific Rd. Corp.	156.0	R
Bklyn. Union Gas Co.	123.7	U
Consolidation Coal Co.	94.0	N
Loew's Inc.*	124.2	N
Cen. Pub. Ser. Co.*	199.5	U
Midland United Co.*	298.1	U
Associated Telephone Util. Co.	95.9	U
Hudson Manhattan Rd. Co.	131.7	U
Stone & Webster, Inc.	400.0	N
Third Ave. Ry. Co.	110.0	U
Utd. Rys. & Elec. Co. of Balt.	96.7	U

	Size	Social Policy	Sector
Allied Chemical & Dye Corp.	277.2		N
Cuban Cane Products co.	101.3		N
Glen Alden Coal Co.	300.0		N
S.S. Kresge Co.	109.5		N
Ohio Oil Co.	110.6		N
Paramount Publix Corp.	236.7		N
Phillips Petroleum Co.	145.3		N
Pittsburgh Plate Glass Co.	101.6		N
U.S. Realty & Improvement Co.	124.6		N
Warner Bros. Pictures, Inc.	167.1		N

ACKNOWLEDGMENTS

The author wishes to thank Professors Gerald C. Wright and Russell Hanson, as well as the Department of Political Science data lab, Indiana University.

NOTES

1. W. B. Gallie, "Essentially Contested Concepts," *Proceedings of the Aristotelian Society* 56 (1955-6), p. 169: According to Gallie there are conceptual disputes which, "although not resolvable by argument of any kind, are nevertheless sustained by perfectly respectable arguments and evidence.. . .There are concepts which are essentially contested, concepts the proper use of which inevitably involves endless disputes about their proper uses on the part of their users."

2. Sources for social policy are Latimer, National Industrial Conference Board (1928, 1929), and Williams and Croxton.

REFERENCES

Bachrach, P. *The Theory of Democratic Elitism: A Critique.* Boston: Little, Brown & Company, 1967.

Baran, P., and P. Sweezy. *Monopoly Capital.* New York: Monthly Review Press, 1968.

Berle, A. *Economic Power and the Free Society.* New York: The Fund for the Republic, 1957.

————*Power without Property.* New York: Harcourt Brace & Co., 1959.

————*The Twentieth Century Capitalist Revolution.* New York: Harcourt Brace & Co., 1954.

———— and G. Means. *The Modern Corporation and Private Property.* New York: Macmillan Co., 1932.

Blackburn, R. "The New Capitalism" in P. Anderson and R. Blackburn, (Eds.), *Towards Socialism.* New York: Cornell University Press, 1966.

Blair, M. *Economic Concentration.* New York: Harcourt Brace Jovanovich, 1972.

Boudreaux, K. "Managerialism and Risk-Return Performance." *Southern Economic Journal* (January 1973).

Bremner, R. H. *American Philanthropy.* (Chicago: The University of Chicago Press, 1960.

Burch, P. *The Managerial Revolution Reassessed.* Lexington, MA: Lexington Books, 1972.

Chevalier, J. "The Problem of Control in Large American Corporations." *Antitrust Bulletin* (Spring 1969).

Dahrendorf, R. *Class and Class Conflict in Industrial Society.* Stanford: Stanford University Press, 1959.

Elliot, J.W. "Control, Size, Growth, and Financial Performance in the Firm." *Journal of Financial and Quantitative Measures* (January 1972).

Foerster, R. "Employee Stock Ownership," *Encyclopaedia of Social Science* (1931).

Galbraith, J. K. *The New Industrial State* New York: Mentor, 1971.

Gordon, R. *Business Leadership in the Large Corporation.* (Washington: The Brookings Institution, 1945.

Green, M. *The National Civic Federation and the American Labor Movement 1900-1925.* (Washington: Catholic University Press of America, 1956.

Habermas, J. *The Legitimation Crisis.* Boston: Beacon Press, 1975.

Herman, E. S. *Corporate Control, Corporate Power.* Cambridge, MA: Cambridge University Press, 1981.

Hicks, C. *My Life in Industrial Relations.* New York: Harper & Bros., 1941.

Holl, P. "Effect of Control Type on the Performance of the Firm in the U.K.." *Journal of Industrial Economics* (June 1975).

Kamershen, D. "The Influence of Ownership and Control on Profit Rates." *American Economic Review* (June 1968).

Kania J., and J. Mckean. "Ownership, Control, and the Contemporary Corporation: A General Behavior Analysis." *Kyklos* (1976).

Keynes, J. M. "The End of Laissez-Faire," in *Essays in Persuasion.* New York: Harcourt Brace and Company, 1963.

Kotz, D. "The Significance of Bank Control over the Large Corporation." *Journal of Economic Issues* (June 1979).

Larner, R. *Management Control and the Large Corporation.* New York: Dunellen, 1971.

Latimer, M. *Industrial Pension Systems in the United States and Canada.* New York: Industrial Relations Counsellors Incorporated, 1932.

Miliband, R. *The State in Capitalist Society.* New York: Basic Books, 1969.

Monsen, J., Jr., and A. Downs. "A Theory of Large Managerial Firms." *The Journal of Political Economy* June 1965.

Monsen, R.J., Jr., J.S. Chiu, and D.E. Cooley. "The Effect of the Separation of Ownership and Control on the Performance of the Large Firm." *Quarterly Journal of Economics* August 1968.

Monthly Labor Review March 1927.

National Industrial Conference Board. *Elements of Industrial Pension Plans.* New York: NICB, 1931.

National Industrial Conference Board. *Employee Stock Purchase Plans in the United States.* New York: NICB, 1928.

National Industrial Conference Board. *Industrial Group Insurance.* New York: NIBC, 1929.

Nevins, A. *Ford: The Times, The Man, The Company.* New York: Scribners, 1954.

Nyman, S., and A. Silberston. "The Ownership and Control of Industry." *Oxford Economic Papers* (March 1978).

Ozanne, R. *A Century of Labor-Management Relations at McCormick and International Harvester.* Madison: The University of Wisconsin Press, 1967.

Palmer, J. "The Profit-Performance Effects of the Separation of Ownership from Control in Large U.S. Industrial Corporations." *The Bell Journal of Economic and Management Science* (Spring 1973).

Radice, H. K. "Control Type, Profitability and Growth in Large Firms." *The Economic Journal* (September 1971).

Rathenau, W. *In Days to Come.* New York: Alfred Knopf Inc., 1921.

Rubinow, I. M. "Group Insurance." *Encyclopedia of Social Science* (1931).

Seider, M. "Corporate Ownership, Control and Ideology: Support for Behavioural Similarity." *Sociology and Social Research* (October 1977).

Sheehan, R. "Proprietors in the World of Big Business." *Fortune* (June 15, 1967).

Sorensen, R. "The Separation of Ownership and Control and Firm Performance: An Empirical Analysis." *Southern Economic Journal* (July 1974).

Stano, M. "Monopoly Power, Ownership Control, and Corporate Performance." *The Bell Journal of Economic and Management Science* (Autumn 1976).

Temporary National Economic Committee. *Investigation of Concentration of Economic Power*, Monograph No.29. Washington: U.S. Government Printing Office, 1940.

Todd, A. J. *Industry and Society*. New York: Henry Holt & Company, 1936.

U.S. Bureau of Labor Statistics. "Welfare Work for Employees in Industrial Establishments in the United States." USBLS Bulletin #250. Washington, D.C., 1919.

U.S. Congress, House Committee on Banking and Currency, *Commercial Banks and their Trust Activities, Emerging Influence on the American Economy*, 90th congress, 2nd Session. Washington: 1968.

Villarejo, D. "Stock Ownership and the Control of Corporations." *New University Thought* (Autumn 1961, Winter 1962).

Veblen, T. *The Engineers and the Price System*. New York: Viking, 1940.

Williams, P., and F. Croxton. *Corporate Contributions to Organized Community Welfare Services*. New York: National Bureau of Economic Research Inc., 1930.

Zeitlin, M. "Corporate Ownership and Control: The Large Corporation and the Capitalist Class." *American Journal of Sociology* (March 1974).

ORGANIZATIONAL DECISION-MAKING AND THE "ECONOMIC GATE":
A CASE STUDY OF NUCLEAR POWER

James E. Stacey

Analysis of organizational decision-making follows two widely-divergent streams, depending upon whether the analyst assumes that the underlying process is economic or social. The economic approach, whether descriptive or prescriptive, assumes that organizations reach decisions by weighing alternatives, costs and benefits, against some pre-determined set of criteria in search of an optimum. By contrast, the social approach, although not excluding the impact of "good reasons" on organizational decision-making, shows how environmental and behavioral variables interact and lead to results that are other than "optimal." Contemporary work based on the social approach has been highly influential, but the myth of the economic rationality of organization survives as a serious impediment to both analytical work and public policy making. In this study elements of each approach will be developed into contrasting specific models of organizational decision-making, which will then be applied in a case study of an important decision by a private electric utility company. Results from the

Research in Corporate Social Performance and Policy, volume 5, pages 231-256 case study will be used to extend the implications of the social model of organizational decision-making where appropriate.

ECONOMIC AND SOCIAL APPROACHES TO ORGANIZATIONAL ANALYSIS

Nowhere is the concept of the economic organization more strongly ingrained than in the private electric utilities, where technocratic myths still dominate the perception of organizational activities by outside analysts, the lay public, and even the actors themselves. According to Sporn (1969), there is an explicitly economic decision-making process operating within private electric utilities. Sporn's model of utility decision-making relates in particular to his concept of the role of engineers in utilities.

> . . . science by itself and the work of the scientist is ineffective in advancing human welfare. For that technology and engineering are required. It is the engineer's function to bring together resources, tools (in the broadest sense), energy, and labor and to combine them in a productive entity to achieve or produce something wholly new or previously impossible, to achieve an improvement that yields a better product at the same cost or the same product at a lower cost, or even a better product at lower cost. Unless or until these factors are brought together in a productive combination, no social or economic benefit results (Sporn, 1969, p. 10).

The engineer's role in the decision-making of a utility and similar organizations has traditionally been pivotal. As a charter member of what Galbraith calls the technostructure, the engineer is in a powerful position with regard to determining the future of the company. It is only recently that the preeminence of engineers in utility decision-making has been challenged. This challenge is not being made by top management, outside consultants, or public service commissions, but by a new group of technocrats, the corporate planners (Gándara).

In Sporn's model, the preeminence of economic criteria is reflected in the extended range of economic impacts. Not restricted to simple benefit/cost models of choice, economics also may serve to stimulate technological advance and the inventive process. In this model, economic criteria assume an independence and sovereignty beyond all other motivations and suggest an underlying economic rationality to the decision-making process.

> In short, a sound economic evaluation of any major capital project is independent of the social, political, or other motivations, and is independent of the particular economic system on which a society is organizezd. If a given society is not to be led astray and if it is not to make a mess of the indispensable business in the proper allocation of its limited total resources, it is important that the proper—and this means total—costs be used in the evaluation. Having done this, the society is then in an excellent position to assign priorities. This does not prevent it from upgrading the priority of any socially desirable project at the expense of another less costly. But the intelligence and sound judgement with which this will finally be

done will always be materially enhanced by having properly determined values and costs. Subsidies, desirable and granted, do not change costs (Sporn, 1969, p. 26).

In Sporn's image of the decision-making process, the engineer, at a specific point in time, calculates an all-encompassing benefit/cost ratio that determines the choice among alternatives. An additional assumption of the model is that all technically feasible alternatives have been brought into the benefit/cost calculation or the decision-making situation.

For economics to maintain its primacy in decision-making, the total costs of alternatives must be evaluated. To Sporn, the study of alternatives must go beyond the critically important and immediately relevant capital costs to include operating and maintenance costs. Included in those costs should be an analysis of the effects of changes in the social-economic environment such as inflation or deflation, income tax structures, and likely changes in ecological regulations. All future economic and social developments that will likely affect a proposed project should also be taken into consideration.

Much of Sporn's model conflicts with other literature on decision-making in organizations. The differences between the two theoretical approaches are significant and lead to major differences in public policy orientations and perspectives on internal organizational control. Recent descriptive theory is based upon analysis of how people actually make decisions, what prevents them from making rational decisions, and under what conditions they will make comparatively rational decisions. The work of Simon and March is of particular relevance— Simon's *Administrative Behavior*, first published in 1945, and *Organizations* by March and Simon. The rationality of humans, in March and Simon's view, is limited by personal and organizational capacities. People lack complete knowledge of their actions, so unanticipated and unintended consequences will occur. Complete knowledge of the alternative courses of action open to the individual or the organization is either not available or it is too expensive to acquire. Even when alternatives exist, people are often unable to rank them in terms of preference. Since the "economic" model of decision-making is suspect, what do individuals do when confronted by the need to make decisions? The decision-maker tends to use solutions that have been used before and are therefore "routine." To an engineer this would be akin to finding an "off-the-shelf" solution— a technology that requires minimum research and development for its use in solving a specific problem. The decision-maker rarely engages in problem solving but when forced to do so conducts a limited search for alternatives along relatively familiar paths and selects the first satisfactory solution that comes along. Hence the decision-maker in the March and Simon model "satisfices" instead of "optimizes." And, within the context of an organization, the decision-maker's standards for satisfactory solutions are a part of a definition of the problem and are subject to manipulation by and the influence of the organization (March and Simon, Perrow, and Simon).

Other authors have also challenged what they feel is the naiveté of traditional economic decision-making models. Perhaps the most controversial of these is John Kenneth Galbraith. Galbraith's view of the modern corporation, in particular what he calls the "technostructure," and the manner in which decisions are made in a mature organization is decidedly at odds with more traditional views of corporate hierarchical decision-making. The stereotype of organizational decision-making, to Galbraith, is influenced by the organization chart, with its clean and clear lines of hierarchical authority.

> At its top is the board of directors and the chairman of the board; next comes the president; next comes the executive vice-president and other viceregal figures; thereafter come the department or divisional heads—those who preside over the Chevrolet division, the large-generators division, the computer division. Power is assumed to pass down from the pinnacle. Those at the top give orders; those below relay them on or respond (Galbraith, p. 68).

No doubt that from a legalistic point of view, power in the corporation does flow along the lines of the organizational chart. However, Galbraith notes that this top-down or hierarchical type of decision-making structure exists (if at all) only in very simple organizations. In more mature and complex organizations, information flow becomes a dominant factor, and group decision-making becomes the norm. The need for a modern organization to draw on, or appraise, the information of numerous individuals comes from the technology, the use of capital, the need for planning (with its accompanying control of the external factors bearing on this planning) and the need for coordination.

In the following sections, elements of the economic and social models will be developed into contrasting models which will then be applied to a case study of decision-making in a private electric utility. Findings of the case study will be used to extend elements of the social model where appropriate.

Two Models of Organizational Decision-Making

In the following analysis, Sporn's economic model will be contrasted to an alternative social model of decision-making. The effort here is not to prove or disprove elements of the competing models, but to determine which elements come closest to describing the decision-making experience of a particular organization. Elements of the models will be discussed as they might apply to private electric utilities, since this is the subject of the research presented later. Major elements of the Sporn model are outlined as follows:

1. Engineers dominate the decision-making process;
2. the primacy, independence, and sovereignty of economic considerations will be maintained beyond all other motivations;
3. all economic studies conducted will be all-inclusive and all-encompassing, involving a global benefit/cost analysis; and

4. the final decision will reflect the economic analysis. That is, at a specific point in time there will be *one* major decision taken, after careful scrutiny of all benefits and costs, both to the organization and to society at large, and before major commitments have been made by the organization.

The key elements of the Simon and March social model also focus on issues that also can be explored with regard to private utilites. The social model expects:

1. satisficing behavior;
2. sequential and limited search processes that are only mildly innovative;
3. specialization of activities and roles, so that attention is directed to "a particular restricted set of values;"
4. "attention-directors that channelize behavior;"
5. Rules, programs, and repertoires of action that limit choice in recurring situations and prevent an agonizing process of optimal decision-making at each turn;
6. a restricted range of stimuli and situations that narrows perception;
7. training and indoctrination enabling the individual to "make decisions, by himself, as the organization would like him to decide;" and
8. the factoring of goals and tasks into programs that are semi-independent of each other so as to reduce interdependencies.

Sporn's economic model is not intended to be a 'straw man,' but represents an ideal that may be productively used to analyze organizational behavior. To an extent, Sporn's model represents what engineers are trained to do, even though actual behavior may be different, and reflects the lay public's impression of what engineers do. Comparing and contrasting these two models may lead to improvements in understanding organizational behavior.

STUDY DESIGN

Case Study

Of the five basic methods (Lijphart; Yin & Heald) for establishing empirical propositions, the case study has been described as the most popular way of discovering how individuals and, in our case, organizations act and how they are likely to act in the future (Wiseman and Aron). The other four methods, the comparative, the experimental, the statistical, and the case survey method (as well as certain forms of the case study) seek a scientific explanation based on the establishment of general empirical relationships among a set of variables while holding other variables constant. Although some would feel that the distinctions made among the four are arbitrary and all could be subsumed in a grand general statement about the purpose and methods of science, the distinction is useful in defining what this research is trying to accomplish.

The case study method is an attempt to study an individual, institution, organization, or community in a broader, more in-depth manner than is possible with other research methods. The basic assumption behind the case study is that the attitudes and behavior patterns of the people in and around the organization have evolved out of their attempts to deal with important events or decision-making points and that modifications in the present affect future behavior. The response to the issue or critical events is also conditioned by the environment within which the organization operates, and by constraints, whether real or imagined, operating on the organization. While avoiding the "additive" approach of survey research, the case study is holistic in its attempt to understand the behavior of individuals and organizations in context (Wiseman and Aron).

Many of the problems with case studies are well known: difficulty of generalization, problems of forgetfulness, inadvertent or purposeful falsification of data, distortion in certain types of documents, inadequacy/excess of material, and inability to disprove an established generalization. Yet, with the proper controls, case studies offer important advantages over other methods. They may guide further research by formulating hypotheses, they may be used to see how actions and attitudes interact over time, the integrity of the unit under study is preserved, they allow the dynamics of change to be studied closely, they make use of detailed data, they maximize limited research sources, and they may help to explain relationships found or hinted at by other methods. The intention here is not to impose a black or white choice between the "good" and "bad" methods, but to see the methods as being on a continuum. Case studies, instead of being a step-child of the social sciences, are seen as having the potential for furthering the developement of theory.

Subjects/Unit of Analysis

In order to explore the elements of the models discussed in the foregoing section, a private electric and gas utility, Niagara Mohawk Power Corporation, was chosen for intensive research using the case study method. Niagara Mohawk Power Corporation is located in Syracuse, New York, and is a member of that small group of 60 utilities that generate the overwhelming bulk of electricity for America. An understanding of Niagara Mohawk's behavior with respect to nuclear power should be of use in understanding the experience of other companies, and also in understanding the general process of decision-making in organizations.

Niagara Mohawk Power Corporation is an investor-owned electric and gas utility, regulated by the New York State Public Service Commission, and serving most of New York State other than the metropolitan area, which is served by Consolidated Edison. Demand for Niagara Mohawk power has consistently increased since World War II, although the rate of increase has slowed in recent years. Projections indicate a continued but lessening rate of growth for electricity generated and/or sold by Niagara Mohawk. Niagara Mohawk operates in several segments of the electric energy cycle—as a purchaser of energy from the Power Authority of the State of New York and other smaller suppliers, as a generator of electricity through several modes of production (coal, hydro, nuclear, etc.), as a transmitter of energy to other distribution companies and, finally, as a distributor of electrical energy to final users.

Because of its size, its coverage, and the variety of generating modes and commercial operations it engages in, and due to the current political environment, Niagara Mohawk has been often involved in controversies, ranging from traditional rate cases to debates about nuclear power. It is the latter subject, nuclear power, that will be the focus here; specifically, what factors led to Niagara Mohawk's involvement in nuclear power, and the changes in strategic decision-making that occurred as result of the organization's environment and its experience with nuclear power. The historical time perspective of the case study will help us to explain how the decision to build a nuclear reactor was made.

Data Collection Procedures

The depth interview was the primary technique for the case study of the decision-making surrounding Niagara Mohawk's entry into nuclear-powered electric generation. The interview protocol followed the normal procedures of going from general to specific questions in order to focus increasingly on the information needed.

The validity and reliability of this case study is high due to the variety of informants and materials made available for the study. Nearly every surviving individual who was even remotely associated with the decision-making surrounding Niagara Mohawk's first nuclear-powered electrical generation plant, Nine Mile Point One, was interviewed. This included all surviving directors, the corporation counsel, and other corporation officers and engineers. Documents, including the original engineering studies and reports, were made freely available to the researcher. This excellent entry to Niagara Mohawk was arranged through a professor who had once worked with the corporation and through the corporation's historian. This developed rapidly into excellent coverage of the events and attitudes surrounding the decision-making.

The procedure for this case study was as follows: An initial contact was made with a company executive to explain the nature and information needs of the study and to ask a series of questions relating the informant's experiences to the research task. The first meeting was also used, when the source was useful, to set up further meetings with the executive or to arrange for access to needed documents. Interviews with other possible company sources were often explored during this and subsequent meetings.

More detailed or in-depth interviews and research usually followed the initial meetings. Varying amounts of corporate materials (histories, studies, reports, and the like) were made available for the study. Some additional information was obtained from the New York State Public Service Commission.

ENVIRONMENTAL INFLUENCES ON NIAGARA MOHAWK'S DECISION-MAKING

Niagara Mohawk's initial interest in nuclear power began in the early 1950s. Niagara Mohawk had a serious interest in nuclear power by 1953 (Philipp, 1979), and this interest coalesced during 1953-59 into a program of training, research, and development in anticipation of the probability of building a nuclear-powered electrical station (Machold). Niagara Mohawk officials noted that there was considerable general interest in nuclear power and that several government programs, in particular the Eisenhower Atoms for Peace Program, were starting. Officials began to look at nuclear power as a possible major source of electrical energy, particularly since all other sources, except hydroelectric power, were felt to be finite and nonrenewable. They were subject to inflationary pressures, as well as pressure from diminishing supplies, and there was fear that costs would increase exponentially (Pratt).

Although many people at that time were claiming that nuclear power would be so cheap that you would not need to meter it, those involved directly in the use of nuclear power for generating energy did not make such claims (Pratt). It was obvious to the officials involved that it would not be a free source of energy, but that it *probably* would be competitive with other energy sources given the proper development program (Pratt).

The engineers of Niagara Mohawk began to explore nuclear power with an eye toward developing it as an energy source to be competitive with other energy sources. The first major step they took was to send the top officers and a number of key people from engineering and operations to California for a month-long crash course with General Electric. While they were there they also visited one of G.E.'s early experimental reactors at Vallecitos. After that experience Niagara Mohawk began to participate in the Enrico Fermi Project of Detroit Edison, an experience that was formative in creating a nuclear power commitment at Niagara Mohawk.

The Enrico Fermi Project

Niagara Mohawk began its more formal commitment to nuclear power early in 1953 when it joined Atomic Power Development Associates (APDA) under the leadership of Walker Cisler of Detroit Edison. APDA created the Power Reactor Development Company (PRDC), which was formed to build the Enrico

Fermi liquid metal-cooled breeder reactor. Although this plant, in hindsight, was ahead of its time (it is now closed due to costs and technical problems), it provided an opportunity for the member companies to look at nuclear power and see the organization needed to build a reactor (Niagara Mohawk, 1953). The Enrico Fermi Project provided experience for new personnel and marked a nascent developmental period for Niagara Mohawk's nuclear power program.

Peach Bottom Reactor

Along with many other utilities, Niagara Mohawk also participated in the development of the high-temperature gas-cooled graphite reactor (HTGR), later designated the Peach Bottom Reactor. This project was directed by Philadelphia Electric Company and built by General Atomics Division of General Dynamics.

High-Temperature Reactor Development Associates, Inc. (HTRDA), composed of over fifty electric companies, was formed in 1959 for the purpose of developing, researching, and constructing the HTGR (Dawson; Niagara Mohawk, 1959). Peach Bottom was completed in 1964 and, despite a long delay in starting up, was in operation until 1974.

Utilities, including Niagara Mohawk, provided engineers for projects being constructed by one of the two large equipment suppliers, Westinghouse and General Electric. Rochester Gas and Electric, New York State Electric and Gas, and Central Hudson, for instance, loaned engineers for several years to work on the ESADA Vallecitos Experimental Super Heat Reactor project in California (Hammer, Lempges). Others were sent to Saxton, the Westinghouse training facility (Arthur). Through such experiences the utilities provided their engineers with skills that were to prove indispensable later on.

The utilities provided other learning opportunities for their engineers in addition to those with the organized groups. One method was to simply send them back to school, either to a university with a special reactor program or to one of the Atomic Energy Commission (AEC) training programs at the Oak Ridge National Laboratories (Arthur, Novarro, and Mangan).

It is important to realize that during the early period of interest in nuclear power, nuclear engineers as such did not exist. Engineering schools across the nation were just beginning to set up programs for training students in nuclear engineering. The utilities, instead of hiring new graduates as is the normal course, were forced into retraining mechanical and electrical engineers in the new discipline. There were some advantages to this; namely, the companies could use seasoned operating personnel who knew intimately the design and needs of the existing system. Resistance to retraining appears to have been negligible. After all, few would pass up an opportunity to be in on the ground floor of a new technology which appeared to be the wave of the future. Later, beginning in the middle 1960s, the utilities began hiring engineers who had graduated from nuclear engineering programs. Moreover, all of the engineers participating at Niagara

Mohawk in the development of nuclear power seemed to have shared a common thread of experience with "total system design." This can be contrasted with the current practice of greater specialization among engineers performing design work for the utility.

The Federal Government

During Niagara Mohawk's early experience with nuclear power, direct contact with the federal government was minimal. Even though in the late 1950s three was considerable government interest in nuclear power, most of the federal impact on Niagara Mohawk's programs was indirect. New legislation and programs facilitated Niagara Mohawk's involvement in nuclear power by allowing private utilities to own nuclear fuel, changing security classifications, providing an insurance pool, and providing a stimulus to the nuclear reactor industry (Mangan). Still, actual contact with AEC and its staff was nonexistent; this came only just prior to the decision to build the first Niagara Mohawk reactor—Nine Mile Point One (Pratt; Philipp, 1980). The federal government's only direct impact on Niagara Mohawk's nuclear power activity came through the U.S. Navy nuclear submarine program. Niagara Mohawk's use of the U.S. Navy's experience in developing nuclear power will be discussed later.

Consultants

Consultants typically form an important part of the social networks involved with the development of nuclear power. But in Niagara Mohawk's case, consultants were to play a relatively minor role. Among the few consultants hired by Niagara Mohawk for its Nine Mile Point One nuclear program were two for radiological measurements and meteorological surveillance. Whipple and Associates, a three-person firm, provided the radiological measurements. Niagara Mohawk no longer has such a radiological surveillance program and does not use consultants for the measurements that they occasionally take. Niagara Mohawk uses its own staff to perform measurements when needed. Maynard, Smith, and Singer performed the meteorological measurements for Niagara Mohawk.

The Nuclear Engineering Social Network

It is apparent that beginning with the Enrico Fermi project and throughout Niagara Mohawk's work on nuclear reactors, a base of contacts with outside consultants and governmental agencies had been slowly growing. With many such contacts, it is difficult to determine who contacted whom. The contacts arose from the environment in which the engineers and company executives worked. These engineers (all of the early nuclear power engineers) grew up professionally together. They went to the same federal training and research facilities such as Oak Ridge or one of the AEC test reactors; they participated together in one of the "classic" early projects such as the Enrico Fermi Project or the HTGR project of General Atomics (Stacey).

The Nuclear Engineering Section

The late 1950s was an important period for Niagara Mohawk in terms of interest and commitment to the development of nuclear power. Long discussions about nuclear power began in the Board of Directors (Jaekle, Maull, Terry). In 1959 information about nuclear power began to flow into the company from federal agencies and suppliers (Jaekle). Along with their participation in the two groups mentioned earlier (APDA and HTGR), Niagara Mohawk Power Corporation established a separate Nuclear Engineering Section (NES) within the company's System Project Engineering Department. This section was to make engineering studies and analyses in order to determine the best type of reactor for the Niagara Mohawk service area (Niagara Mohawk, 1959).

The NES followed the old Niagara Mohawk tradition of doing most of its own architectural and engineering work on its generating stations. As a relatively large utility, Niagara Mohawk was able to use services of its engineering design sections on the smaller power plants of that period. The System Project Engineering Department (SPED) was responsible for all but a small fraction of the architectural and engineering work for the Niagara Mohawk system power plants. The System Project Engineering Department (SPED) was traditionally broken down into three sections, civil, electrical, and mechanical (Mowers).

Eventually the NES, along with the other engineering sections initially operated out of the company's offices in Buffalo, New York, was to do all the architectural and engineering services for the Nine Mile Point One nuclear reactor. This approach was relatively unique among utilities (Pratt; Philipp, 1980; Maul; and Martin). The usual pattern was for a utility to contract out architectural and engineering services and to oversee the operations but not to do the actual engineering and architectural work. The construction work for Nine Mile Point One was done by Stone & Webster, Inc., of New York City. It is indicative of the importance of nuclear power to Niagara Mohawk that the company established a separate section (the Nuclear Engineering Section) within the Department rather than break up the section and subsume it under the existing breakdown of civil, electrical, and mechanical sections.

Bud Pratt was responsible for the establishment of the Nuclear Engineering Section (Philipp, 1979; Rhode). Having been appointed recently as vice-president and chief engineer, Pratt was very interested in nuclear power and had grave concerns about the future of Niagara Mohawk's fuel resources. Among Pratt's concerns, expressed on several occasions, was the realization that the company could no longer hope to build additional hydroelectric power facilities and that, over the 30 or more years that oil and coal plants had to operate, the future indicated declining and finite resources for those fuels (Philipp, 1979; Pratt). Philipp was then placed in charge of the Nuclear Engineering Section with the intent of building up the section within the department as an autonomous engineering unit.

In that time period, it was a bold step to set up such a unit and to believe that a utility could engineer a nuclear reactor on its own. It was an early period for a utility to be involved in nuclear power at all, for only a few power reactors were built or even started—Shippingport, Indian Point One, Dresden, Yankee (Dawson). However, shortly after the Enrico Fermi people came back from Detroit, another major event led to an acceleration of Niagara Mohawk's nuclear timetable and level of experience in designing nuclear power systems. The Power Authority of the State of New York (PASNY) had been constructing, under the direction of Robert Moses, two major power projects: the St. Lawrence and Niagara Falls hydro-facilities. These facilities were completed in record time, and around 1960 they came on line releasing tremendous amounts of power onto the New York State power grid. This made some of Niagara Mohawk's smaller plants unnecessary, and they consequently had to be decommissioned. The period from 1961 to 1969 "was an era of marketing the abundant power and natural gas then available, so that power from the Niagara project could be absorbed and system facilities would be utilized at high efficiency levels as well" (Niagara Mohawk, 1974). Although PASNY paid the fixed and other charges for the power plants that were decommissioned, the question remained as to what to do with the System Project Engineering Department which at that time amounted to a staff of about 300 individuals (Pratt; Philipp, 1980; and Lempges). An effort to go outside the Niagara Mohawk system to find work for this highly trained staff to do began. Rather than just letting the professionals go, and realizing that the steam station design engineers should get some experience in nuclear power, Philipp began to look for new jobs for the engineers in the nuclear field, and he convinced Niagara Mohawk's management to allow the engineers to start designing a hypothetical reactor and power plant. This reactor-power plant combination would be based on guidelines and procedures set up in the SPED (Philipp, 1979).

The engineers were well into the hypothetical plant design when another important event occurred: Niagara Mohawk won a contract to build the power plant portion of a new nuclear power reactor test facility to be run by General Electric (Lempges). G.E. had just won a contract from the federal government and Empire State Atomic Development Association, Inc. (ESADA) to build a superheated steam reactor at Vallecitos in California. This was an effort to improve the efficiency of light water reactors and had been an approach promoted by M. H. Pratt and Philipp.

After a one-month intensive briefing at General Electric (not to be confused with the earlier course taken at Vallecitos), Niagara Mohawk engineers began designing the power plant for the Vallecitos Boiling Water Reactor built by

General Electric. It was essentially an experimental reactor used to test different core designs. Although the plant is closed today because of fears aroused by its location on a geologic fault, the data generated are still used as a basis for some current reactors and even for liquid-metal fast breeder reactor (LMFBR) designs (Mangan; Philipp, 1980; Dawson).

From 1960 to about 1964, the Nuclear Engineering Section was built up to about 25 professional engineers, all operating out of the Buffalo office. The section was developed to such levels in hope of a continued level of business sufficient to keep the section going (Philipp, 1979).

Plant Cost Evaluation

In 1959 Niagara Mohawk officials reached a point when they began to look seriously at developing their own nuclear power generating station in upstate New York. It was in that year that the engineers on loan to other projects were called back to the company and studies were begun to determine the specific choice of plants at a specific site. The important decision remaining was *when* it might be feasible to produce power from atomic energy at cost economically competitive with other fuels. That decision came in 1963, and construction began immediately thereafter. In the interim, Niagara Mohawk continued its related interests and participation in nuclear power development (Niagara Mohawk, 1974).

Prior to the decision in 1963 to build the Nine Mile Point One plant, extensive and detailed cost comparisons were undertaken to determine the costs of all the components as well as to determine the best supplier and the cost of the nuclear facility relative to other power sources. Many items, including many things that were not going to be used in the plant, were costed out during this period in order to get a picture of the industries involved (Mangan; Niagara Mohawk, 1963).

Several vendors of nuclear reactors were explored in-depth along with their associated technologies. General Electric, Westinghouse, Atomic International, General Atomic, and a consortium of Stone and Webster and Babcock and Wilcox were considered during this phase (Niagara Mohawk, 1960). These firms represented the broad spectrum of reactor types then available for a utility including boiling water reactors (BWR), pressured water reactors (PWR), sodium graphite, spectrum shift PWR, BWR with separate superheat, and the high-temperature gas-cooled reactor (HTGR) (Niagara Mohawk, 1960).

An important aspect of Niagara Mohawk's decision-making shows up in the documents supporting the reports prepared during this period—consistent and long-term inter-utility support. Niagara Mohawk engineers, in preparing the cost estimates for the various reports of this period, relied heavily upon the cost experiences of other utilities and suppliers. Cost estimates were provided from Consolidated Edison and other utilities who had had experience with the systems

Niagara Mohawk was then considering. A network of engineers also resulted from an arrangement called the Empire State Utilities Power Resources Associates (ESUPRA). Originally formed to study and expedite commercial nuclear power, ESUPRA gradually evolved into the present day Empire State Electric Energy Research Corporation (ESEERCO).

After the initial studies were completed, Niagara Mohawk opted for the light-water reactor technology. The reasons for this are set forward in the major summary document appearing in 1963.

> Water-cooled nuclear reactors are the only type recommended at this time for commitment to construction on the Niagara Mohawk system. Several more advanced reactor types, generally employing nonaqueous coolant systems and producing higher pressure and temperature steam, have reached various stages of development including construction of power plant prototypes. However attractive the future potential for these advanced systems may be, none have been developed anywhere near the extent of water-cooled reactors and operational experiences on a power plant scale is virtually nonexistent. For this reason, operating cost and performance estimates for any of these advanced plants are not reliable at this time (Niagara Mohawk, 1963).

Time and again the importance of the U.S. Navy's submarine reactor program for the development of Niagara Mohawk's nuclear-powered generating station program emerged throughout the course of the case study. It surfaced not only in the literature surrounding the history of nuclear power but also in the reports generated by Niagara Mohawk and in the interviews held at Niagara Mohawk (Bupp and Derian, Stacey).

The major summary report emphasized the gains to be obtained from the light-water reactor technology, as opposed to others which might eventually turn out to be more efficient or cheaper but which were more complex or needed much more development.

> Historically, water-cooled power reactors are an outgrowth of the nuclear Navy program and their development was continued to an unprecedented extent by the U.S. Atomic Energy Commission under the Civilian Nuclear Power Program. In recent years, research and engineering refinements by reactor manufacturers, and construction and operation of commercial scale plants by private utilities has furthered their development (Niagara Mohawk, 1963).

Although Niagara Mohawk had an early and active involvement with other reactor technologies, such as the breeder (Fermi) and the high-temperature, gas-cooled, it also had an intimate knowledge of the progress and success of the submarine reactor program. In 1955 Niagara Mohawk became the first New York State utility to obtain nuclear power generated electricity from the Sea Wolf test facility run by General Electric in West Milton, New York. Although this was only for a short period of time (about a year and a half), Niagara Mohawk had evaluated the facility and the electricity it generated as to its suitability for the Niagara Mohawk system (Stacey).

The number of vendors under consideration was then narrowed down to three—General Electric, Westinghouse, and General Atomic. General Electric and Westinghouse were offering light-water technology while General Atomic was a vendor of gas-cooled reactors. The light-water reactor had the edge over the other systems because of its relative simplicity and also in terms of track record and reliability (Rhode).

As part of the economic studies performed by the engineers, a comparison was made between nuclear power costs and those of fossil fuel plants. The traditional dichotomy between the two, based on low fuel costs for nuclear versus lower initial capital costs for fossil plants, emerged.

Based on Niagara Mohawk data and future projections, a report concluded that a sizeable nuclear fuel advantage would prevail for all conceivable fluctuations in delivered coal prices (Niagara Mohawk, 1963).

The conclusions of the study, which was one of the major summary documents leading to the 1963 board of directors' decision to build a nuclear-powered generating plant, conveniently ignored the cost comparisons that formed the background from the report and were summarized in a cost comparison table. There one would find at least one option, the expansion of an existing coal-fired steam station, cheaper than any of the nuclear options. The other options (all were variations on building new coal-fired facilities) were more expensive by 2.5 percent to 10.6 percent over the nuclear options (Niagara Mohawk, 1963). Considering the level of financial risk and technological uncertainty one might expect from nuclear power, which at that time had no track record as an electrical generating technology, these figures were hardly superior enough to make nuclear power an outstanding alternative.

Since the last major review of nuclear power plant costs in 1960, costs had been reduced substantially by federal research programs, ESADA research, more experience in reactor construction by the vendors, and intense competition among the major suppliers of reactor systems. But, as Sporn has noted (Sporn, 1962, 1964, 1966, 1969), coal technology was and is a moving target. As costs were being reduced in the field of nuclear power, costs were also being reduced in coal-fueled plants by improved technology, the unit train concept, and more competitive coal prices in the Middle Atlantic region (Gándara).

Financing

In order to build a power plant, particularly a nuclear power plant, a utility must raise the needed capital. This is usually done through selling bonds or issuing stock. The rate at which the bonds sell and the interest rate that they bear is usually a rough indicator of how the financial community at large views the risks involved in the project.

The expected cash requirements for the Nine Mile Point One nuclear power plant came to approximately $90 million (Niagara Mohawk, 1963; Philipp, 1980). This capital need was met by Niagara Mohawk by issuing mortgage bonds and stock. Niagara Mohawk had no problem selling its bonds and the interest rate was normal for that period. Likewise, the company had no problem selling its stock at or above book value. The financial community, as expressed through its willingness to invest in stocks and bonds to cover the cost of construction for the Nine Mile Point One nuclear power station, had no reservations about the new technology nor about Niagara Mohawk's capability to engineer the plant (Jensen). Until the late 1970s, utilities had no problems obtaining financing for their nuclear power plants. Some would say this attests to the faith of the financial community in either nuclear power or in the utilities themselves (Jensen).

Impact of the Experience

Niagara Mohawk's first experience with constructing and using a nuclear-powered generating station of its own had two major impacts. The first, a reorganization, was a result of the plant running over budget. Nine Mile Point One was completed for $120 million, roughly one third over estimated cost. In terms of hindsight, this would represent a bargain; in the environment of that period it represented a serious error. One must realize that utilities during that period had a long and successful track record with coal- , oil- , and gas-fired and hydroelectric generating plants, and, in general, were extremely successful in forecasting final budgets and construction schedules. The norm for that period was for a plant to come in under budget and ahead of schedule (Sporn, 1969; Gándara). In addition to being over budget, Nine Mile Point One experienced some delays in scheduled completion. Although the company did not discard the use of nuclear power, the shock was such that it led to a disbanding of the Nuclear Engineering Section and an internal reorganization of Niagara Mohawk. First, engineering added a Generation Department that was broken down into sections dealing with coal, oil, hydro, and nuclear generation sources. Second, as a result of some prompting by the engineers, Niagara Mohawk began to expand the number and types of internal officials involved in generation plant decisions, adding such specialties as planners, economists, and lawyers. This move from a specialized and separate section for nuclear engineering services is a pattern found for mature nuclear technologies in other utilities (McAnally and Peoples).

The second major effect of Niagara Mohawk's initial success with nuclear power was to push the company into trying to build additional nuclear-powered plants at a time when the external environment, both financially and socially, was beginning to experience profound changes that would affect the viability of nuclear power plant plans across the nation. Niagara Mohawk initiated plans for an additional nuclear-powered generating facility at Easton-on-the-Hudson, a site on the Hudson River north of Albany, before the first plant had been finished. The utility ultimately was unsuccessful in completing its plant at the upper Hudson site due to financial problems and conflict with the federal requirements protecting landscape views from National Monuments. The proposed site was across the Hudson River from the Saratoga Battlefield National Monument, and the Central Hudson Scenic Preservation Society objected to its being built there.

Niagara Mohawk had been relatively unscathed in terms of opposition to its plans for nuclear power plants. Although other New York utilities, notably New York State Electric and Gas Corporation, had been confronted on their nuclear power plant construction plans, until recently opposition was oblique to the central issues of nuclear power (Nilkin). Opposition focused then on peripheral issues such as cooling water discharge or, in Niagara Mohowak's case, scenic values disruption, issues that were not intrinsic to nuclear power and could be raised with virtually any other type of generation plant. At the point that Niagara Mohawk actually abandoned its plans for nuclear power at the Easton-on-the-Hudson site, utilities were beginning to be stressed financially as a result of entering the turbulent 1970s, when rising fuel prices, inflation, and regulatory lag began to work against the companies.

Niagara Mohawk's continuing commitment to nuclear power is indicated by its present (1982) efforts at constructing, with other utilities, a second unit at Nine Mile Point and by its recent efforts, in conjunction with other New York utilities, to build a nuclear-powered generating station at Sterling, New York. The Sterling plant application failed because the New York State Public Service Commission felt that the utilities had not fully justified the plant in light of a decreasing population base and a slowing rate of increase in electrical energy demand. Current controversies have focused on whether or not to finish the Nine Mile Point Two unit is to be finished, who should have to pay for the enormous construction cost overruns.

Summary

Niagra Mohawk Power Corporation's active interest in nuclear power began as far back as 1953. In 1954 that interest intensified with Niagara Mohawk's participation in Detroit Edison's Enrico Fermi Project. The Enrico Fermi project, and the subsequent high temperature gas-cooled reactor (HTGR) project led to a series of decisions and activities for Niagara Mohawk that would culminate in the construction of its first nuclear-powered generating station, Nine Mile Point One. Niagara Mohawk has remained, in the contest of a diversified fuel strategy, committed to nuclear power, and in particular, to light-water technology. The utility is scheduled to complete its second nuclear power plant at Nine Mile Point in 1986. From a relatively closed decision-making environment, Niagara Mohawk has moved into a more open strategic policy environment. That openness has brought a wide range of technical, social, and economic factors as well as a greater range of participants into Niagara Mohawk's internal and external environment.

CRITICAL FACTORS IN STRATEGIC DECISION-MAKING

Niagara Mohawk's experience with nuclear power demonstrates the way in which environmental and social considerations interact with economic and technical factors in shaping strategic decisions within organizations. The experience also indicates some limits and possibilities for improving public policy surrounding new technologies and complex social problems. This review of findings and conclusions will discuss the environmental factors which were found to have influenced Niagara Mohawk Power Corporations's decision to innovate with nuclear power.

One of the background factors that tends to be slighted in studies of organizatioanl decision-making is the general condition of the United States economy. During the early stages of nuclear power development and its innovation by Niagara Mohawk, the United States economy was in a period of strong growth, and inflation was substantially less than it is now. A healthy, growing economy helped to create a positive environment for the decisions that Niagara Mohawk was about to make.

In addition, prior to Niagara Mohawk's entry into nuclear power, New York was experiencing strong population growth and strong increase in electrical energy demand. However, it was more important that the engineers at Niagara Mohawk *expected* that demand to continue its strong increase. And throughout the 1950s and 1960s demand did continue to increase, fueled not only by increased population growth but also by changes in American life-styles toward "All Electric Living."

The many nuclear power programs of the federal government also boosted the development of nuclear power as a potential option for private electric utilities. These programs included several that have traditionally received attention, such as the U.S. Atomic Energy Commission's reactor development programs, the Eisenhower Atoms for Peace programs, and the various efforts of the government to proivde technical and economic incentives to private electric utilities (Dawson). But the various U. S. Navy nuclear submarine programs appear to have been very important for the early development of nuclear power generally and specifically at Niagara Mohawk. The Nautilus program provided a relatively tested technology, and the Sea Wolf program gave Niagara Mohwak direct experience with the production and transmission of electrial generated at nuclear-powered stations.

At the state level, Governor Rockefeller had develped an environment strongly supportive of nuclear power (Salmansohn). In addition, regulatory lag in New

York was generally working in the utility's favor (MacAvoy). The regulatory lag, in addition to the rising energy demand, gave Niagara Mohawk additional slack resources (Stacey). In addition to the role played by the federal and state governments in promoting nuclear power, many utilities were aggressive in creating and taking advantage of opportunities to use the new technology. Niagara Mohawk Power Corporations's early and extensive experiences with nuclear power through the Enrico Fermi, HTGR, Vallecitos, and Knolls Laboratory projects gave the utility a positive outlook toward and extensive training in the new technology. This experience was used in the construction of the Nine Mile Point One plant, but the social network established through that experience also helped in the design, costing, and decision-making associated with the power plant. The willingness of the board of directors to undertake a risky technology bespoke its faith in the future of nuclear power. Its unanimous and enthusiastic support for nuclear power probably communicated nuclear power's importance immediately to the staff of the company.

The interest in nuclear power on the part of President Machold and the aggressive pursuit of nuclear power by Chief Engineer Minot Pratt were critical factors in Niagara Mohawk's entry into nuclear power. Downs, in his study of innovations, notes that the chief executive officer's attitudes play a vital role in the acceptance of an innovation. In Niagara Mohawk's case, President Machold was described as an enthusiastic supporter of nuclear power. Directors and company officers who were interviewed described his mood, and consequently the company's, with regard to innovating with nuclear power as the "thing to do" or "wave of the future."

At the time that many utilities, including Niagara Mohawk, were becoming actively interested in nuclear power, several major and prestigious studies had been done that helped create an environment accepting new ideas for providing energy and generally supportive of nuclear power specifically. In 1953, during the time that Niagara Mohawk had begun its interest in nuclear power, the Paley Commission had issued its report evaluating the future potential of all resources, including energy, in the United States. Palmer C. Putnam, who had authored sections of the Paley Commission report, produced *Energy in the Future* in 1953, which indicated a problematic future for traditional fuels and a positive, though potentially costly, future for nuclear power. Chief Engineer Pratt's evaluation in the early 1950s of existing energy suppliers was an apparent outgrowth of this general concern with the nonrenewable nature of most traditional energy sources and the potentially renewable energy source of nuclear power.

Like other utilitites, Niagara Mohawk's fuel diversification policy was an important factor in innovating with nuclear power. Niagara Mohawk had a long tradition of striving for a diversity of power sources and was located in a region where it could maintain a mix of the four primary fuel sources (oil, coal, hydro, and natural gas). This fuel diversity tradition was seen as being strengthened by the addition of nuclear power to the generation types. This experience stands in contrast to Gándara's finding that fuel diversity was a consideration absent for most of the light-water reactor's commercialization period. Fuel diversification only became important for other utilities in recent years, hinging on fuel supply history relating to the utility's regional location. Although fuel costs may not have been as important as they might have been expected to be, other fuel-related issues influenced the decision to go with nuclear power. For many years coal had been an interruptable source of fuel due to chronic labor strife (Davis), with projected company growth threatened by the effects of strikes. Company executives also perceived a future performance gap in terms of the finite nature of fossil fuels and saw nuclear power as a future resource of infinite capacity.

In New York, up until the early 1960s, industry studies indicated that nuclear power was not competitive with other fuels but should be given further research and development. The utilities within New York then formed an organization to pursue a research and development program to make nuclear power more competitive.

A number of confounding factors need to be considered in determining the role that economics played in the decision to buy a nuclear power plant. During the early period of commercialization of the light-water reactor (LWR), coal prices were generally declining. As Sporn (1967) has pointed out, coal-fired plant technology is a moving target in which *both* fuel costs and equipment costs fluctuate. Technological developments as well as competitive practices among the coal and railroad companies kept the price of coal decreasing during most of the period Niagara Mohawk was innovating with nuclear power. The coal industry engaged in competitive bidding practices (except in New England, which the coal industry generally wrote off) to keep coal a more attractive fuel in the face of a potential nuclear power threat (Gándara). In addition, the costs of nuclear power were kept artificially low, due to under-pricing of power plants by major vendors and the governmental subsidies built into the research and development of nuclear power plants (Bupp and Derian).

The "Economic Gate"

Nuclear power, for Niagara Mohawk Power Corporation, was not economical enough for economics to be a necessary *and* sufficient reason to build Nine Mile Point One. However, nuclear power was economical enough to allow it to be an option for Niagara Mohawk to consider. Throughout the late 1950s and early 1960s Niagara Mohawk was committed to innovating with nuclear power and it was only waiting for the price of nuclear power to come down into range where it could be reasonably considered as an option to coal-fired power plants. Other factors were more influential in determining Niagara Mohawk's actual entry, and the timing of the entry, into nuclear power. Economics certainly played a major role but one which tends to be overemphasized. This coincides with a pattern found on a nationwide level (Gándara, Perry et al.). Other factors have been found which influenced the decision of utilities to innovate with nuclear power. Although fuel costs of nuclear power were lower than those of coal-fired power plants, capital costs were much higher. Point of delivery costs for coal and other fuels can be misleading as an indicator for whether or not a utility will use nuclear power. The total costs of various power plant alternatives, as determined over the life of the plant, are better indicators of the role that economics must play in a utility's decision to pick one mode of generation technology over another.

In Niagara Mohawk Power Corporation's case, the proposed Nine Mile Point One nuclear power plant was not the most economical alternative available to the company. Nuclear power in general was also not significantly more economical than most of the other options available to the company. Economics acted as a "gate" for Niagara Mohawk as it pursued nuclear power. Rather than acting as the major decision variable, the "economic gate" merely allowed a certain range of alternative projects to pass through, in effect passing some minimum efficiency criterion. Once the alternatives were past that gate, then other environmental variables determined which alternative would be chosen. However, even prior to passing through the gate, environmental factors influenced which alternatives would be considered for economic analysis and which, if found wanting, would be pursued through further research and development.

The Changed Environment of Strategic Decision-Making

From the late 1950s and the early 1960s to the late 1970s and into the 1980s the environment of strategic decision-making for private electric utilities has changed radically. What was once a sleepy backwater of decision-making inhabited by engineers supposedly making efficient decisions based on rational calculations has become turbulent and filled with a variety of actors and stages which influence the content and direction of decision-making. Niagara Mohawk Power Corporation has, like other private electric utilities, been influenced by these changes, although its adjustment is still taking place and is slower than that of some other utilities.

The first major change to affect Niagara Mohawk was the switch from making decisions in a closed environment to decision-making in an open environment. This has been the trend for many other utilities and has sometimes been referred to by industry participants as a trend towards "management in a fishbowl." In the earlier decision-making period, strategic decision-making at Niagara Mohawk has a distinctly "seat-of-the-pants" quality about it. This is not to say that the decisions were necessarily poorer or that research was not done. Rather the type of research done during that period was more limited in scope and purpose. Its scope was limited to a relatively few power generation alternatives and its purpose was generally to support decisions that had already been made some time earlier. Documentation of all aspects of the decision-making process during this period was much less than that of the later period of open decision-making. Few notes were kept at board of directors meetings and the general nature of documentation was limited to engineering reports and other legal or contractual documents normally associated with a typical construction project. As the environment changed for the utility, so did the documentation needs, so much so that whereas the formal documents surrounding the decision to make Nine Mile Point One were minimal and would fit comfortably on a desk corner, the documentation concerning Nine Mile Point Two would fill a small room.

Several factors led to this explosion in documentation. One of the most important was a change in the internal decision-making environment of Niagara Mohawk. With the inclusion of additional actors, the need for documentation increased. With the advent of the National Environmental Protection Act and its requirements for environmental impact statements and public hearings, a big boost was given to the number and types of documents needed to make a decision. Finally, boards of directors in general have become more concerned in recent years about their liability in the event of poor decisions, and have consequently sought to keep more accurate or appropriate records of their strategic decision-making activities. Again, it should be emphasized that just because there is more documentation, it does not mean that strategic decision-making is of higher quality than in the past or that documents are now something more than the post hoc justifications that they tended to be in the past.

As Niagara Mohawk has moved from a closed to an open decision-making environment, both internally and externally, the number and types of participants involved in a decision have increased. Whereas in the past decisions were made internally and engineers predominated, with a role for the board and a minimal role for the Public Service Commission, now we find a wide range of participants. At the insistence of the engineers, Niagara Mohawk added additional participants internally such as economists, financial analysts, planners, and lawyers to the decision-making process for new generation plants. Externally as well as internally, the strategic decision-making environment became much richer. At the federal level the old Atomic Energy Commission was split into two separate agencies charged with promotion (the Department of Energy) and enforcement or regulation (the Nuclear Regulatory Commission). The New York Public Service Commission has begun to take a more active role in utility decisions and its role has increased significantly with the addition to the commission of two commissioners who are consumer activists. A recent Public Service Commission hearing investigated the cost and schedule overruns on the Nine Mile Point Two project. The PSC staff, however, remains unreformed, and rather than being an independent critic of utility decision-making, tends to be more supportive of utility interests. A variety of nontraditional intervenors have also entered the decision-making scene. The New York State Bureau of Consumer Affairs is now a regular participant in rate-making and other types of hearings. A variety of consumer, environmental, and energy user groups have also invaded the traditionally sacrosanct environment of the utilities. But, as with documentation, more and different types of participants do not necessarily guarantee "better" decisions, only that they will probably be longer in coming and possibly more frustrating to the consumer and citizen. Events surrounding the recent hearings on the Nine Mile Point Two project indicate that the results of decision-making have changed minimally despite the addition of numerous participants to the decision-making process.

SOCIAL FACTORS AND
DECISION-MAKING MODELS

The research indicates strong support for a modified version of March and Simon's decision-making model. The participants clearly initiated a limited search for alternatives that was heavily biased at the beginning in favor of nuclear power. That nuclear power was used indicates that some innovation did take place but of a rather limited variety, constrained as it was by the professional orientation of the engineers, the social and political environment which was supportive of nuclear power at that time, and the private utility concept which limits the range of alternatives open to society for solving energy problems.

Once the decision was made to go with nuclear power the utility was gradually reorganized to mobilize the bias toward that mode of generation. Opportunities to extend the range of stimuli and situations were ignored in favor of activities that narrowed the perception of alternatives. Both Sporn and Galbraith appear to be correct in their assessment that engineers or technocrats dominate the process. But the rest of Sporn's model is not borne out by the Niagara Mohawk experience. Instead it appears that the Sporn model was used for post hoc rationalization of decisions that had been made previously on essentially social grounds. Even with the use of economic analysis to justify the project, it is clear that the alternative chosen was not the cheapest available. Economics was not the primary, independent, and sovereign motivation that Sporn's model predicts. The economic studies conducted were not all-inclusive and all-encompassing but were limited to a simple capital investment, operations and maintenance costs model.

The "economic gate" concept should be thought of as a supplement to the March and Simon model of satisficing behavior. As a basic efficiency test, it allowed for a small range of alternatives to emerge from which the utility could choose its preferred alternative. In this instance, nuclear power was chosen not because it was the cheapest alternative but because it was the alternative that the engineers wanted. And the engineers worked hard to get nuclear power past that "economic gate" of minimum efficiency, so that other social and psychological environmental factors could intervene on its behalf.

The research lends support to the notion that in organizational decision-making, external and broadly "social" criteria, as contrasted with internal and narrowly "economic" criteria, will be major determinants. If one includes in the social criteria the preference of engineers for professionally stimulating and challenging solutions, rather than pedestrian or mundane solutions, then the social model of strategic decision-making is strengthened further. And in the case of Niagara Mohawk Power Corporation's decision to build a nuclear-powered generating station, social criteria colored the decision-making from the start so that economics retained a much reduced role as an "economic gate." Hence, social considerations worked to undermine any attempt to divorce economic analysis of technological alternatives from the social context. Contrary to Sporn's argument, economic analysis of technologies is invariably colored by the social context in which such analysis is carried out, and nowhere is this clearer than in Niagara Mohawk's decision to innovate with nuclear power.

ACKNOWLEDGMENT

This research was partially supported by the Snow Foundation, Syracuse University.

REFERENCES

Arthur, John. Chief Engineer, Rochester Gas and Electric Co., Rochester, New York. Interview, 1 May 1979.

Bupp, Irwin C., and Jean-Claude Derian. *Light Water: How the Nuclear Dream Dissolved*. New York: Basic Books, Inc., 1978.

Davis, David H. *Energy Politics*, 2d ed. New York: St. Martin's Press, 1978.

Dawson, Frank G. *Nuclear Power: Development and Management of a Technology*. Seattle: University of Washington Press, 1976.

Downs, George W., Jr. *Bureaucracy, Innovation, and Public Policy*. Lexington, MA: D.C. Heath and Co., 1976.

Galbraith, John Kenneth. *The New Industrial State*, 3rd ed., revised. Boston: Houghton Mifflin Co., 1978.

Gándara, Arturo. *Electric Utility Decision-making and the Nuclear Option* (R-2148-NSF). Santa Monica, CA: Rand, 1977.

Hammer, Stephen. *The Rochester Gas and Electric Story*, Vol. 2., 2d. ed. Rochester, N.Y.: Christopher Press, Inc., 1967.

Jaekle, Edwin F. Member, Board of Directors, Niagara Mohawk Power Corporation. Interview, 27 February 1981.

Jensen, Harry. Member (Retired), Board of Directors, Niagara Mohawk Power Corporation. Interview, 4 March 1981. Jupiter, Florida.

Lempges, Tom. Vice-President, Nuclear Generation, Niagara Mohawk Power Corporation, Syracuse, New York. Interview, 19 January 1981.

Lijphart, Arend. "Comparative Politics and the Comparative Method." *American Political Science Review* 65 (September 1971): 682-693.

MacAvoy, Paul W. *The Regulated Industries and the Economy*. New York: W. W. Norton & Co., 1979.

Machold, Earle J. Letter to John T. Conway, Executive Director, Joint Committee on Atomic Energy. Reprinted in *Nuclear Power Economics—Analysis and Comments—1964*, pp. 40-43.

Joint Committee on Atomic Energy, Congress of the United States, 88th Congress, 2nd Session, October 1964.

Mangan, Charles V. Chief Engineer, Niagara Mohawk Power Corporation, Syracuse, New York: Interview, 28 March 1979.

March, James G., and Herbert Simon. *Organizations*. New York: John Wiley & Sons, Inc., 1958.

Martin, Laumann. Senior Vice-President and General Counsel (Retired), Niagara Mohawk Power Corporation, Syracuse, New York. Interview, 8 January 1981.

Maull, Baldwin, Member, Board of Directors, Niagara Mohawk Power Corporation. Interview, 27 February 1981, New York, New York.

McAnally, James L., and Denton L. Peoples. "Organizing for Nuclear Power." *Public Utilities Fortnightly* 95 (March 27, 1975): 31-36.

Mowers, Jack L. Company Photographer and Historian (Retired), Niagara Mohawk Power Corporation, Syracuse, New York. Interview, 23 April 1979.

Nelkin, Dorothy. *Nuclear Power and Its Critics: The Cayuga Lake Controversy*. Ithaca, N.Y.: Cornell University Press, 1971.

Niagara Mohawk Power Corporation. *Annual report*. Syracuse: Niagara Mohawk Power Corporation, 1953.

―――. *Annual report*. Syracuse: Niagara Mohawk Power Corporation, 1959.

―――. Evaluation of ESUPRA phases I and II nuclear power plant proposals. September 22, 1960, System Project Engineering Department.

―――. Untitled and undated summary report. (Graph of cumulative costs is dated April 1, 1963). Syracuse, N.Y.: Niagara Mohawk Power Corporation.

―――. *The Niagara Mohawk Story (1823-1973): A Reference Manual of 150 Years of Niagara Mohawk Power Corporation and Its Predecessor Companies*. Syracuse, N.Y.: Niagara Mohawk Power Corporation.

Novarro, Joe. Project Manager, Shoreham Nuclear Power Plant, Long Island Lighting Company, Wading River, New York. Interview, 16 July 1979.

Paley Commission. *Resources for Freedom*, Summary and Volumes I-V. The President's Materials Policy Commission, June 1952.

Perrow, Charles. *Complex Organizations: A Critical Essay*, 2d ed. Glenview, Ill.: Scott, Foresman and Co., 1979.

Perry, Robert, et. al. Development and Commercialization of the Light Water Reactor, 1946-1976 (R-2180-NSF). Santa Monica, CA: Rand, 1977.

Philipp, Howard D. Director, Research and Development Department, Niagara Mohawk Power Corporation, Syracuse, New York. Interview, 31 July 1979.

―――. Interview, December 1980.

Pratt, Minot H. Vice-President and Director (Retired) Niagara Mohawk Power Corporation, Syracuse, New York. Interview, 23 May 1979.

Putnam, Palmer C. *Energy in the Future*. New York: D. Van Nostrand Co., Inc., 1953.

Rhode, Gerald K. Vice-President, Engineering, Niagara Mohawk Power Corporation, Syracuse, New York. Interview, 6 June 1979.

Salmansohn, Peter. Nuclear Energy, Rockefeller, and Big Business. Unpublished Masters Thesis, Goddard College, 1976.

Simon, Herbert A. *Administrative Behavior: A Study of Decision-Making Processes in Administrative Organization*, 3rd ed. New York: The Free Press, 1976.

Sporn, Philip. Statement by Philip Sporn, Chairman, System Development Committee, American Electric Power Co., submitted for the record of the 1962 Hearings on development, growth, and state of the atomic energy industry. In *Nuclear Power Economic—Analysis and Comments--1964*, pp. 45-51. Joint Committee on Atomic Energy, Congress of the United States, 88th Congress, 2nd Session, October 1964.

―――. A post-Oyster Creek evaluation of the current status of nuclear electric generation—1964.

In *Nuclear Power Economics—Analysis and Comments—1962 through 1967*. Report of Joint Commmittee on Atomic Energy, Congress of the United States, February 1968. Washington: U.S. Government Printing Office, 1967.

———. Nuclear power economics: An appraisal of the current technical economics position of nuclear and conventional generation—1966. In *Nuclear Power Economics—1962 through 1967*. Report of Joint Committee on Atomic Energy, Congress of the United States, February 1968. Washington: U.S. Government Printing Office, 1967.

———. Nuclear power economics--Analysis and comments--1967. In *Nuclear Power Economics--1962 through 1967*. Report of Joint Committee of Atomic Energy, Congress of the United States, February 1968. Washington: U.S. Government Printing Office, 1967.

———. *Technology, Engineering, and Economics*. Cambridge, MA: The M.I.T. Press, 1969.

Stacey, James E., Jr. New Technology and Organizational Innovation: Niagara Mohawk Power Corporation and Nuclear Power. Unpublished Doctoral Dissertation, Syracuse University, August, 1981.

Terry, John. Senior Vice President, General Counsel and Secretary, Niagara Mohawk Power Corporation, Syracuse, New York. Interview, 9 March 1981.

Wiseman, Jacqueline P., and Marcia S. Aron. *Field Projects for Sociology Students*. Cambridge, MA: Schenkman Publishing Co., Inc., 1970.

Yin, Robert K., and Karen A. Heald. Using the Case Survey Method to Analyze Policy Studies. *Administrative Science Quarterly* 20 (September 1975): 371-381.

Research in
Corporate Social Performance and Policy

Edited by **Lee E. Preston**
Center for Business and Public Policy
University of Maryland, College Park

Volume 3, 1981, 250 pp.
ISBN 0-89232-184-9

CONTENTS: **Editor's Introduction,** *Lee E. Preston, University of Maryland.* **Corporate Power and Social Performance: Approaches to Positive Analysis,** *Lee E. Preston, University of Maryland.* **The Process of Corporate Social Involvement: Five Case Studies,** *Michael J. Merenda, University of New Hampshire.* **Implementing Affirmative Action: Impetus and Enabling Factors in Five Organizations,** *Marilyn L. Taylor, University of Kansas.* **Corporate Law Violations and Executive Liability,** *S. Prakash Sethi, University of Texas—Dallas.* **Economy-Ecology Conflict: Analysis, Examples, and Policy Approaches,** *John F. Striener, California State University and Stahrl W. Edmunds, University of California—Riverside.* **The Context of Social Performance: An Empirical Study of Texas Banks,** *Banwari L. Kedia, Louisiana State University, and Edwin C. Kuntz, S.E. Missouri State University.* **Public Issues Scanning,** *John E. Fleming, University of Southern California.* **Employer Policies and the Older Worker,** *Lois Farrer Copperman, Portland State University.* **MNC Responses to Equity-Sharing Policies: The Indonesian Experience,** *Robert B. Dickie, Boston University.* **Corporate Political Participation: From Tillman to the Eighties,** *Carl L. Swanson, University of Texas—Dallas.*

Volume 4, 1982, 300 pp.
ISBN 0-89232-259-4

CONTENTS: **Introduction,** *Lee E. Preston, University of Maryland.* **Case Research in Corporation and Society Studies,** *James E. Post and Patti N. Andrews, Boston University.* **Conceptual Frameworks and Strategies For Corporate Social Involvement Research,** *Robert J. DeFillippi, Fordham University.* **The Thompson-Page Contribution to Social Issues Research,** *John F. Mahon, Boston University.* **Strategic Planning Systems For A Politicized Environment,** *Duane Windsor and George Greanias, Rice University.* **Structure Culture and Performance in Public Affairs: A Study of the Forest Products Industry,** *Jeffrey A. Sonnenfeld, Harvard Business School.* **The Public Affairs Function: Report on a Large Scale Research Project,** *Edwin A. Murray, Jr., Boston University.* **Ethical Investment Policies and Activities of Catholic Religious Orders,** *Richard E. Wokutch, Virginia Polytechnic Institute and State University.* **Strategic Action in the Regulatory Environment the Case of the Firestone "500",** *Elliot Zashin, University of Illinois.* **The Two-Part Problem Regulatory Compliance: Compliance Reform in Strip Mining,** *Barry M. Mitnick, University of Pittsburgh.* **Corporate Social Reporting: Eight Decades of Development at U.S. Steel,** *Robert Hogner, Florida International University.*

 JAI PRESS INC., 36 Sherwood Place, P.O. Box 1678 Greenwich, Connecticut 06836
Telephone: 203-661-7602   Cable Address: JAIPUBL

Research in
Organizational Behavior

An Annual Series of Analytical Essays and Critical Reviews

Edited by **Barry M. Staw**
School of Business Administration, University of California, Berkeley
and **L.L. Cummings**
J.L. Kellogg Graduate School of Management, Northwestern University

Volume 1, 1979, 478 pp.
ISBN 0-89232-045-1

Edited by **Barry M. Staw,** *Graduate School of Management, Northwestern University*

CONTENTS: **Editorial Statement,** *Barry M. Staw.* **Beyond Open System Models of Organization,** *Louis R. Pondy, University of Illinois and Ian I. Mitroff, University of Pittsburgh.* **Cognitive Processes in Organizations,** *Karl E. Weick, Cornell University.* **Organizational Learning: Implications for Organizational Design,** *Robert Duncan and Andrew Weiss, Northwestern University.* **Organizational Design and Adult Learning,** *Douglas T. Hall and Cynthia V. Fukami, Northwestern University.* **Organizational Structure, Attitudes and Behaviors,** *Chris J. Berger, Purdue University and L. L. Cummings, University of Wisconsin - Madison.* **Toward a Theory of Organizational Socialization,** *John Van Maanen and Edgar H. Schein, Massachusetts Institute of Technology.* **Participation in Decision-Making: One More Look,** *Edwin A. Locke and David M. Schweiger, University of Maryland.* **Leadership: Some Empirical Generalizations and New Research Directions,** *Robert J. House and Mary L. Baetz, University of Toronto.* **Performance Appraisal Effectiveness: Its Assessment and Determinants,** *Jeffery S. Kane, Advanced Research Resources Organization and Edward E. Lawler, III, University of Michigan.* **Bibliography. Index.**

Volume 2, 1980, 368 pp.
ISBN 0-89232-099-0

Edited by **Barry M. Staw,** *Graduate School of Management, Northwestern University and* **L.L. Cummings,** *Graduate School of Business, University of Wisconsin*

CONTENTS: **Editorial Statement,** *Barry M. Staw, and L.L. Cummings.* **Construct Validity in Organizational Behavior,** *Donald P. Schwab, University of Wisconsin.* **Rationality and Justification in Organizational Life,** *Barry M. Staw, Northwestern University.* **Time and Work: Towards an Integrative Perspective,** *Ralph Katz, Massachusetts Institute of Technology.* **Collective Bargaining and Organizational Behavior Research,** *Thomas A. Kochan, Cornell University.* **Behavioral Research on Unions and Union Management,** *Jeanne Brett, Northern University.* **Institutionalization of Planned Organizational Change,** *Paul S. Goodman and Max Bazerman, Carnegie-Mellon University and Edward Conlon, Georgia Institute of Technology.* **Work Design in the Organizational Context,** *Greg R. Oldham, University of Illinois and J. Richard Hackman, Yale University.* **Organizational Growth Types: Lessons from Small Institutions,** *A. C. Filley and R. J. Aldag, University of Wisconsin.* **Interorganizational Processes and Organizational Boundary Activities,** *J. Stacy Adams, University of North Carolina.*

Volume 3, 1981, 356 pp.
ISBN 0-89232-151-2

Edited by **L.L. Cummings,** *Graduate School of Business, University of Wisconsin and* **Barry M. Staw,** *School of Business Administration, University of California, Berkeley*

CONTENTS: Editorial Statement, *L.L. Cummings and Barry M. Staw.* **Management as Symbolic Action: The Creation and Maintenance of Organizational Paradigms,** *Jeffrey Pfeffer, Stanford University.* **Relative Deprivation: A Theory of Distributive Injustice for an Era of Shrinking Resources,** *Joanne Martin, Stanford University.* **The Politics of Upward Influence in Organizations,** *Lyman Porter, University of California, Irvine, Robert W. Allen, University of California, Irvine, and Harold L. Angle, University of Minnesota.* **Organization as Power,** *David J. Hickson, University of Bradford, England, W. Graham Astley, University of Pennsylvania, Richard J. Bulter, University of Bradford, England, and David C. Wilson, University of Bradford, England.* **An Attributional Model of Leadership and the Poor Performing Subordinate,** *Terrence R. Mitchell, University of Washington, Stephen G. Green, University of Washington, and Robert Wood, University of Washington.* **Employee Turnover and Post-Decision Accommodation Processes,** *Richard M. Steers, University of Oregon, and Richard T. Mowday, University of Oregon.* **Attitudinal Processes in Organizations,** *Bobby J. Calder, Northwestern University, and Paul H. Schurr, University of North Carolina.* **Cultural Contingency and Capitalism in the Cross-National Study of Organizations,** *John Child, University of Aston, England.*

Volume 4, 1982, 364 pp.
ISBN 0-89232-147-4

Edited by **Barry M. Staw,** *Graduate School of Business Administration, University of California, Berkeley and* **L.L. Cummings,** *J.L. Kellogg Graduate School of Management, Northwestern University*

CONTENTS: Editorial Statement, *Barry M. Staw and L.L. Cummings.* **Organizational Life Cycles and Natural Selection Processes,** *John Freeman, University of California, Berkeley.* **The Evolution of Organizational Forms: Technology, Coordination and Control,** *Howard Aldrich and Susan Mueller, Cornell University.* **Bureaucratic Versus Profit Organization,** *Marshal W. Meyer, University of California, Riverside.* **The Meanings of Absence: New Strategies for Theory and Research,** *Gary Johns, Concordia University and Nigel Nicholson, University of Sheffield.* **Workers Participation in Management: An International Perspective,** *George Strauss, University of California, Berkeley.* **Unidimensional Measurement, Second Order Factor Analysis, and Causal Models,** *John E. Hunter, Michigan State University and David W. Gerbing, Baylor University.* **A Matrix Approach to Literature Reviews,** *Paul Salipante, Case Western Reserve University, William Notz, University of Manitoba and John Bigelow, Oregon State University.*

Volume 5, 1983, 350 pp.
ISBN 0-89232-271-3

Edited by **L.L. Cummings,** *J.L. Kellog Graduate School of Management, Northwestern University* and **Barry M. Staw,** *Graduate School of Business Administration, University of California, Berkeley*

CONTENTS: Editorial Statement, *L.L. Cummings and Barry M. Staw.* **Interactional Psychology and Organizational Behavior,** *Benjamin Schneider, University of Maryland.* **Paradigm and Praxis in Organizational Analysis,** *J. Kenneth Benson, University of Missouri.* **Time and Behavior in Organizations,** *Joseph E. McGrath and Nancy L. Rotchford, University of Illinois.* **The Use of Information in Organizational Decision Making: A Model and Some Propositions,** *Charles A. O'Reilly, University of California, Berkeley.* **Performance Appraisal: A Process Focus,** *Daniel R. Ilgen, Purdue University and Jack M. Feldman, University of Florida.* **Social Comparison Processes and Dynamic Conservatism,** *Ken K. Smith, Univeristy of Maryland.* **Employee Owned Companies,** *Arnold S. Tannenbaum, University of Michigan.* **Sex Bias in Work Settings: The Lack of Fit Model,** *Madeline E. Heilman, New York University.* **Organizational Drmography,** *Jeffrey Pfeffer, Stanford University.*

**JAI PRESS INC., 36 Sherwood Place, P.O. Box 1678
Greenwich, Connecticut 06836**
Telephone: 203-661-7602   Cable Address: JAIPUBL